TOTALLY
TENDERLY
TRAGICALLY

TO

T

Also by Phillip Lopate

TOTALLY TENDERLY TRAGICALLY

Essays and criticism
from a lifelong love
affair with the movies

PHILLIP LOPATE

ANCHOR BOOKS/A DIVISION OF RANDOM HOUSE, INC.
NEW YORK

ANCHOR BOOKS EDITION

Grateful acknowledgment is made to Andrew Sarris for permission to
excerpt from his book *Confessions of a Cultist*. Copyright © 1970 by
Andrew Sarris.

Library of Congress Cataloging-in-Publication Data
Lopate, Phillip, 1943–
        Totally, tenderly, tragically: essays and criticism from a
    lifelong love affair with the movies / Phillip Lopate.

            p.   cm.
        Includes index.
        1. Motion pictures.   I. Title.
    PN1995.L627   1998
    791.43—dc21   98-6829
                                                      CIP

ISBN: 978-0-385-49250-8

Book design by Cheryl L. Cipriani

www.anchorbooks.com

144912319

CONTENTS

Contents

CAN MOVIES THINK?

To Lorenzo Semple, Jr.
and Kent Jones,
whose friendship helped me
in the dark

INTRODUCTION

All my life I have been movie-mad. The condition started in childhood (my parents sent us to Saturday matinees to get us out from underfoot), caught fire in adolescence, and has stayed with me ever since. Those friends who shared my celluloid fever in college mostly graduated to higher things— opera, ballet or the theater, whereas for me it was the opposite: other performing arts were fallback options when I could not find a movie to see. If you ask me today what I want to do on my birthday, the answer is, "Go to a movie." New Year's Eve? "Maybe we can take in a double feature." Valentine's Day? "How about the new Almodóvar, I hear it's not so bad, or the Minnelli retrospective—"

I approach moviegoing seriously, and no longer feel shame about that. I remember during the early eighties, in that reverse-snobbish backlash against film studies, how people used to make fun of you for using words like "film" or "cinema" (which they would pronounce with mock British nasality as "the cinem*ah*"). Proper form, apparently, was to say "movies" or "flicks"; anything else was considered unbearably pretentious. I could never bring myself to say "flicks," which seemed a *faux*-populist way to disparage the chance of receiving sublimity onscreen. For me, film is and always will be a ravishingly important art form. Ever since I saw *The Passion of Joan of Arc*, I realized I could be equally transported by a Dreyer, Mizoguchi, Tati or John Ford picture as by a Mozart opera or a Vermeer exhibit.

So I have sought out precisely those films that would take me to a place where the uncanny, the sublime, the tragic, the ecstatic, the beautifully resigned, all converge. Often enough, that search has led me to the American past—tracking down George Cukor's *Little Women*, say, because the director's *A Star Is Born* or *The Marrying Kind* made such an impression on me, then delving into delightful obscurities like *The Model and the Marriage Broker* (a great Thelma Ritter performance) or *Rockabye*, gagging a bit on *Susan and God*, until I had all fifty-odd Cukors under my belt. I'd do the same with favorite foreign or experimental filmmakers. Sure, I kept up with the big Hollywood studio product, same as everyone, year after year, but with nowhere the same "completist" zealotry as I did my favorites. Like a book collector who can afford to bide his time until just the right first edition comes along, I would patiently wait for the chance to fill in my cinematic gaps—then pounce.

Over the years, I have put in my fifty thousand hours in the dark, with the inevitable result that I think I now know a lot about movies. What that means, at its most superficial, is that I can have those nostalgic dialogues with other film buffs (some of whom don't even speak English!) which consist mostly of movie titles, sighs, raised eyebrows. It also means that I have the privilege of feeling alienated at a dinner party when the conversation turns to film, and I get to squirm silently in the presence of middlebrow wisdom that attacks Jerry Lewis or Clint Eastwood while overpraising the latest *Masterpiece Theatre* type adaptation—silently, because it would take too long to explain my premises, and in the end, they would only think me perverse.

When it comes to movies, everyone regards himself as an

expert. With reason: 1) the average adult has seen thousands of motion pictures, and 2) mass entertainment promotion reassures the audience that no special expertise is required to appreciate its product. In most cases that is even true. Nonetheless, I am convinced that it adds another level of depth, or dimension, to the appreciation of a film if one knows the conventions surrounding the genre, the stylistic tics of the director, the past performances of some actors and how their present role stretches or constricts them, something about the historical context in which the story takes place, the main attributes of the national cinema which this work represents, the technologies of lighting or film stock or screen ratio available to the filmmakers at the time.

I have often been asked: "Doesn't it *ruin* the experience of simply enjoying the film, to be thinking about all that?" No: surprisingly not. Or perhaps I am so used to being detached that I no longer experience that division as negative. When the plot in *Vertigo* turns romantic, and the camera starts swimming around Kim Novak and James Stewart like a happy fish, I swoon into the arc, wanting it never to end, at the same time knowing this particular sequence was filmed with a turntable, etc. Rightly or wrongly, I believe myself to have developed a sixth sense about composition and framing, and I take an extra pleasure when it seems to me the camera has been placed at the best possible vantage point for a scene. Conversely, I will start to bail out on a film, even before its plot elements turn banal, if the cutting looks choppy or the color murky or the approach to camera movement inconsistent. No one is minding the store; there is no artist at the helm.

Part of the reason I write about movies is to try to articulate some of these flickering judgments, which are so difficult to put into words. The bigger reason I write about movies, I suppose, is simply that I am a writer. I write about the things I care about: cities, friendship, family life, books and films.

Many artists develop a strong, aficionado's interest in another medium (such as Mondrian's for jazz), allowing its contrasting and comparable elements to cast an illuminating sidelight on their careers. Ironically, I have written much more about movies than about my own artistic practice, literature. I think the reason is that I can be more tolerant and catholic in my cinematic tastes, where a competing aesthetic isn't as much of a challenge. If a writer's style doesn't interest me, or I find his mind irritating, I am likely to put down the book quickly, thinking, "This guy has nothing to teach me." On the other hand, I may stick around to watch a film by an equally off-putting sensibility; after all, it's only an hour and a half, I can let my mind wander. If my mind starts to wander when I'm reading a book, I don't get very far.

It's not easy to write about movies. (I'm not complaining, just stating a fact.) Every frame is packed with a million dots of visual information, and the images keep changing. How do you do justice to the acting, cinematography, screenplay, directing—and say something not only about this particular film, but how it fits into a larger pattern of the filmmaker's/actor's/scriptwriter's/cinematographer's career, as well as the genre, the historical period, the *Zeitgeist?*

You start to recount the story—you've got to tell some of the plot—and pretty soon you're swamped by the way one scene leads to another, and it all seems *indicative* of this amazing wholeness which keeps eluding your powers of description. If it's a bad movie you can be curtly dismissive; but if it's one you admire, you can easily get lost in admiration of the way each little detail of form and content reinforces the general effect, so that the piece you write can end up taking longer to read than watching the movie itself. You're in danger of smothering a movie with your appreciation: a subtle form of murder, the critic enviously trying to displace the creator with more and more refined commentary. Best to launch a quick, bold attack—get in, get out—summarizing like a lyric poem the essence of your yearning to encapsulate the loved one's personality, while always guiltily aware that so much has been left unsaid.

This book is, in part, an attempt to capture the variety of different approaches to writing about movies—the straight review, the mosaic of fragments, the diary, the letter, the interview, the short story, the reflective genre study, the memoir piece, the biographical essay—which I, sometimes with my back to the wall, have been driven to employ. It's a variety that itself is testimony to a kind of dilettantish stance. Put bluntly, I'm not really a professional film critic. Though I've written on the subject for movie journals, newspapers and general magazines, I have never held a regular post, one that would offer the opportunity to comment on every major release but also oblige me to review movies for which I had no feeling (such as *E.T.* or *Star Wars*). The result is that I've tended to write where my somewhat arty cinematic interests took me, or where they converged sufficiently with the needs of a harried editor.

This makes me both an outsider and an insider in the film-critic world—a unique, and, I hope, useful vantage point. I am an outsider in two respects, being neither a "regular" film critic nor an academic scholar. Indeed, the field of film theory has grown so specialized in the past thirty years that I've gone from being one of the cognoscenti to a rank amateur. I'm sure that many film professors, exposed to the contents of this book, would smile disdainfully at its impressionistic naïveté, its lack of a systematic relationship to theory. It isn't that I'm opposed to film theory; actually, I've read lots of it, and even been quite stimulated by it (when I wasn't bored silly), but I can't seem to make it a permanent part of my brain.

Beyond that, I've already developed my own style of writing and it's too late to change. In that sense, the volume you hold in your hands may bear more of a family resemblance to my three previous personal essay collections than to a standard work of film criticism. Those collections of mine were an attempt to write a discontinuous memoir in the form of personal essays. I see the present collection as another disguised autobiography: the story of my adult life, indirectly reflected by my obsession with one constant, the movies. The italicized afterthoughts I've attached to many of the pieces often try to uncover the personal thread behind these writings about film.

The book is autobiographical, too, in another crucial sense: the accidents of personal history that inform my movie biases play such a large part. One reason I didn't try to become a regular film critic was that I could never convince myself that my take on a picture was necessarily correct, or should become universally adopted: I was all too aware of how the peculiarities of my social background—that I come from a working-class (eventually lower-middle-class) urban Jewish household, was born during World War II, have three siblings, went to college in the early 1960s (the *auteur* era), that my autodidact father spoke highly of Stroheim's *Greed*, that my mother is dark-haired and I tend to be most moved by brunettes onscreen and in life (were she a blonde, I might have devoted myself as passionately to Scandinavian cinema as I did to Japanese)—all subconsciously shape or warp my appreciation of a film.

Finally, the book is autobiographical in the sense that it reflects the changes I have gone through, emotionally and physically, over the years. When I was a young man I could be more easily seduced by the pure sensuousness of the visual: give me an Ophulsian camera movement and you had me in your pocket. Later, these blandishments affected me less, partly because a whole younger generation of Hollywood filmmakers came to power who had technique galore, who were masters of the gratuitously gorgeous shot, but whose knowledge of human nature sometimes seemed painfully thin. Over the years (perhaps because I wrote a few myself), I have become increasingly attuned to the screenplay: the language in the dialogue, the construction of plot and character. Now, when I watch a movie, I can almost imagine I am reading along, as though the text of the script were superimposed over the images. And what I want—and am often stymied in getting—is complexity, wit, nuance.

I remember once reading a piece by Manny Farber (there never was a better American film critic) about Jean-Luc Godard, in which he seemed to be taking Godard to task for some callow viewpoint. Besotted as I was with Godard, I found it hard to imagine a perch from which anyone could look down and judge such a world-genius as immature. I have now arrived at that perch: it is called middle age. I too have become impatient with callow flash: I have a hard time accepting Leonardo di Caprio in *Titanic* as a mature male lead, and the picture's stale, silly dialogue gets on my nerves— never was there a greater disjunction between elegance of visuals and inelegance of language. Again, when I left the theater after seeing *Pulp Fiction*, I thought to myself, "Clever lad. . . . I'd like to check in on him ten years from now when he's learned something about real life." (As it happened, I couldn't wait, and saw his very next film, *Jackie Brown*, which I loved! Who would have expected from Tarantino a film about a tender relationship between a fifty-six-year-old man and a forty-four-year-old woman?)

One of the life experiences that has most affected my moviegoing sensibilities was being appointed to the New York Film Festival selection committee. This was as "insider" as you can get: there must have been some critics around town who were miffed at being passed over for the honor by a non-regular, but overall, the community of film curators and writers embraced me warmly. In four years I saw at least a thousand art films, went to film festivals like Cannes and Berlin, talked the talk, buzzed the buzz, and learned to trust none of my predispositions. As a lay film buff, I never understood how the NYFF could have the nerve, the gall to reject the latest movie by a major filmmaker such as Godard, Rohmer, Fellini, Satyajit Ray, Angelopoulos, Makavejev, Chantal Akerman. As a member of the committee, I found myself voting against all these titans—when the film in question was weak. So much for auteurism. Being on the selection committee helped to broaden my grasp of world cinema, especially those works from corners of the globe that had hitherto seemed dark corners, such as Iran, Taiwan, South Korea, Burkina Faso. Nowadays I look forward to the latest movie by Iran's Abbas Kiarostami or Taiwan's Hou Hsiao-Hsien with as much excitement as I do the newest French picture by Maurice Pialat or André Téchiné. None of the aforementioned, I realize, are household names; but that is more the result of the decline of film culture and foreign film distribution in this country than the fault of these directors. The important point is that there are still brilliant filmmakers, in America as well as abroad, and there are still mature, engrossing, surprising, essential films being made. I remain a happy captive of the movie screen.

MEMORIES

ANTICIPATION OF *LA NOTTE:*
The "Heroic" Age of Moviegoing

One has to guard against the tendency to think of one's youth as a time when the conversations were brighter, the friends truer and the movies better. I am quite willing to let go of the first two, but it does seem to have been my luck to have come of age during a period of phenomenal cinematic creativity. I like to think of the early sixties as the "heroic" age of moviegoing, if one can call heroic an activity that consists of sitting on one's bum and letting one's thoughts be guided by a parade of cinematic sensations.

It was in 1959, while a junior in high school, that my craving for celluloid and my avocation as a film buff began. Certainly I had always liked going to movies; my parents had sent us off, when we were children, to the neighborhood double feature every Saturday morning. But the notion of motion pictures as an art form only struck me when I was about fifteen. I bought Arthur Knight's survey, *The Liveliest Art*, and went about in my thorough, solemn way trying to see every movie listed in the index. One thing that attracted me to film history was that it was relatively short, conquerable, compared to other artistic fields. The Thalia theater's repertory schedule became my summer school catalogue that year, and I checked off nearly everything as a must-see, still happily unable to distinguish beforehand between the worth of an *M* and a *Captain from Koepenick.*

I went so far as to subscribe to a series of Russian silent films at the Kaufman–92nd Street Y, defiantly attending *Earth* the night before an important exam. But Dovzhenko's poetic style put me to sleep; even now I have only to picture waving wheat and apple-cheeked, laughing peasants for my eyes to start to close.

In my last two years of high school I was restless and used film showings as a pretext to get out of Brooklyn, away from my family, and explore the city. The 92nd Street Y, the Sutton, and the Beekman introduced me to the posh East Side; the Art and the 8th Street Theater were my ports of entry to Greenwich Village; I learned the Upper West Side from the Thalia and the New Yorker. It was a Flaherty revival at Columbia University that first gave me the idea, walking through the campus afterward, to apply there for admission.

Sometimes a film club ad would lead me to some church basement in Chelsea, to watch an old Murnau or Preston Sturges, projected by a noisy Bell & Howell set up on a chair in the back of a rec room. Often I was the youngest member of that film addict crowd, whose collective appearance made me wonder what I was getting myself into. They were predominately male, lower middle class, with the burdened look of having come straight from work with their rolled-up *New York Posts* and ink-stained trousers; they had indoor faces with pendulous eye bags, sharp noses ready to sniff out the shoddy, and physiques that seemed at once undernourished in some parts and plump in others, the result of hasty delicatessen meals snatched before screenings. They looked like widowers or young men who had never known love—this was the fraternity I was about to join. Some seemed abnormally shy; they would arrive a few minutes early and sit as far away from everyone else as they could; at "The End" they would leave without a word. Occasionally, one of the old, bald-headed veterans would engage me gregariously in spasmodic conversation—an exchange of film titles, punctuated with superlatives, snorts, complaints about the projection or the sight lines—and I would come away touched by his kindness for having talked to an ignorant kid like me, and perhaps for this reason would feel sorry for him.

Whether the film had been glorious or dull barely mattered, so long as I could cross it off my list. The development of a taste of any sort requires plodding through the overrated as well as uncovering the sublime. If the movie had been genuinely great, I would leave the screening place inspired and pleasantly conscious of my isolation, and wander the streets for a while before taking the subway home. I came to love the way the gray city streets looked after a movie, the cinematic blush they seemed to wear. When the film had been a disappointment—well then, all the more was it a joy to get back the true world, with its variety and uncanny compositions.

At Columbia, I discovered the general appetite for films was much higher than it had been at my high school; even the average student was willing to experiment with difficult fare. I remember going down to the Village one Friday night with a bunch of other dateless freshmen to see Kurosawa's *Ikiru*, part of a memorable season of Japanese premieres. Before the movie, just to get in the mood, we ate cross-legged on the floor at a Japanese restaurant. I adored *Ikiru*, with its perversely slow framing scene of the wake and its heart-wrenching flashbacks; but it also meant a lot to be sitting before it in a row of studious boys who I hoped would remain moviegoing friends. My own gang, as in *I Vitelloni*—except it didn't happen with this bunch. It took a while before I found my real film companions.

From time to time, film criticism would appear in the *Columbia Daily Spectator* by an upperclassman, James Stoller.

His articles were so stylistically mature and so informed that they seemed to me to be written by a professional quarterly critic rather than a college student. I developed an intellectual crush on this Stoller: if his opinion differed from mine, I would secretly revise my own. I had been, for example, avoiding Satyajit Ray's films because their packaging suggested what Andrew Sarris called "dull UNESCO cinema." But Stoller wrote that the *Apu* trilogy was great, so I went, and he was right.

Finally I decided I had to meet James Stoller. Palms sweating, I summoned the courage to call his room from the phone downstairs in his dormitory. I explained that I was a fellow film lover. Could I stop by sometime and talk with him? Sure, come on up, he said.

It shocked me to see the great critic living in so tiny and shabby a room: a double-decker bed; a narrow desk, which he shared with his roommate; a single chair; and books. We had no place to sit but the lower bunk bed. It always surprised me—having come from a ghetto—that parts of Columbia should look so seedy and run-down. I suppose I was expecting the Ivy League to be a step upward.

Stoller himself gave an impression of fastidious hesitation and social awkwardness. I had come prepared to play the role of the freshman ignoramus and so was puzzled when he reacted incredulously to my praise of his articles, retreating into a modest shrug. When I asked if he had been yet to Michelangelo Antonioni's *L'Avventura*, the *cause célèbre* that had just opened and which I was dying to see, he said he had, and fell silent. "Well, what did you think of it?" I prodded, expecting him to erupt with the equivalent of one of his articles. "It's—terrific, I guess, I'm not sure, I need to watch it a few more times. . . . Go see for yourself." He was uncomfortable being put on the spot.

I rushed to see *L'Avventura*. It was the movie I had been preparing for, and it came at the right time in my development. As a child, I had wanted only action movies. Dialogues and story setups bored me; I waited for that moment when the knife was hurled through the air. My awakening in adolescence to the art of film consisted precisely in overcoming this impatience. Overcompensating, perhaps; I now loved a cinema that dawdled, that lingered. Antonioni had a way of following characters with a pan shot, letting them exit and keeping the camera on the depopulated landscape. With his detachment from the human drama and his tactful spying on objects and backgrounds, he forced me to disengage as well, and to concentrate on the purity of his technique. Of course the story held me, too, with its bitter, world-weary, disillusioned tone. The adolescent wants to touch bottom, to know the worst. His soul craves sardonic disenchantment.

I rushed back to Stoller, now ready to discuss the film. He listened patiently and with quiet amusement to my enthusiasm. Indeed, this turned out to be our pattern: I, more ignorant but more voluble, would babble on, while he would offer an occasional objection or refinement. It was only by offering up chatter that I could get him to correct my misconceptions and to educate me cinematically.

This was not yet the era of film appreciation courses. Nor would we have dreamed of taking any offered; it was a point of pride to gather on our own the knowledge of our beloved, semiunderground subject, like the teenage garage-band aficionados of today.

Stoller introduced me to his friend Nicholas Zill, a film-obsessed sophomore, and we soon became a trio. Zill was a mischievous, intelligent boy of Russian Orthodox background who was given to sudden animated inspirations. The three of us took long walks together in the Columbia neighborhood, leapfrogging in our conversation from one film to another. Once, coming to a dead stop on the sidewalk, Zill asked me in horror, "You mean you haven't seen *Diary of a Country Priest?*" At such moments I felt like the baby of the group.

Zill and I both shared a zest for the grotesque, or what has been somewhat ponderously called "convulsive cinema," "the cinema of cruelty." I must say, these predilections were kept to the level of aesthetic appreciation; in our daily lives we were squeamishly decent, even if Zill, a psychology major, seemed to like cutting up rats. Nothing pleased us more than to talk about the beggars' orgy in *Viridiana*, or the maiming finale in *Freaks*, or choice bits in *Psycho*. We would go on in this perverse vein until Stoller was forced to remonstrate (which was probably why we did it). Stoller always championed the humane, the tender, the generous, and domestically observant moviemakers: Renoir, Ophuls, Truffaut, Satyajit Ray, Cukor, Borzage. It was typical for a powerless student like me to be drawn to Buñuelian fantasies of surrealist immorality and Raskolnikovian license. Much rarer was it to find balanced humanity in a nineteen-year-old, like Stoller. If I have come around over the years to his point of view, at the time I was looking for antisocial shivers, sliced eyeballs.

Nick Zill wanted to make movies—as I suppose we all did—but he went further in imagining bizarre film scenarios. He had already shot a film in high school, I remember it only as a disorganized romp of him chasing pretty girls, or was it pretty girls chasing him? In any case, he had registered an organization called Filmmakers of Columbia with the Campus Activities Office, so as to be able to borrow equipment and accept university funds should one of his projects ever get going. Filmmakers of Columbia existed only on paper; there were no meetings, even the title was pure wish fulfillment. As it happened, there *were* a number of "isolated" Columbia filmmakers (i.e., not in our circle) around, the most notable being young Brian De Palma. We did not know whether to consider De Palma's hammy experimental shorts like *Wotan's Wake* intentional or unintentional jokes, but we agreed that he had no future as a film director and that he was not a seriously knowledgeable, rigorous *cinéaste* like ourselves.

•   •   •

Sometimes I would go over to my friends' rooms and pass the time looking through their film magazine collections. Stills on glossy periodical stock particularly fascinated me. To stare at a shot from *Gilda*, say, with Rita Hayworth in her sheath dress before a palm-treed nightclub stand, was to enter a fantasy as satisfyingly complete, in its own way, as having seen the movie. A single frame, snatched from twenty-three others per second, is not intended to possess the self-complete wholeness of an art photograph, but for that very reason it evokes more the dream of continuing motion. Stills from the silent era, with their gestural intensity and powder-white ingenues' faces; soft-lit glamour shots from the thirties; the harsh key lighting and seamy locales of the forties—all were infinitely suggestive of the way the reigning fashions, film stock, decor, directorial style, and technology blended to produce a characteristic period image.

The desultory quality of these browsing sessions showed we were perhaps not so far removed from that age when we'd collected comic books and baseball cards. The point was not to read the articles straight through (one could always go back for that), but to be splashed by a sea of information: film festival roundups, news of film productions, historical rediscoveries. By leafing through these magazines together we shared a mood of sweet latency, imagining the films we had in store, like provincials dreaming of life in the capital. Cinema was a wave originating elsewhere, which we waited to break over us. This waiting had something to do with the nature of adolescence itself; it also reflected the resurgence of European films at the time.

To be young and in love with films in the early 1960s was to participate in what felt like an international youth movement. We in New York were following and, in a sense, mimicking the cafe arguments in Paris, London and Rome, where the cinema had moved, for a brief historical movement, to the center of intellectual discourse, in the twilight of existentialism and before the onslaught of structuralism.

In retrospect, I may have undervalued the American studio films of the early sixties. At the time, having just lived through the Eisenhower fifties, I was impatient with what seemed to me the bland industrial style of most Hollywood movies (then symbolized by the much-maligned Doris Day); I could spot Art much more easily in foreign films, with their stylized codes of realism (sex, boredom, class conflict, unhappy endings) and their arty disjunctive texture. It took a certain sophistication, which I did not yet have, to appreciate the ironies behind the smooth-crafted surfaces of the best Hollywood genre movies. Our heroes in the French New Wave explicitly credited Hollywood films with the inspiration for their own personal styles, of course, but I accepted this taste partly as a whimsical paradox on their part without really sharing it, except in the case of rebels like Samuel Fuller or Frank Tashlin, whose shock tactics made them "almost" European.

Sometimes, instead of studying, I would end up in the film section of the college library poring over books on movies by writers like Béla Balasz, Raymond Spottiswoode, Siegfried Kracauer, Hortense Powdermaker—even their names were irresistible. Or I would struggle through the latest *Cahiers du Cinéma* in the periodicals section. As if my French were not imperfect enough, the *Cahiers* critics confounded me further with their profundity-mongering style, rarely passing a simple judgment without at the same time alluding to Hegel. I was never sure that I fully understood anything in *Cahiers*, except for the interviews with salty old Hollywood directors, and the rating system, with stars like a Michelin guide: ** *à voir,* *** *à voir absolument,* and a black dot • for *abominable.*

Sight and Sound was a breeze in comparison, although I was ashamed to admit to my friends how much I got from the

English journal. It was considered stodgy and rearguard, perhaps because it was the official organ of the British Film Institute, but probably more because it took issue with *Cahiers du Cinéma*'s *auteur* line—and we were deeply devoted auteurists. (I am using this term as shorthand for a critical approach recognizing the director as the main artist of a film, and looking at the body of a director's work for stylistic consistencies.)

I hesitate to raise a last-ditch defense of the *auteur* theory, so tattered has its flag become in recent years. Suffice to say that I remain loyal to the ideals of my youth. Say what you may against the *auteur* theory, it was good for adolescents: it gave us a system, and—more important—it gave us marching directions; it encouraged hero worship; it argued for the triumphant signature of selfhood in the face of conformist threats; it made clear distinctions between good and bad; and it blew the raspberry at pious sentiment.

Andrew Sarris's auteurist breakdown of American directors, which first appeared as a special issue of *Film Culture*, spring 1963, influenced us deeply partly because of its ruthlessly hierarchical ranking system: Pantheon Directors, Second Line, Likable But Elusive, Esoterica, Less Than Meets the Eye, and that most sinisterly fascinating of categories, Fallen Idols. It was here we learned to curl our lips at respected names like Fred Zinnemann, David Lean and Stanley Kramer—liberal directors whose hearts and themes may have been in the right place but whose earnestly conventional handling of *mise en scène* seemed unforgivable.

Ah, *mise en scène!* That camera style that favored flowing tracking shots and pans, wide angles and continuous takes; that followed characters up staircases and from room to room, capturing with rich detail their surroundings: the unfolding-scroll aesthetic of Mizoguchi, Ophuls, Murnau, Dreyer, Welles, Renoir and Rossellini. Not only did this style seem deeper and more beautiful because it allowed more of a spiritual, contemplative feeling to accumulate than the rapid montage style, it was, if you bought all the arguments (and I did), more ethical. Why? Because it was less "manipulative." It offered the viewer the "freedom" to choose what to pay attention to in a long shot, like a theater spectator, rather than forcing the point with a close-up detail. The deep-focus style could also be seen as sympathetic to a progressive, left-wing political view, because it linked the characters inextricably to their social contexts. In retrospect, some of these claims seem contradictory, a result, perhaps, of the admirable critic André Bazin's need to reconcile his own Catholicism and Marxism and film tastes, however farfetched the synthesis. There also seems something curiously puritanical about the austere aesthetic of refraining from making cuts—something finally self-defeating, as well, since movies will always be assembled from pieces of spliced film.*

Nevertheless, I was so impressed by the style of slow cutting that each time a shot, having started to build up a pleasurable suspense in me, was broken by what seemed to me a "premature" cut to change the angle, I would wince, as if personally nicked. Watching television at home with my parents, during a filmed series like *Maverick*, I would call out the cuts, just to prove my thesis that the editing followed a predictable metronomic pattern of one shot every four seconds or so. Threatened with bodily harm if I kept up this obnoxious routine, I maintained the practice silently in my head.

It would infuriate me when the *Times*'s critic, Bosley Crowther (our favorite arch-Philistine), based his argument solely on content without saying a word about a film's visual style. How could he reject a film because he found the characters unsympathetic, or because of its "controversial" treat-

---

*This antagonism toward montage was carried to extremes by the auteurist *New York Film Bulletin*, which swore that it would trade all of Eisenstein for any one sequence in a Stanley Donen musical.

ment of violence, organized religion, sexuality? Clearly, the real ethical questions were things like: Why did the director cheat with so many reaction shots? Why that gloopy slow-motion sequence?

For a certain kind of youth, the accumulation of taste becomes the crucible of self, the battleground on which character is formed. I must mention how much we hated Ingmar Bergman. Although his films had done more than anyone else's to build an audience for art films, his own popularity condemned him in our eyes: he was the darling of the suburbs and the solemn bourgeoisie who ate up the academic symbolism of *Wild Strawberries*. I once debated a fellow student for six hours because he called *The Seventh Seal* a great movie. Now I have come to love certain Bergman films (especially the early ones, like *Monika* and *Illicit Interlude*), but then, no, impossible. It was precisely because Bergman was so much an *auteur*, but not "our kind," that he posed such a threat. Like political radicals who reserve their greatest passion for denouncing liberals, we had to differentiate ourselves from the Bergmanites.

Our man was Godard. His disruptive jump cuts and anarcho-classical sensibility spoke directly to our impatient youth. Belmondo in *Breathless* was our heroic mouthpiece, whether talking to the camera or lying on the pavement: underneath that fierce hoodlum's exterior we recognized a precocious, wounded film addict. With their cinematic self-referentiality, Godard's films showed me my brothers, those equally unhappy captives of shadows. I confess I also found solace in Godard's portraits of women as either fickle betrayers or masochistic victims, which dovetailed nicely with my own adolescent fears of the opposite sex.

Even when Godard seemed momentarily to flirt with the Right, this didn't bother me. At the time I was fairly apolitical: one should not confuse the early sixties with the late. By 1968, the students at Columbia would have more important things to argue about than the merits of Gerd Oswald's *Screaming Mimi*. But in 1960–64, our politics *were* the *politique des auteurs*. We looked for our morality in form: "The angles are the director's thoughts; the lighting is his philosophy" (Douglas Sirk).

It may seem arrogant to identify more with the directorial/camera viewpoint than with the protagonists', but that was precisely what the *auteur* theory encouraged us to do. Besides, if I could take the position of "I am a camera," this identification had less to do with superiority and more with fear and shyness, that shyness which in adolescence cooks up to pure alienation. If I went to a party, I would pretend to be filming it because I was too timid to approach the girls I liked. In classrooms where the professor droned on, I would escape by thinking, "Where would I place the camera if I were making a documentary of this?" Always my camera would start well back from the action, not only because of a preference for the long-shot aesthetic, but also because I felt so far apart from the vital center of life. Around this time I even had a dream in which I was directing a movie sequence inside a greenhouse: I was sitting behind the camera on a mechanical dolly, and I kept calling for the camera to be pulled farther and farther back, against the technicians' murmured warnings, until finally I crashed through the glass. Had I been perceptive, the dream might have warned me that I was on the edge of losing control; instead, I accepted it as a satisfying omen that I was going to become a film director.

It is a truism that moviegoing can become a substitute for living. Not that I regret one hour spent watching movies, then or now, since the habit persists to this day, but I would not argue either if someone wanted to maintain that chronic moviegoing often promotes a passivity before life, a detached tendency to aestheticize reality, and, I suppose, a narcissistic absorption that makes it harder to contact others. "Only connect," people were fond of quoting Forster at the time. For me, "connect" meant synchronizing my watch with the film schedules around town.

Often I would cut classes to catch an afternoon matinee at one of the little art houses in the Carnegie Hall area. Putting my feet up in the half-empty theater during intermission, I would listen in on the conversation of the blue-haired matinee dowagers: "I couldn't make head or tails of that movie the other day!" "I'm glad you said that. And they don't need to show such explicit stuff onscreen." Many an afternoon I shared with those old ladies, wondering what they were making of the capricious, Hitchcockian 360-degree tracking shots in, say, Chabrol's *Leda*. Or I would roam around Times Square, up and down 42nd Street (then a mecca of cinema gold, both foreign and domestic), enjoying the reverse chic of seeing a sacred Melville, Franju, Walsh, Losey or Preminger film in such sordid surroundings.

In retrospect, the mystery to me is, how did I pay for all those movies? Even taking into consideration student discounts, early-bird specials and the fact that movies were so much cheaper then, I must have spent a good part of my food money on tickets. But at least I could keep up with Stoller and Zill.

Nick Zill had been living in a railroad flat on West 106th Street, along with three other roommates. Since one of Nick's roommates worked in an art film distribution company, he was able to bring sixteen-millimeter prints home to screen. The first time Nick invited me over for a screening in their living room, I stumbled over bodies and wine bottles to find a space on the floor. The idea of being part of a small, "invited" group watching a bona fide rare movie, Renoir's *La Marseillaise*, was heaven. I had been infected early on by the mystique of the lost, the rare, the archival film; one had only to advertise a movie as "forgotten" and I could barely stay away.

Like an epicure dreaming of delicacies he has never tasted, I would fantasize being elected President just so I could order a screening in the White House den of Visconti's *Ossessione* (then tied up in litigation) or Eisenstein's *Bezhin Meadow,* or all of Louise Brooks's films, or that Holy Grail of *cinéastes,* the eight-hour *Greed.* And here I was, ensconced in a similar lucky place, the very hardness of Nick's wooden floor a mark of privilege. Most of the West 106th Street audience had a less reverential attitude, drawn simply by the lure of a free movie.

When Nick told me he was moving, and that I could take over his room if I wanted, I jumped at the chance to become a resident member of the West 106th Street film club. Perhaps I should have thought twice about it. In this dilapidated tenement building, which the city has since torn down, the rooms were so dark and closetlike that Zill once used one for a sensory deprivation experiment, locking his younger brother in and covering the windows. My own room looked out on a brick wall, and its only light source was a naked bulb that hung from the ceiling like a noose.

I mention the squalor of our living conditions because it seems somehow connected to the movie hunger. Not only did the silver screen offer a glamorous escape, it sometimes did just the opposite, held up a black-and-white mirror to our grainy, bleakly uncolorful lives. One found romantic confirmation in the impoverished locations of Italian neorealist and French New Wave pictures. If the hero in *Diary of a Country Priest* (which I had since seen) could die in a humble room like mine, the shadows forming a cross on the cracked walls above his pallet, then my own barren walls were somehow blessed, poeticized.

Do what I might, however, I was unable to find more than a few moments a week of daily life charged with that poetic transcendence I had come to expect from the movies. I wanted life to have the economy and double meaning of art.

But more often I simply felt torn by a harsh, banal pain that had no cinematic equivalent. As the unhappiness increased, I began, almost in mechanical response, to think of killing myself.

If I reflect back to what brought on this crisis, I have to admit that it all feels very remote by now; I am no longer the teenager I once was; every cell in my body has since changed, biologically if not cognitively. Still, I can try to piece together the reasons. Some of my pain, I suspect, came from the fact that I had been a "star" in high school, while my first year at Columbia, surrounded by other high school stars, plunged me into such anonymity as to make me misplace all sense of self-worth. Too, I was living on my own for the first time. Though I had run away from home, I think I felt "abandoned" by the ease with which my parents had let me go. They were too financially strapped to help me, and I was wearing myself out at odd jobs while studying full time. In the process I managed to lose forty pounds: a six-footer, I had gone from 165 pounds to a gaunt 125, as though trying to prove, against my own assertions of independence, that I was unable to take care of myself properly. Malnutrition may have affected my mental outlook more than I realized; in any event, I began to feel utterly hopeless and tired with life. I saw patterns of despair everywhere: in the street, in the sky. The arguing and drug taking of my roommates filled me with distress, contempt and self-contempt for failing to forgive them. The urge to destroy myself took on an autonomous momentum and ironclad logic of its own. In retrospect, I was suffering from a kind of disease of logic, predicated on an overestimation of my reasoning powers; another way of putting it is that I was living entirely in my head.

Some of my unhappiness had to do with virginity. I was unable to break through to women—not only sexually but on all levels—to ask them for the least human companionship. Going to Columbia (an all-male school at the time), and immersed in this milieu of latent homosexuality, which was threatening my identity in its own way, I was frightened of women yet filled with yearning for them. It pained me even to see lovers taking liberties on the screen. Movies, saturated with the sensual, mocked me by their constant reminder that I was only a spectator.

At the same time, movies helped push me deeper into a monastic avoidance of the body. In the cinematic postulant, there is an ascetic element that exists, paradoxically, side by side with the worship of beauty: a tendency to equate the act of watching a film with praying.* One day I was at my job at the library, cataloguing book slips, when, light-headed with overwork and lack of sleep, I heard someone address me from behind. "Are you a Benedictine?" I turned around and no one was there. It seemed I had had an auditory hallucination, but even if I had merely overheard a scrap of conversation, I was spooked by the sense that someone was mocking me, unmasking my shameful monkish nature.

In Godard's *Masculin-Féminin* there is a scene with the hero, Paul (Jean-Pierre Léaud), sitting in a movie theater watching a Swedish film. On the sound track are his thoughts: "This wasn't the film we'd dreamed of. This wasn't the total film that each of us carried within himself . . . the film that we wanted to make or, more secretly, no doubt, that we wanted to live." Paul's confusion between movies and reality, his yearning for an alternate existence, his absorption of all the social distress and pain around him and his inability to connect with women, driving his chic girlfriend away with his gloomy overseriousness, add up to the fate of many Godard heroes: suicide. Unless I am mistaken, suicide was in the air,

---

*Years ago, the Anthology Film Archives even constructed a Temple of Cinema in which each seat was separated from its neighbors by a black partition, not unlike a stiffened monk's cowl, which made contact with one's companion nigh impossible and forced the viewer into solitary contemplation of the mysteries.

in the cinematic culture of the early sixties; perhaps it was no more than a facile narrative solution for movies made by young men who were fond of indulging their existential self-pity. In any event, I fell right in with the mood.

Between screenings of Vigo's *L'Atalante* and *Zéro de Conduite* at West 106th Street, I told my older brother that I was thinking of killing myself. Distressed, he counseled patience, but it was too late to listen. Vigo's dream of a man and a woman drifting down the Seine in a houseboat, touching each other, seemed insultingly unreachable.

A few nights later I swallowed twenty sleeping pills with the aid of a quart of Tropicana orange juice. I had already written a suicide note with quotes from Paul Goodman and Freud—I can laugh at it now—and I lay down to die in my sleep. But stomach pains kept me awake: the beef stew I had eaten earlier at Columbia's dining hall (it is that wretched institutional food I have to thank for being alive today) and the acidic orange juice refused to digest. After an hour's uncomfortable attempt to ignore the stomach and think easeful, morbid thoughts, I leaned over the side of my bed and vomited—whole chunks of beef stew and carrots in a pool of orange juice. Then I called out to my roommates and told them what I had done. They rushed me to St. Luke's Hospital, where my stomach was pumped—so unpleasant but revivifying an experience that when the resident asked me in the middle of it why I had tried to do myself in, I was unable to think of a single reply. I stayed in the hospital's psychiatric ward for two weeks.

The afternoon I was released, my brother met me at the hospital and we went straight downtown to see a double bill at the Bleecker Street Cinema: *Grand Illusion* and *Paths of Glory*. Still movie-hungry after a two-week drought—or else piggishly overindulgent, like a tonsillitis patient demanding all the ice cream he can eat—I insisted we race uptown to see *Zazie dans le Métro*, the Malle film that Stoller had praised in a recent review. What an orgy! I had gotten suicide out of my system, but not cinema.

I must backtrack a little. Before the suicide attempt, at the beginning of my sophomore year, Stoller, Zill and I had agreed that Filmmakers of Columbia should run its own film series at the college, both to show movies we wanted to see and to raise money for future productions. Zill had surprised me by proposing that I be made president of the organization. Granted, his fear of being held fiscally responsible for our new venture may have had something to do with offering me this honor, but I accepted it with pride.

We began sending away for film rental catalogues and, when they arrived, poring over them like kids let loose in a candy store. We were free to order any movie we wanted to see, provided it was available in sixteen millimeter—and provided we occasionally considered commercial factors. It might be interesting, for instance, to rent all of the Brandon catalogue's Eastern European arcana, but if nobody came to *Ghetto Terezin* or *Border Street*, we would still have to shell out the seventy-five dollars' rental. The decision was made to balance our schedule with obscurities like Griffith's *Abraham Lincoln* and *Border Street* on the one hand, and moneymakers like Hitchcock's *Notorious* and *Rock Around the Clock* on the other. We booked the films, wrote the blurbs, ground out a flyer and held our breaths.

Nick called me at the hospital, unable to believe, among other things, that I had attempted suicide two weeks before the opening of our Filmmakers of Columbia series. Shouldn't that have been enough to live for? No, I insisted stubbornly. Nevertheless, I got swept up immediately and fortunately into the venture, making business phone calls from the psychiatric ward while Zill and Stoller ran around town distributing flyers.

The first night of the film series drew a sellout crowd for Kurosawa's *Drunken Angel* and Kenneth Anger's *Fireworks* (a homoerotic short that had not been seen in New York for many years). I was so excited counting the money we made that I couldn't watch the movies. The next day, the dean called me into his office and told me he had heard about *Fireworks*, and to "keep it clean from now on."

A happier period began for me. Stoller introduced me to a woman named Abby, and we started going out together. Though the affair lasted only three months, it served its purpose. I also began writing film reviews for the *Columbia Daily Spectator* and stories for *Columbia Review*, the literary magazine, and no longer felt so neglected on campus. Moreover, the film series was a big hit, and was to continue successfully for years—helping to put me through college, in fact. Susan Sontag, who was then a religion professor at Columbia and already a force in the New York cultural life—especially to us *cinéastes*—gave her blessing to the series by periodically attending. Stoller and Zill gradually withdrew from the activity, although they continued to offer programming suggestions. And Jim Stoller provided one of our most memorable evenings by agreeing, after lengthy persuasion, to play piano behind Pabst's *The Love of Jeanne Ney*; it was a treat to see him overcome his compulsive modesty and perform in public.

We were all waiting impatiently for the sequel to *L'Avventura. La Notte* was said to feature a dream cast of Jeanne Moreau, Marcello Mastroianni and Monica Vitti. Meanwhile, the art theaters kept our excitement at a boil by showing some of Antonioni's early films, like *Il Grido* and *Le Amiche*, which only deepened our admiration for our own "Michelangelo."

By the time the first ads appeared announcing the premiere of *La Notte*, I had worked myself into such a fit of anticipation that my unconscious mind jumped the gun: I began dreaming, for several nights in a row, preview versions of *La Notte*. When I finally saw it, the film became a normal extension of my dream life. Several of us went on opening night, waiting in line for an hour for tickets. I was with Carol Bergman, a Barnard girl whom I'd fallen in love with (and would marry a year later), and I held her throughout the film, perhaps undercutting the full impact of Antonioni's despondent message. It was great to see an Antonioni movie through the comfortable bifocals of being in love; when one is happy, one can look at both comedy and tragedy with equanimity.

Primed to adore *La Notte*, I did. Especially the ending, with the camera pulling away from Moreau and Mastroianni groping each other desperately in the lush grass at dawn. We left the theater quoting the Master's latest koan: "Sometimes beauty can lead to despair."

It was Jim Stoller, as usual, who saw problems with Antonioni's new direction before the rest of us did. After voicing objections, in his *La Notte* review, about the "sloppily paced" party sequence, the "leaden and insistent" symbolism, and the academic "discontinuous editing" in the walk sequence which was "used to develop a series of explicit, one-to-one meanings as in Eisenstein," Stoller went on to raise a more telling objection. Antonioni, he felt, had stacked the cards by denying any reference to a worthy model of behavior, any "point worth aspiring to," if only in the past, and any real engagement between the characters.

Of course I disagreed at the time, finding Stoller's demand sentimental. More to the point, this was disloyalty! I tried to argue him out of his position. But the words "card stacking" continued to roll uneasily around my brain.

My own disappointment with Antonioni came later with *Blow-Up*, though that derived partly from a misunderstanding, having wrongly elevated him to the level of philosopher in the first place. I had followed the lead of the press, which trumpeted his every quote as a weighty pronouncement: "Eroticism the Disease of the Age: Antonioni." Even his interview silences were reported as evidence of deep thought. It was partly the burden placed on Antonioni to be the oracle of modernity that forced him into ever more schematic conceptions. When his subsequent films exhibited signs of trendy jet-setting, hippie naïveté, and sheer woolly-headedness— even if the visuals remained stunning—I, like many of his fans, felt betrayed. It took me years to figure out that most film directors are not systematic thinkers but artistic opportunists. Maybe thanks to Coppola, Cimino & Company, we have reached a more realistic expectation of directors today; we are more used to the combination of great visual style with intellectual incoherence. But at the time we looked to filmmakers to be our novelists, our sages.

Film enjoyed as never before (or since) the prestige of high culture. English professors with whom I had difficulty making office appointments would stumble across my legs in Cinema 16 showings; they would interrupt themselves in class to gush about a movie; they would publish essays comparing Resnais's ordering of time to Proust's.

The euphoria and prestige that surrounded films in the early sixties seem, in retrospect, deserved. The French New Wave—Godard, Truffaut, Varda, Chabrol, Rivette, Resnais, Malle, Rohmer—had all burst on the American scene at once; Antonioni, Visconti, Rossellini, Fellini, Buñuel, Bergman, Welles, Minnelli, Satyajit Ray, Wajda, Losey, Torre Nilsson and the Brazilian Cine Novo group were already operating in high gear; the New American Underground of Brakhage, Mekas, Warhol, Anger etc. was in its heroic phase; and the lingering activity of such old masters as Renoir, Dreyer, Ford, Hawks, Lang, Hitchcock and Ozu provided a sort of benign historical link to the golden age of silent cinema. A whole apparatus had sprung up to support this moviemaking renaissance; the art-house circuit, new movie journals, museum and university studies, and, like a final official seal of legitimacy, the establishment of the New York Film Festival.

I covered that first New York Film Festival in 1963 for the *Columbia Daily Spectator*. The air at Lincoln Center on opening night was alive with high hopes, with the conviction that we were entering a fat time for movies. Everyone, from dignitary to hungry film buff, seemed grateful to the ones who had given us a film festival; New York City was finally linked with Europe.

It was a banner year. The festival premieres included Buñuel's *Exterminating Angel*; Olmi's *The Fiancés*; Polanski's *Knife in the Water*; Ozu's *An Autumn Afternoon*; Bresson's *Trial of Joan of Arc*; Resnais's *Muriel*; Losey's *The Servant*; Rocha's *Barravento*; Mekas's *Hallelujah the Hills*; Marker's *Le Joli Mai*; Kobayashi's *Harakiri*; ROGOPAG by Rossellini, Godard, Pasolini and Gregoretti; Blue's *The Olive Trees of Justice*; De Antonio's *Point of Order*; and Melville's *Magnet of Doom*. There were also first-shown retrospectives of the uncut Ophuls's *Lola Montes*, Mizoguchi's *Sansho the Bailiff*, Kurosawa's *I Live in Fear*. At the time, I did not appreciate what an unusually fortunate confluence of circumstances was reigning in the cinematic heavens; I thought it would go on forever with the same incandescence.

At college, I was still struggling with the question of whether to become a writer or a filmmaker. While writing came easily to me, I felt I had to try to make my own movie. I could not remain always a sponge for others' celluloid visions. So I adapted one of my short stories to a screenplay, took the profits from the film series, and gathered volunteer actors and technicians.

Orson Welles once said that *Citizen Kane* succeeded because he didn't know what could or couldn't be done in motion pictures. I wish to report that my movie didn't work for the same reason. I chose an impossibly complicated scheme: three unreliable narrators in the space of a twenty-minute film. Completed in my senior year, 1964, *Saint at the Crossroads* was "over two years in the making": in addition to the usual problems with a tiny budget and a volunteer crew— camera leaks, personality clashes, absenteeism, inappropriate weather—the fancy synch-sound equipment we had rented for the dialogue scenes failed to synchronize. Sound was our undoing; in the end we had to rent a dubbing studio. The visuals, however, were very pretty, largely due to my camera-man, Mark Weiss, who alone on the set knew what he was doing. There was an obligatory Antonioniesque sequence in Riverside Park where boy and girl, walking together, grow farther apart with each shot. They reach the pier where an elaborate tracking shot surrounds them as they kiss, then shows each looking away moodily at the water. . . .

I stayed up all night with the sound man to do a final mix, rushing to complete the film for its scheduled premiere. We finally got the mix done at eight o'clock Saturday morning—just in time for me to grab a taxi to my job as a weekend guard at the Metropolitan Museum. As the cab approached the museum, I looked out, blinking my eyes in the morning light, and saw Susan Sontag and three men in tuxedos, laughing with champagne glasses in their hands as they tripped around the fountain. Right out of *Last Year at Marienbad.*

Saint at the Crossroads premiered at Columbia, paired with Fellini's *Il Bidone.* Many of the exiting spectators were heard to remark "The sound was a problem," then lower their voices as they saw the filmmaker standing by. Once more Stoller came to the rescue, salving the pain with a positive review of *Saint at the Crossroads* in the *Spectator.* Admitting there were some "technical infelicities and rather disorienting violations of film grammar," he went on with a friend's partisan eye to discover "some very considerable achievements. If

Lopate continues making films—as he should—he will soon, or next, give us something of surprising originality and power." No thanks: I had had my fun; I would become a writer. It was easier and cheaper to control pens and paper than actors. Besides, I could not stand the prospect of again disappointing so many volunteers because of my inexperience. Making that one twenty-minute film had taught me the enormous difference between having an aesthetic understanding of film and being confronted with the demands of transferring three dimensions into two on an actual set.

Gershom Scholem once characterized youth movements by their chatter, as distinguished from true language: "Youth has no language. That is the reason for its uncertainty and unhappiness. It has no language, which is to say its life is imaginary and its knowledge without substance. Its existence is dissolved past all recognition into a complex flatness." I am not sure I agree, even looking back with memory's foreshortened lens, that this period of my youth was complexly flat; it seems in some ways to have been unusually rich. But certainly we had no real perspective, which is why we called on movies to be our language and our knowledge, our hope, our romance, our cause, our imagination and our life.

THE FIRST NEW YORK FILM FESTIVAL— 1963

"It's the greatest thing that ever happened to New York," said one of my friends about the first New York Film Festival, held from September 10–19 while most Columbia students were still on vacation. Another, who had been a movie addict for years and was about to start a film magazine, told me disgustedly that he had "given up on films."

My own opinion comes closer to the first: the festival was an exciting, frequently rewarding experience, and I see no reason to be ungrateful for the opportunity of seeing so many interesting films. However, it should be noted that my second friend had gone to every one of the events in the festival—a fact which makes his reaction of disgust considerably more understandable. Of the twenty-one films presented at Lincoln Center I saw eight and attended only two of the ten programs at the Museum of Modern Art. Perhaps this makes me unqualified to write an article on the festival. At the time, ten movies in ten days seemed like a lot. Lack of both time and money forced me to make a limited selection. But I still think it was better to have enjoyed what I saw while regretting the loss of a few good films than to have glutted myself with celluloid and suffered the inevitable aftereffects.

From what I saw, there were no masterpieces in the festival—no single film that satisfied on all levels. A few of the young directors—Polanski, Olmi, Mekas and Patroni-Griffi (whose works I am unfortunately unable to discuss because of lack of space)—provided some of the most exciting moments. Polanski's *Knife in the Water* may have been the most consistently successful film shown in the entire festival. The great veteran directors—Buñuel, Bresson, Kurosawa and Ophuls—were represented by works which proved to be fascinating, challenging, technically brilliant and somehow less powerful than the masterworks of their previous careers.

Luis Buñuel's *Exterminating Angel* opened the festival at Lincoln Center. This is the most recent work in a lifetime of magnificent filmmaking which includes *Viridiana, This Strange Passion, Los Olvidados* and *Un Chien Andalou.* The story depicts a group of wealthy, high society guests at a party who suffer a paralysis of will and are unable to leave the living room. Thrown together without food or water and held there by an insane power of inertia, the guests resort to violence, pettiness and suicide. Every facet of their degeneration is illustrated with loving irony by Buñuel. Outside the house, preparations are being made by the army and the police to rescue the guests from their prison, while curious onlookers collect at the scene of the disaster. All this time we know that the inhabitants have only to take a few steps in order to free themselves from the room!

A fascinating idea, unfortunately marred by two flaws in Buñuel's execution. First, the characterizations are almost uniformly weak, with only a few of the principals managing to convey individual personalities. This is usually one of Buñuel's strongest talents, and I can't understand how he could have slipped from the brilliant characterizations in *Viridiana* to the confused, uneven ones in this film. Silvia Pinal, who was riveting as the heroine in *Viridiana*, leaves no impression in *The Exterminating Angel*. Secondly, the plot, having nowhere to turn, ends in a terribly disappointing

"Here we go again" formula, reducing the whole film to an extended joke.

Still, there is something so extraordinary and disturbing about the film that it must be regarded as a partial work of genius. Buñuel has managed to create so vivid a sense of being trapped that the audience begins to feel just as uncomfortable as the people in the film. I think that the director consciously set out to construct a mirror of the spectators who would be seeing his movie. Both are, after all, captive audiences. A stronger, more direct and complex relationship between spectator and film is the result, such as one frequently finds in twentieth-century theater experiments but rarely in movies. If this was Buñuel's aim, he has succeeded tremendously—so much so that the Lincoln Center audience could not help making nervous jokes, after the film had ended, about whether or not they would be able to leave the building.

But more important is the question of how Buñuel brought about that wholly believable sense of claustrophobic terror which is the real achievement of the movie, and which every action, every character, every image has no other purpose but to nourish. For the mood itself—and not any one character or object—is the hero of this movie. Buñuel has built it up with a tremendous imagination for details: a man shaving his legs, a woman squeezing a pimple, repetitions of groans and self-pitying statements—little eccentricities which grate on the nerves of the other characters and the audience. "Obsessional" is the best way to describe *The Exterminating Angel*; the most characteristic and telling image in the film is of a woman pulling out clumps of hair.

Strangely enough, the very lack of characterization, while weakening interest in the action, contributes to the overall mood of murky, hellish confinement without hope of escape. In fact, it is precisely because the party-goers trapped within the room are rather shallow and mean that they cannot retreat to private worlds for some sort of emotional escape. Even eroticism cannot provide a healthy release; as depicted by Buñuel, it becomes inextricably combined with the forces of sickness and destruction. To add to this unrelenting sense that "there is no way out," the photography, brilliantly controlled by Gabriel Figueroa, remains hard and unsparing, devoid of much of the standard "beauty" of most foreign art films (the one exception here, a powerful and ironic shift to soft romantic focus, shows the two lovers after their double suicide).

A cruel fatality hangs over the movie, as if the characters were slowly sinking into quicksand. It is this feeling which makes one think that something other than a paralysis of will is responsible for their imprisonment. At a relatively early stage in the movie, one of the guests, who is dying of a heart attack, expresses thanks that he has been spared the sight of the awful destruction which God is planning for the rest of the visitors. One is never really sure, especially considering Buñuel's strong antireligious views, how seriously to take this statement, and it adds to the richness and complexity of the film. Perhaps it is nothing but human failure and weakness which holds them there, but on the other hand it might very well be a fierce avenging angel, who, as the title states, has come to exterminate them all.

Robert Bresson, like Buñuel, is an eccentric in the world of films—a man who continues to work in a completely individual way outside of the stream of contemporary cinema. Both men are schools in themselves, embodying entire realms of human experience. But whereas the Spanish-Mexican focuses on cruelty, shock and bitter satire, Bresson's concerns are more in the direction of spirituality and religious faith. In his latest film, *The Trial of Joan of Arc*, Bresson repeats his interlocking obsessions with criminals, outcasts, prisoners and martyrs. He is the most careful film artist working today, and when he dies, critics will find themselves having to evaluate his work in its entirety. Each of Bresson's films feeds the others, because his themes remain remarkably consistent while his technique develops with a theoretical seriousness and logic which is beautiful to watch. Out of five previous attempts, he has already made two great films, *Pickpocket* and *Diary of a Country Priest*, as well as an exceptionally good one, *A Man Escaped*. (His first two films have never been shown in the United States.)

Bresson's style, from the beginning rather sober and austere, has become increasingly simplified throughout his career, ridding itself of any excessive, unnecessary elements. Every cut or camera movement seems justified and takes on meaning. Editing for Bresson is never merely a convenient way of putting together a scene, but an additional way of conveying the point or drama. For instance, in the cross-examination of Joan of Arc, Bresson could have easily included both judge and defendant in a single shot (which would have immediately shown the reaction of each character's words on the other), then inserted close-ups. Instead, he uses two separate medium shots of Joan and the interrogator, and these two shots, taken from the same angle and distance, are practically the only ones employed throughout the many courtroom scenes. The pattern of repetition (intercutting from one face to the other) emphasizes the agonizing, drawn-out nature of the questioning. At the same time, the separation of the two characters underscores Joan's complete isolation from anyone she might appeal to, while also indicating that these two antagonists represent entirely different world-systems and can never come together in the same image.

The Trial of Joan of Arc shifts between the courtroom and her cell, in which the questioning is occasionally continued. The interrogation has been taken verbatim from the actual transcript of the trial. Bresson has written new material for many of the scenes in prison, lines which have no relation to the legal proceedings but which point up the hostility of

Joan's enemies and the soldiers who guard her. Still, the reliance on the trial transcript has forced Bresson to make a movie which, in many ways, breaks with the style and feeling of his three other movies seen in the United States.

While the changes might be welcomed as indications of growth, I feel they take away from the emotional involvement and final satisfaction which his previous films made possible. His entire sense of sin, a kind of diabolical, metaphysical force, is absent. The bureaucratic stubbornness of the judges seems a poor substitute. Gone also is the feeling of a powerful struggle in the air as invisible angels and devils wrestle for domination of the protagonist's soul.

The struggle is no longer apparent because the entire mechanism of interior doubt has been removed. Its absence can be explained by the parallel absence of a narrative track spoken by the protagonist, which had brought the audience closer to the thoughts of the protagonist in Bresson's previous films but which has been omitted in *Joan of Arc*. And it has been omitted because Bresson, rightly, could not venture to reconstruct the thoughts of a historic personality. His imagination has been constrained by a factual strait-jacket, and the result is a movie seen much more on the surface than any of his previous films. Without the addition of a narrative track, Bresson's forbidding images, as well as the rather neutral, inexpressive face of the actress playing Joan, do not invite much penetration or psychological awareness of the interior drama.

The plain truth, irreverent as this may sound, is that the writing in the trial transcript simply does not measure up to the high quality of Bresson's own screenwriting (as evidenced in *Pickpocket, Diary of a Country Priest* and *A Man Escaped*). The director, who had obviously fallen in love with the actual court transcript, seemed to have become aware of its inadequacies as a film script somewhere along the line and tried to "juice it up" in his added material with curses and lecherous talk about her virginity. A good try, but the combination proves faintly embarrassing.

The beauty of the original transcript is, in any case, in the subtle wordings which Joan and the interrogators employ to get the better of each other. These nuances, however, were lost in the worst set of subtitles I have ever encountered. It is not enough for the author of subtitles to indicate the general direction of a speech; he must try to convey as faithfully as possible the exact text of the original. In other words, ten spoken words should not be translated as "No." This particular set of subtitles also violated the beautiful shadows and greys of Bresson's images with the most glaring bluish-white words imaginable.

The *Times*'s Bosley Crowther's moronic attacks on subtitles have perhaps made us too defensive and too willing to accept anything projected on the bottom of the screen. I don't agree with his solution of dubbing, but it is time they stopped spoiling the beauty and purity of the images as directors intended them to be seen. Perhaps, although this sounds too visionary, an extra strip might be attached to the bottom of the regular screen, onto which the subtitles might be projected, simultaneously with the film's projection on another reel. Until some such solution is reached, subtitle companies will have to rediscover their long-lost consciences. This means proofreading the titles to put a halt to sloppiness, and keeping the words small, neat, readable and in harmony with the tones of the original images.

The subtitles were not Bresson's fault, of course, but he must be held responsible for a rather unrealistic sound track, in which much of the dialogue was obviously dubbed, while unconvincing cries of "Burn the witch!" and murmurs from a make-believe, invisible crowd were later added. However, the images, aided by the absolutely appropriate, subdued photography of L. H. Burel, are as brilliant and impressive as anything in Bresson's previous works. The director sets up about ten basic shots and returns to them continually within the course of the film. His sparse use of images infuses each one of them with a greater value and significance. The repetition of shots does become tiresome, but it is exactly those ten or so shots that we leave the theater remembering. The burning of Joan at the stake is magnificent: a rare, completely beautiful moment in films that justifies the promise of the rest of the movie. *The Trial of Joan of Arc* is an impressive work, but one which seems probably more satisfying when one considers the film afterward than while one is actually viewing it.

At the same time that Lincoln Center was running its program of "the best of the year's best films selected from other festivals," the Museum of Modern Art presented "ten programs of distinguished films of the recent past," none of which had ever been shown publicly in New York. One of them, *I Live in Fear*, by Akira Kurosawa, I had been waiting to see for years, and it is a little embarrassing to anticipate a great film for so long and then to discover that it was actually rather silly. I say this as someone who has loved almost every film made by Kurosawa, from *Ikiru* and *The Lower Depths* to *The Magnificent Seven*, *Rashomon*, *Throne of Blood*, *Yojimbo* and *Sanjuro*.

The theme in *I Live in Fear*—the threat of nuclear destruction—is handled with simplemindedness and heavy significance. Kurosawa neglects almost everybody in the film while lavishing great attention on the protagonist—an interesting, eccentric old businessman who fears the bomb and tries to convince his family and mistresses to move with him to Brazil before it's too late. Most of the film is concerned with his desperate attempts to talk them into leaving Japan.

Kurosawa has a tendency to dissipate half of his artistic tension when working in a contemporary setting (*The Bad Sleep Well, Drunken Angel*). His greatest film, *Ikiru*, takes place in modern Japan, so this generalization is not completely valid, but it does apply to *I Live in Fear*, the first two thirds of which are talky, static, repetitive and cinematically boring. The director tries to cover up the lack of plot development or good supporting characters with typical Kurosawa shenanigans—screamings, thrashings, etc.—but the failure is only accentuated.

Then something happens. The last third of the film suddenly comes alive with an eerie power; the plot veers off and the technique changes with it, as one instinctively feels a new tension and artistic discipline seizing control of the direction. The old man sets fire to his plant in an effort to tear his sons away from their home, confesses the arson to a group of angry workers and is sent to a madhouse where he actually does go crazy, mistaking the glare of the sun for a huge atomic explosion.

Finally everything begins to fall into place; the parallel which Kurosawa has been wanting us to feel all along, between his protagonist and King Lear, takes hold. In the final third of *I Live in Fear*, Kurosawa has done the impossible: he has broadened his little drama and transformed his protagonist into a great tragic hero with a peculiarly modern temperament. It is a remarkable achievement; but why did it have to come after all that junk?

The complete, restored version of *Lola Montes*, which closed the festival at the Museum, maintained a much more consistent level of quality and artistic control than did the Kurosawa film. It was the last and most spectacularly impressive work of the late, brilliant director Max Ophuls, whose works never gained the widespread public recognition they merited. His films, including the beautiful *Letter from an Unknown Woman* and *Earrings of Madame De . . .* , were justly respected and loved by intellectual film critics for their elegant polish and opulent style, their completely individual and fluid use of camera movement, and the romantic aura which surrounds them.

An Ophuls film is always visually delightful to watch, but *Lola Montes* exceeded all expectations in the constant succession of overwhelmingly lovely images. So much "beauty," using the term in its most traditional and unambivalent sense, was crammed into the movie that it became almost painful to watch. It may well be the most beautiful color CinemaScope movie ever made.

Ophuls uses color with a dazzling, kaleidoscopic imagination, and manipulates the CinemaScope screen so that it becomes alternately larger, more spacious than it has ever seemed before, and capable of confining the most intimate love scenes. Occasionally his technique falters, possibly as a result of trying to do too much: the use of a masking device to block off the sides of the screen for certain flashbacks becomes an unnecessary distraction. However, his overall success with the sometimes unwieldy CinemaScope frame can be ascribed not only to his undeniable ability to devise beautiful compositions, but to the care and attention he devotes to backgrounds. The most consistent mistake made by directors working in CinemaScope is to place the main actors in the center of the frame and forget about the sides. Ophuls imparts a strong sense of reality to both luxurious settings and tawdry circus scenes by building up the background through hundreds of small details (especially in the furnishings and costumes).

The film unrolls in a dreamily fluid manner, carried along by Ophuls's smooth, stately tracking and crane shots, and his breathtaking use of dissolves, gracefully superimposing sometimes three or even four images on a single frame. Unfortunately, all this magnificent technique has been mounted for a slender and disappointing story that cannot possibly sustain the burden. The heroine, a famous courtesan, is taken through her countless love affairs, including one as the mistress of Ludwig I of Bavaria, and finally ends up a curiosity attraction in an American circus. The story is sheer romanticism—a glorification of love wherever it can be found, tempered by an awareness of the dissatisfaction and sadness which inevitably cloud a life of continual amours.

Romanticism is fine, but it must be backed up by more content than a somewhat boring string of Technicolor affairs depicted in a drastically superficial and undeveloped manner. The characterizations, including Lola herself as played ineffectually by Martine Carol, are all on the level of standard Hollywood costume pictures. I left the theater wondering what Lola Montes was really like, but more importantly, what had taken place of any importance during the span of this extremely watchable two-and-a-half-hour movie. The director, fascinated with the technical possibilities of the film, seems to have stretched the plot line for the sole purpose of including a few more dazzling visual effects. *Lola Montes* may have been Ophuls's most technically advanced film but, compared to a movie like *Letter from an Unknown Woman*, it was certainly not his most human.

It is a pity that the Museum of Modern Art's selections of revivals and rarities were so uneven. I wish they had included such hitherto unreleased films as Buñuel's *Nazarin*, Renoir's *The Testament of Dr. Cordelier*, Chabrol's *Les Bonnes Femmes*, Ichikawa's *Burmese Harp*, Visconti's early films, *La Terra Trema*, *Senso* and *Ossessione*, Munk's *Eroica*, Rouch's *Moi un Noir* and *La Pyramide Humaine*, Antonioni's *Cronaca di un Amore*, Brook's *Moderato Cantabile* and Godard's *Le Petit Soldat*. Let us hope that someone, perhaps Dan Talbot of the New Yorker Theater, will get around to reviving these films; certainly no "high class," first-run art house will touch them as long as they continue to follow a policy of rejecting all films over two years old no matter how great they happen to be.

As for the series presented at Lincoln Center, one can only hope that its organizers will continue to bring to America as many exceptional films as they did this year. One added request might be that they search out those good films which did not find their way into previous festivals.

This was the first extended film criticism I ever published. It appeared in my college newspaper, Columbia Daily Spectator, *on November 1, 1963, two weeks before my twentieth birthday. (The newsprint has turned auburn and crumbly.) I probably should be more embarrassed by it as a piece of juvenilia than I am. Certainly I can see passages which convey a callow bluff at authority; but what amazes me is how much of the style, the syntax, the argumentation resemble the way I write today. This is a case of either precocious or arrested development!*

In reconsidering my earlier opinions, I am certainly less picky about The Exterminating Angel, *which looks very good today; but I would stick to my guns about the Bresson, Kurosawa and Ophuls films. Over the years, I tried very hard to hypnotize myself into believing I loved* Lola Montes; *I even succeeded at moments, but in the end I have lapsed into the honesty of my first, teenage response. The fatal miscasting of Martine Carol in the central role prevented it from being more than the noble ruins of a great film.*

THREE ON A COUCH:
Jerry Lewis Adjusts

It is always an interesting moment when the great comic, with some impatience, announces that he can no longer take on the burden of being Everyman, that he has changed, his dignity has caught up with his insecurity. Charlie Chaplin's last speech in *The Great Dictator*, with its polysyllabic moralisms, must have been such a moment, dampening the public's identification with the Little Fellow. The bond of mass identification can become a nightmarish strait-jacket for the performer and honesty may impel him to break out of it, as Chaplin did even more strenuously in *Monsieur Verdoux*. Jerry Lewis's time has come to leave his "Little Fellow" behind, but the transition has been managed so tactfully that few have noticed. American critics continue to mumble about "typical fare for a sub-12-year-old mentality" while he has set about preparing his audience for the moment when he can no longer be their patsy, and when the new, accomplished personality which he has been evolving off-camera will have to serve as sufficient metaphor for their experience.

Over the last six years Lewis has directed a series of re-markable pictures *(The Bellboy, The Errand Boy, The Ladies' Man, The Nutty Professor, The Patsy, The Family Jewels)*, ex-hibiting a daring and craft which make him one of the most imaginative filmmakers in Hollywood. Spiraling out from his basic character of the disoriented, clumsy Jewish teenager, Lewis has also been at work assembling from film to film the fragments of a more up-to-date self-portrait. Behind his recent efforts can, in fact, be detected the maneuver to force people (his adoring public, his wife*or himself) to see certain character traits of his which are either ugly or intimidating, and then prompt an acceptance of them by showing other characters in the film accepting the new combination. At the end of *The Family Jewels*, the little girl chooses the cynical, repellent clown as her guardian, knowing that it is really her gentle friend in disguise: in a sense, she agrees to take on both of them. The last scene of *The Nutty Professor* shows Stella Stevens walking off with the maladroit scientific genius, while her pockets are cautiously packed with Buddy Love serum.

In *Three on a Couch*, Jerry Lewis has finally taken the brave step of discarding the whole schizoid apparatus and giving himself the role of a man with a creative, integrated personality. Even at his most precarious moments, the character serves as an indication of Lewis's realistically heightened respect for himself. Lewis plays an abstract painter who has just been awarded an important mural commission in Paris. It is no accident that recognition of his creative talent comes from Paris, as it did for Lewis the director, and he returns the favor by treating the city as the artistic center of the world.

With this commission he will be able to marry and spend a honeymoon year vacationing and painting in Paris. He rushes off to his fiancée, a psychiatrist (Janet Leigh), and she is pleased, but not as perfectly happy as he had imagined the realization of their marriage plans would make her. She reasonably counters: "But my patients *need* me. Lives depend on

---

*Lewis, in an interview with *Cahiers*, revealed that his wife had hated the character of Buddy Love, and refused to let her younger children see their daddy in *The Nutty Professor*.

me." She feels particularly reluctant to leave three of her female patients, all of whom she has been unable to shake from their bitter mistrust of men.

Christopher comes to Dr. Elizabeth Accord's office not as a neurotic to be helped, but as the privileged one who gains access to the most sacred ark, the therapist's private life. Unlike the traditional Jerry Lewis character, who had gone out with high school girls *(The Nutty Professor)* or paired off with a kid *(The Family Jewels)*, Christopher has already won the love of a formidably mature woman.

As portrayed by Janet Leigh, Elizabeth is the embodiment of the tightrope walker that medicine and other professions expect of its women practitioners today: assured, strong-willed but not domineering, and feminine in a Chanel-suited, sensibly dressed way. In a delicious and gently cutting detail, she is shown to have a color dial which regulates the lighting from deep shades to pastels—a nice status symbol for the woman psychiatrist who wants to satisfy her decorative urge—which also allows the director to use simple backgrounds of projected color for the stylized, intimate therapy sequences.

Both appearing to be in their thirties, Christopher and Elizabeth must have either cherished their independence or been married and divorced earlier: in any case, they seem about to form a union of two strong individuals who know what they're doing—not a partnership, exactly, since they will be working in dissimilar fields, but an alliance of brains and attractiveness. However, the first thing that Christopher asks of her is to leave her practice and follow him to Paris, where they can both rejoice in his talent. Although art-making has its validity, he must be made to realize that it occupies a lower rung in the scale of social necessity than healing. The fact that she carries her point, and he must wait until the patients show some breakthrough in their therapy, reflects the argumentative strength of a more selfless position. Janet Leigh's superbly restrained performance conveys the requisite obstinacy. She has always been a calm actress, well composed both emotionally and physically, like a trim machine in her famous white bra. Hitchcock and Welles each took delight in violating her working woman's put-togetherness. Lewis has respected it, and the results are just as forceful.

Elizabeth speaks always in terms of her obligations, which confuses Christopher, who is used to the language of artistic egoism. She has mastered the technique of covering up emotions with a professional evenness of expression. Thus, at no point in the film is there a statement of the idea that Elizabeth does not look forward to leaving her practice for the sake of marriage and honeymoon: no, she maintains throughout that it is just what she wants . . . but outside circumstances are wrong at the moment. Although Elizabeth has been accepted into the medical profession, and performed as well as any man, she acts as though she fears that this "honeymoon" will soon have to end. The contradictory pressures placed on intelligent career women today, encouraged to use their brains to the fullest, but to defer to their male bosses or lovers at key moments, encourage wile. Elizabeth's deviousness takes the form of an overscrupulous sense of obligation to cure her girls of misanthropy, when she is actually using them to hold off her own man.

Christopher's failure to convince Elizabeth that she should give up everything and come with him wounds his masculine self-respect, and he chooses an equally devious method to get her to agree, at the same time reinstating his masculine self-respect. He appears to each of the three girl patients in the guise of her ideal man: the athletic one makes him feign an interest in track-running; the Southern botanist turns him into a shy, effeminate scientific prodigy; and for the French girl who loves all things Western, he becomes a Texas rodeo star. His aim is to get them cured faster than she could have, through the magnetism of his personality—but to cause them to fall in love with him only to a point: the point at which they will feel warm enough toward all men to start dating again. This course approximates one of the most delicate tasks of psychiatry: how to bring the analysand to have faith in relationships by establishing the therapeutic one as a model and, at the same time, not seem the solution itself, the all-satisfying lover. It is, of course, cruel of Christopher to think he can help them all by winning their affection and then leaving them in the lurch. But his only interest is in getting his fiancée on the boat for Europe, and if he manages to create an illusion of well-being in the three patients sufficient to satisfy Elizabeth, it is no concern of his whether they hang themselves the day after he sails.

The portrayal of the three women minimizes this ethical issue: they are all cute and sweet and a little dazed (starlets, in short), but one-dimensional, so that one sees each of the courtships essentially from Christopher's point of view, which stresses his herculean efforts, rather than the girls' valiant attempts to come out of their shells. While Lewis stays clear of driving the film into a tragicomedy of meddling, that direction is indicated just casually enough to suggest the abyss. As it is, Christopher remains strangely impervious to the desirability of, say, Mary Ann Mobley: he courts the girls with no intention of falling in love himself, or inducing them to fall irretrievably in love with him, and in this he succeeds. Some men would have been less satisfied.

Each of the girls comes to Elizabeth with happy reports of a new man in her life, and the doctor, believing her therapeutic manner triumphant, announces that she is giving them their "graduation." For the first time Elizabeth seems to lose her tightness and accept with enthusiasm the prospect of following her boyfriend's wishes. That part of her which has always wanted to leave with Christopher seizes on this appearance of miraculous progress as a pretext to terminate her psychotherapies, now that the time for the boat's departure nears.

They celebrate her success with a spontaneous dance around a circle, holding hands; the adult restraint collapses suddenly, and we see that hidden beneath it has been the potential for unspoiled childish pleasure at getting what one wants. Elizabeth has simply learned to defer this childish side until the moment of satisfaction. The victory dance is shot, with poignant distance, from above: it is that giddy joyousness before the fall that all comic artists relish.

Just before leaving for the ship, where the captain is going to marry them on board, Christopher and Elizabeth check in at her office and discover a surprise going-away party. It quickly turns into a debacle for Christopher when each of the three girls, who has been separately invited, shows up. Despite his anguished efforts to rush Elizabeth off to the boat, the hoax gets uncovered and she is furious. Discovering in one blow that her therapeutic success is a sham and that her fiancé has been playing around with other women, she refuses to listen to Christopher's excuses. Meanwhile, the girls' rapid adjustment to the situation gives us some assurance that they are not that emotionally scarred by the hoax. They crowd around her taxi in the last scene, to convince her to leave them and go off with her man. The roles have now been reversed: she mutters between clenched teeth that she will never forgive him, while they retaliate with all her supportive lines about wounds healing, etc. Interestingly, the strength they display seems to come more from her prior therapeutic efforts than from their experiences with Christopher. He sits impotently in the car watching the women argue among themselves. At this point he has no choice but to realize that there are some things beyond his control, either through stratagem or persuasion.

If the plan has backfired, as we knew it must, it is because

Christopher has hubristically overextended himself in re-molding the world to his requirements. The final humiliation of having no way of reaching Elizabeth except through others, who must plead his case, is muted only by his physical exhaustion. He has been through a dizzying round of dating which is not especially funny. An earlier elegiac sequence had intercut shots of the hero squiring each of the girls, with others of him alone, a traveling shot limply and sympathetically following him as he rushes into his apartment, or a shot of him looking bleary-eyed as he puts down a phone and falls into bed. All of the lyrical moments in the film have to do with tiredness. The camera gracefully tracks Elizabeth and Christopher, who seem to be dancing slow-motion around the ballroom floor, but soon it becomes clear that they have not been moving at all; they are standing stock-still, while the camera has been mounted on a turntable. The next moment Christopher crumples stiff-legged with exhaustion onto the floor.

The personal background for this theme may well be Lewis's superhuman schedule of telethon performances, TV specials, starring roles in films and directorial work, during which he famously performs on- and off-camera and whips his crew into a manic circus. He has demonstrated more energy than anyone else: *Three on a Couch* begins to reflect a self-conscious criticism of this tendency. It also demonstrates the difficulty of maintaining one's inner personality in a frantic schedule of juggling multiple roles. Christopher becomes less and less the artist and more the cowboy, athlete, scientist and all-around martyr. Though many of his scenes in disguise are funny to watch, the central focus is on their destructive effect on him. Given the proportionately greater maturity of Christopher to the typical Lewis hero, such quick-change farce naturally appears as something of a regression. The trouble is that Christopher/Jerry's new maturity is not strong enough to win his case: he must resort to the old, zany tricks, with some reluctance, like a retired sorcerer calling on the magic he knows will work.

But it creates a problem of mixed comic styles. At moments the drive for the big physical laugh takes over from the comedy of self-delusion, without resulting in further development of character, and sometimes even undercutting the earlier sense of character. A sudden remembrance of his duty to the millions may have prompted Lewis to insert this farewell scene in a farcical, *Where's Charley* vein.

Until then, the film has been guided by the tightest of pacings. In the surprise party, Lewis opens up the structure with a spectacular flood of chaos which both climaxes and overwhelms the delicate buildup: it is a triumph of comic frustration, and its only fault is that it forces the viewer to lose hold of the more intimate tensions that had been sustained before. As part of this shift, the hero becomes a hopelessly insignificant figure seen from long shot, trying to move against the sea of crushing, happy partygoers. During the episode, all four girls bump into Christopher, make demands on him and expect him to be an escort, while he tries to flee into an elevator which he can never manage to catch. The action circles ritualistically around this same Tati-esque, finally numbing encounter with the elevator door. It is interesting that Christopher's difficulties are no longer of a self-actuating nature, but seem the conspiracy of a technological environment which suddenly turns hostile.

Compared to *The Patsy*, in which Jerry seems utterly lost throughout, surrounded by malevolent, exploding pianos, the characters in *Three on a Couch* use the artifacts of modern life with serene trust. In altering that relationship at the end and reintroducing physical chaos, Lewis seems to be expressing the anxiety he has experienced all along with that suave self-control. Whether his appetite for unleashing anarchy as denouement is a talent or a regression is not entirely clear; but it does suggest the unevenness of his development as an artist.

In *Three on a Couch*, Jerry Lewis has attempted a portrayal of the hangups of intelligent, ambitious, worldly professionals, especially when they try to mate. It is a different sort of movie for him, and he concentrates for the most part on the subtle comedy of character difference and masculine-feminine power struggles. A tangential pleasure of the film is that it presents art and psychiatry without their usual caricatures, taking for granted that there are painters who speak and dress sensibly, and psychiatrists who do not have Viennese accents or nervous facial tics. This alone bespeaks a measure of maturity rare in Hollywood comedies, let alone those by Jerry Lewis.

I wrote this piece in 1966 for a wonderful, short-lived magazine, Moviegoer, *edited by Jimmy Stoller, which folded while my article was still in galleys. Hence this is the first time it's been published. I was twenty-three, a few years out of college, and intended to provoke by defending Jerry Lewis as a serious film artist on this side of the Atlantic. Even then, one heard the xenophobic line that only the perversity of the French could make them pretend to like Jerry Lewis. I thought at the time, and still do, that Lewis had a superb command of film technique—movement in space, art direction, expressive color; the only difference is that then I was more forgiving of his tacky pathos and uneven writing, as a small price to pay for the stylish look of his gloriously artificial universe (see, for instance,* The Ladies' Man*). His physically spastic gestures, which have since been deplored as mocking the disabled, I always felt to be a legitimate comic stylization, to which he had as much right as Tati did to M. Hulot or Harry Langdon to his baby persona. Also, since I was closer to the humiliations of high school, I*

could empathize more with his pariah self-pity. His whiny Jewish klutz seemed utterly recognizable to me; he reminded me of
any number of the Brooklyn kids with whom I grew up. (As for
the charges against Jerry of fostering anti-Semitism, I can only
say that there is a type of Jewish male radically out of touch
with his body.) But when I saw the film, I had already begun to
move away from that spasmodic, adolescent humor toward a
dryer, more character-based irony, so that the transitional film
Three on a Couch fit in perfectly with my own altering tastes.

In retrospect I think I overrated it. Certainly I have had little urge to see it again, after having analyzed its plot turns so
intently. Even today's Lewis scholar-fanatics tend to emphasize
his earlier movies, growing strangely silent when it comes to
Couch. What I could not have anticipated when I wrote the
piece was that Lewis—who seemed at the zenith of his directing career—was about to enter decades of being unproductive.
In fact he would never regain the confident, splashy form of
The Nutty Professor and The Patsy. Three on a Couch, which
I took to be a refreshing, adult change of pace from his delirious, inspired manner, was actually the beginning of his decline.
Partly, Lewis's core audience began to "outgrow" him: the sixties enshrined another kind of inner child, more blandly, radically innocent.

Some of the resonance Three on a Couch had for me was
undoubtedly personal. I had married, at twenty, an attractive,
composed woman, the daughter of a clinical psychologist, who
was herself trained as an anthropologist. I was in love with the
ideal of conjugal maturity, which I had precociously embraced
while repressing like crazy the id-like twinges of my Jerryish underdevelopment. I probably saw myself as the wild, erratic artist
to her responsible social scientist. I was fascinated with the figure of the professional career woman and the compromises to
which she might be subjected. In that pre-feminist era, I wrote
fumblingly of the pressures and power struggles between the
sexes—then still a subject for farce! Both Lewis's and my own

unresolved chauvinism—the presumption that ultimately the career woman would and must give in—diluted the force of his film and the critique I wrote of it.

As for the theme of "maturity," I now see it as part of a curious larger pattern, whereby popular comics of the past thirty years have felt obliged to demonstrate their analysand's lessons of self-actualization and wholeness—from the schlemiel or sadist (Don Rickles) who would end his TV comedy hour with a schmaltzy rendition of "You'll Never Walk Alone," to Albert Brooks's Mother.

CONTEMPT:
The Story of a Marriage

Thirty-four years after its premiere, one of the masterworks of modern cinema, Jean-Luc Godard's *Contempt*, long unavailable, has been ravishingly restored and is back in town. The film has inspired passionate praise—*Sight & Sound* critic Colin McCabe may have gone slightly overboard in dubbing *Contempt* "the greatest work of art produced in post-war Europe," but I would say it belongs in the running. It has certainly influenced a generation of filmmakers, including R. W. Fassbinder, Quentin Tarantino and Martin Scorsese (who paid his own homage by quoting from the Godard film's stark, plangent musical score in *Casino*, and cosponsoring its re-release). Scorsese has called *Contempt* "brilliant, romantic and genuinely tragic," adding that "It's also one of the greatest films ever made about the actual process of filmmaking."

In 1963, film buffs were drooling over the improbable news that Godard—renowned for his hit-and-run, art house bricolages such as *Breathless* and *My Life to Live*—was shooting a big CinemaScope color movie with Brigitte Bardot and Jack Palance, based on an Alberto Moravia novel, *The Ghost at Noon*. It sounded almost too good to be true. Then word leaked out that Godard was having problems with his producers, Carlo Ponti and Joseph E. Levine (the distributor of

Hercules and other schlock), who were upset that the rough cut was so chaste. Not a single nude scene with B.B.—not even a sexy costume! Godard obliged by adding a prologue of husband and wife (Michel Piccoli and Bardot) in bed, which takes inventory of that sumptuous figure through color filters, while foreshadowing the couple's fragility: when she asks for reassurance about each part of her body, he reassures her ominously, "I love you totally, tenderly, tragically."*

Beyond that "compromise," Godard refused to budge, saying: "Hadn't they ever bothered to see a Godard film?"

Ironically, *Contempt* itself dealt with a conflict between a European director (Fritz Lang playing himself) and a crude American producer, Jerry Prokosch (performed with animal energy by Palance), over a remake of Homer's *Odyssey.* Prokosch hires a French screenwriter, Paul (Michel Piccoli), to rewrite Lang's script. Paul takes the job partly to buy an apartment for his wife,† the lovely Camille (Bardot); but in selling his talents, he loses stature in her eyes. Through a series of partial misunderstandings, Camille also thinks her husband is allowing the powerful, predatory Prokosch to flirt with her— or at least has not sufficiently shielded her from that danger. Piccoli, in the performance that made him a star, registers with every nuance the defensive cockiness of an intellectual-turned-hack who feels himself outmanned.

According to Pascal Aubier, a filmmaker who served as Godard's assistant on *Contempt* and many of his other sixties pictures, "It was a very tormented production." Godard, unused to working on such a large scale, was annoyed at the cir-

---

*I say "ominously," because this triumvirate of adverbs signals Paul's absolutist romanticism, his masochistic eagerness to embrace the tragic notion of fate, rather than make the compromises necessary for the mundane everyday balm of growing old together.
† Incidentally, this Rome apartment made more sense in the novel, where all the characters were Italian, than the film, where we never learn why this French couple is so keen on buying a co-op in Rome.

cus atmosphere generated by the *paparazzi* who followed Brigitte Bardot to Capri. B.B., then at the height of her celebrity, arrived with her latest boyfriend, actor Sami Frey, which further irritated Godard, who liked to have the full attention of his leading ladies. The filmmaker was also not getting along with his wife (and usual star) Anna Karina, and seemed very lonely on the shoot, remembers Aubier; "but then, that's not unusual for him. Godard also has a knack for making people around him feel awkward, and then using that to bring out tensions in the script." He antagonized Jack Palance by refusing to consider the actor's ideas, giving him only physical instructions: three steps to the left, look up. Palance, miserable, kept phoning his agent in America to get him off the picture.* The only one Godard got on well with was Fritz Lang, whom he idolized. But Lang was not feeling well, and had to cut short his participation.

No sign of the shooting problems mars the implacable smoothness of the finished product. Godard famously stated that "a movie should have a beginning, a middle and an end, though not necessarily in that order." *Contempt*, however, adheres to the traditional order: it is built like a well-made three-act tragedy. The first part takes place on the deserted back lots of Rome's Cinecittà studios† and at the producer's house. The second part—the heart of the film—is an extraordinary, lengthy sequence in the couple's apartment: a tour de force

---

*Palance also despised his co-star, Bardot, for her diva-like requirement that she be allowed to sleep late and work only in the afternoon. But this hostility worked in the film's behalf: the sexual spark betwen Camille and Prokosch seems all the more based on animalism and attraction to power, stripped as it is of the least tenderness.

†"Italian cinema is not doing so well these days," observes one character. Indeed, the fate of cinema is a persistent theme in the film, from the Lumière Brothers' quote painted on the screening room wall ("The cinema is an invention without a future") to Paul's counterstatement that "I think the cinema will last forever." Godard himself wrote a few years later, in 1965: "I await the end of cinema with optimism."

of psychological realism, as the camera tracks the married couple in their casual moves, opening a Coke, sitting on the john, taking a bath in the other's presence, doing a bit of work, walking away in the middle of a sentence. (This physical casualness is mimicked by a patient, mobile camera that gives the artful impression of operating in real time.) Meanwhile, they circle around their wound: Paul feels that Camille's love has changed since that morning—grown colder and contemptuous. She is indeed irritated by him, but still loves him. With the devastating force of an Ibsen play, they keep arguing, retreating, making up, picking the scab, until they find themselves in a darker, more intransigently hostile space.

The third part moves to Capri—the dazzling Casa Malaparte, stepped like a Mayan temple by a disciple of Le Corbusier—for a holiday plus some *Odyssey* location shooting. Capri is an insidious, "no exit" Elysium where luxury, caprice and natural beauty all converge to shatter the marriage and bring about the inevitable tragedy.*

Part of *Contempt's* special character is that it exists both as a realistic story and a string of iconic metaphors, connecting its historical layers. Palance's red Alfa Romeo sweeps in like Zeus's chariot; when he hurls a film can in disgust, he becomes a discus thrower ("At last you have a feeling for Greek culture," Lang observes dryly); Bardot donning a black wig seems a temporary stand-in for both Penelope and Anna Karina; Piccoli's character wears a hat in the bathtub to imitate Dean Martin in *Some Came Running* (though it makes him

*This tragedy is promised from the first by a multiplicity of signposts: the brooding musical score of Georges Delerue; the allusions to Greek tragedy; the passage Paul quotes from Dante ("Already death looked down from the stars/ and soon our joy was turned to grief"). No attempt is made to prolong suspense over whether things will turn out well or ill; rather, an unhappy fate is asserted with overdetermined insistence, and the only question becomes what form it will take.

resemble Godard himself); Piccoli's bath towel suggests a Roman toga; Lang is a walking emblem of cinema's golden age and the survival of catastrophe, his anecdotes invoking Dietrich and run-ins with Goebbels; the Casa Malaparte is both temple and prison. Meanwhile, the CinemaScope camera observes all; approaching on a dolly in the opening shot, it tilts down and toward us like a one-eyed Polyphemus. Or is it Lang's monocle? ("The eye of the gods has been replaced by cinema," observes Lang.) Primary colors are intentionally used as shorthand for themes. Bardot in her lush yellow robe on the balcony in Capri incarnates all of paradise about to be lost.

What makes *Contempt* so unique a viewing experience today, even more than in 1963, is the way it stimulates an audience's intelligence as well as its senses. Complex and dense, it unapologetically accommodates discussions about Homer, Dante and German Romantic poetry, meditations on the role of the gods in modern life, the creative process, the deployment of CinemaScope (Lang sneers that it is only good for showing "snakes and funerals," but the background-hungry, color-saturated beauty of cinematographer Raoul Coutard's compositions belies this).

It is also a film about language, as English, French, Italian and German speakers fling their words against an interpreter, Francesca (admirably played by Georgia Moll), in a jai alai of idioms which presciently conveys life in the new global economy, while making an acerbic political comment on power relations between the United States and Europe in the *Pax America*. (More practically, the polyglot sound track was a strategy to prevent the producers from dubbing the film.)

"Godard is the first filmmaker to bristle with the effort of digesting all previous cinema and to make cinema itself his subject," wrote critic David Thomson. Certainly *Contempt* is shot through with film buff references, and it gains veracity and authority from Godard's familiarity with the business of moviemaking. But far from being a smarty-pants, self-referential piece about films, it moves us because it is essentially the story of a marriage. Godard makes us care about two likable people who love each other* but seem determined to throw their chances for happiness away.

Godard is said to have originally wanted Frank Sinatra and Kim Novak for the husband and wife. Some of Novak's musing, as-you-desire-me quality in *Vertigo* adheres to Bardot. In her best acting performance, she is utterly convincing as the tentative, demure ex-secretary pulled into a larger world of glamour by her husband. Despite Godard's claim that he took Bardot as "a package deal," and that he "did not try to make Bardot into Camille, but Camille into Bardot," he actually tampered with the B.B. persona in several ways. First he toyed with having her play the entire film in a brunette wig—depriving her of her trademark blondness—but eventually settled for using the dark wig as a significant prop. More crucial was Godard's intuition to suppress the sex kitten of *And God Created Woman* or *Mamzelle Striptease*, and to draw on a more modest, prudishly French-bourgeois side of Bardot† for the character of Camille. In her proper matching blue sweater and headband, she seems a solemn, reticent, provincial type, not entirely at ease with the shock of her beauty.

---

*Do they in fact love each other? Some would argue that they seem to have been merely infatuated enough to get married, but never really knew each other; hence "love" is a misnomer. But the way I read the movie is that there is some genuine love between them (despite their differences) and the potential for lasting love, which makes the outcome all the more sorrowful.

†For instance, when Bardot remarked to Godard that she had trouble saying dirty words aloud, he purposely wrote in a speech for Camille to utter a string of profanities ("*Trou de cul . . . putain . . . merde . . . nom de Dieu . . . piège a con . . . saloperie . . . bordel . . .*"), which she does, but so awkwardly that it only accentuates the character's basically prudish unworldliness. This side of Bardot survives in the doyenne who today proclaims her disgust with modern society's "decadence, moral and physical filth . . . and the spread of pornography," never acknowledging her own contributions to the record of sexual iconography.

When she puts on her brunette wig in the apartment scene, she may be trying to get Paul to regard her as more intelligent than he customarily does—to escape the blond bimbo stereotype. (Her foil, Francesca, the dark-haired interpreter, speaks four languages and discusses Hölderlin's poetry with Lang.) At one point Paul asks Camille, "Why are you looking so pensive?" and she answers, "Believe it or not I'm thinking. Does that surprise you?" The inequalities in their marriage are painfully exposed: he sees himself as the brain and breadwinner, and her as a sexy trophy. Whatever her new-found contemptuous feelings may be, his own condescension seems to have always been close to the surface. "You're a complete idiot," he says when they are alone in Prokosch's house, and later tellingly blurts out, "Why did I marry a stupid twenty-eight-year-old typist?"

On the face of it, her suspicion that Paul had acted as her "pander" by leaving her with his lecherous employer seems patently unjust. Clearly he had told her to get into Prokosch's two-seat sports car because he did not want to appear fool-ishly, uxoriously jealous in the producer's eyes; and we can only assume he is telling the truth when he says his arrival at Prokosch's house was delayed by a taxi accident. Still, under-neath the unfairness of her (implicit) accusation is a legiti-mate complaint: he would not have acted so cavalierly if he were not also a little bored with her, and willing to take her for granted. Certainly he is not particularly interested in what she has to say about the minutiae of domesticity: the drapes, lunch with her mother. All this he takes in as a tax paid for marrying a beautiful but undereducated younger woman. Her claims to possessing a mind (when she reads aloud from the Fritz Lang interview book in the tub) only irritate him, and he becomes significantly most enraged when she has the audac-ity to criticize him for filching other men's ideas (after he pro-poses going to a movie for screenwriting inspiration).

Camille also says she liked him better when he was writing detective fiction and they were poor, before he fell in with that "film crowd." His scriptwork does put him in a more self-abasing position, since screenwriting is nothing if not a school for humiliation. We see this in the way Paul, having watched Prokosch carry on like an ass in the projection room, nevertheless pockets the producer's personal check, after a moment's hesitation. (It is precisely at this moment in a Hollywood film that the hero would say: Take your check and shove it!) Paul compounds the problem by seeming to blame her for turning hack, saying he is only taking on the job so that they can finish paying for the apartment. It is important to remember that we are not watching the story of an idealistic writer selling out his literary aspirations, since "detective fiction" is not so elevated a genre to begin with, and since Paul's last screenplay was some junky-sounding movie called *Toto Contra Hercules* (a dig at Joseph E. Levine), so that, if anything, the chance to adopt Homer for Fritz Lang is a step up.

More important than issues of work compromise is that Camille has come to despise her husband's presumption that he can analyze her mind. Not only is this unromantic, suggesting she holds no further mystery, but insultingly reductive. She is outraged at his speculation that she's making peace for reasons of self-interest—to keep the apartment. As the camera tracks from one to the other, pausing at a lamp in between, Paul guesses aloud that she is angry at him because she's seen him patting Francesca's bottom. Here the lamp is important, not only as an inspired bit of cinematic stylization, but as a means of hiding each from the other, if not from the audience. Camille shakes her head in an astonished no at Paul's misinterpretation, then catches herself. She scornfully accepts his demeaning reading of her as jealous, saying, "Okay, let's admit that it's that. Good, now we're finished, we don't have to talk about it anymore."

After he speculates that she no longer loves him because

of his dealings with Prokosch, she tells him: "You're crazy but . . . you're intelligent." "Then it's true?" he presses, like a prosecutor. "I didn't say that . . . I said you were intelligent," she repeats, as if to link his "craziness" with his intellectual pride, as the thing responsible for his distorted perceptions.

More than anything, the middle section traces the building of a mood. When Paul demands irritably, "What's wrong with you? What's been bothering you all afternoon?" he seems both to want to confront the problem (admirably), and to bully her out of her sullenness (reprehensibly). At first she evades with a characteristically feminine defense: "I've got a right to change my mind." We see what he doesn't—the experimental, tentative quality of her hostility: she is "trying on" anger and contempt, not knowing exactly where it will go.* Her grudge has a tinge of playacting, as though she fully expects to spring back to affection at any moment. She even makes various conciliating moves, assuring him she loves him, but, because of his insecurities, he refuses this comfort. Paul is a man worrying a canker sore. Whenever Camille begins to forgive, to be tender again, he won't accept it: he keeps asking her why she no longer loves him, until the hypothesis becomes a reality. Paul is more interested in having his worst nightmares confirmed[†] than in rehabilitating the damage.

Perhaps we can understand this Godardian dynamic better by referring to a little-known but key short of his, "Le Nouveau Monde," which he shot in 1962 as part of the compilation film *ROGOPAG*.[‡] The protagonist goes to sleep and

---

*Her voice-over interior monologue accentuates this reading: "Why did I talk to him like that? To get revenge somehow. Paul had hurt me terribly. Now it was my turn to make him suffer. So I hinted at this and that . . . without saying anything specific."

†As his own interior monologue confirms: "I had often thought that if Camille left me, it would be the worst possible catastrophe. Now I am in the midst of that catastrophe."

‡The movie's title was an acronym of the participating directors' names: Rossellini, Godard, Pasolini and Gregoretti.

wakes up to find everything looking the same but subtly different. Pedestrians pop pills nervously, his girlfriend tells him she no longer loves him—just like that. "The New World" has a sci-fi component: while our hero slept, an atomic device was exploded above Paris, which may account for his girlfriend's spooky, affectless indifference. But the short is also a dry run for *Contempt:* one day you wake up and love has magically disappeared.

All through the sixties, Godard was fascinated with the beautiful woman who betrays (Jean Seberg in *Breathless*), withdraws her love (Chantal Goya in *Masculin-Féminin*), runs away (Anna Karina in *Pierrot le Fou*) or is faithless (Bardot in *Contempt*). What makes *Contempt* an advance over this somewhat misogynistic obsession with the femme fatale is that here, Godard seems perfectly aware how much at fault his male character is for the loss of the woman's love.

The film's psychology shows a rich understanding of the mutual complicities inherent in contempt, along with the fact that trying to alter another person's contemptuous opinion of yourself is like fighting in quicksand: the more you struggle, the farther in you sink. As William Ian Miller wrote in his book *The Anatomy of Disgust:* "Another's contempt for or disgust with us will generate shame and humiliation in us if we concur with the judgment of our compatibility, that is, if we feel the contempt is justified, and will guarantee indignation and even vengeful fury if we feel it is unjustified." Paul responds both ways to his wife's harsh judgment: 1) he agrees with her, perhaps out of the intellectual's constant stock of self-hatred, 2) he considers her totally unjust, which leads him to lash out with fury. He even slaps her—further damaging her shaky esteem for him. In any film today, a man slapping a woman would end the scene (spousal abuse, case closed); but in *Contempt* we have to keep watching the sequence for twenty-five more minutes, as the ramifications of and adjustments to that slap are digested.

In assessing the film, much depends on whether one regards the director's sympathies as balanced between the couple, or as one-sidedly male. Some women friends of mine, feminists, report that they can only see the male point of view in *Contempt*: they regard Bardot's Camille as scarcely a character, only a projection of male desire and mistrust. I see Godard's viewpoint as more balanced. True, Piccoli's edgy performance draws a lot of sympathy to Paul; even when he is being an ass, he seems interesting. But Camille also displays striking insights; her efforts to patch things up endear her to us; and her hurt is palpable.

Pascal Aubier told me point-blank: "Godard was on Camille's side." In that sense, *Contempt* can be seen as a form of self-criticism: a male artist analyzing the vanities and self-deceptions of the male ego. (And perhaps, too, an apology: what cinematographer Coutard meant when he called the film Godard's "love letter to his wife," Anna Karina.)

Still, it can't be denied that in the end Camille does betray Paul with the vilely virile Jerry Prokosch. It has been Prokosch's thesis all along that Homer's Penelope was faithless. Lang, and Godard by extension, reject this theory as anachronistic sensationalism. Godard, you might say, builds the strongest possible case for Camille through the first two acts, but in Act III this Penelope proves faithless.

Bardot's Camille is a conventionally subservient woman, brought up to defer to her man. "My husband makes the decisions," she answers Prokosch when he invites her over for a drink. Later she tells Paul, "If you're happy, I'm happy." It is her tragedy that, in experiencing a glimpse of independent selfhood—brought about through the mechanism of contempt, which allows her to distance herself from her husband's domination—she assumes she has no choice but to flee into the arms of another, more powerful man.

Contempt is an ironic retelling of Homer's *Odyssey*. At

one point Camille wryly summarizes the Greek epic as "the story of that guy who's always traveling." But Paul's restlessness is internal, making him ill at ease everywhere. In modern life, implies Godard, there is no homecoming, we remain chronically homeless, in barely furnished apartments where the red drapes never arrive. Paul's Odysseus and Camille's Penelope keep advancing toward and retreating from each other: never arriving at port.

But the film also resembles another Greek tale, *Oedipus Rex*. Paul is infantilely enraged at the threatened removal of the nurturing breast, and jealous of a more powerful male figure who must be battled for the woman's love. The way he keeps pressing to uncover a truth he would be better off leaving alone is Oedipal, too. His insistent demand to know why Camille has stopped loving him (even after she denies this is the case) helps solidify a tentative role-playing on her part into an objective reality ("You're right, I no longer love you"). Anxious for reassurance, he will nevertheless only accept negative testimony which corroborates his fears, because only the nightmare has the brutal air of truth, and only touching bottom feels real.

Even in Capri, when the game is up, Paul demands one last time: "Why do you have contempt for me?" She answers: "That I'll never tell you, even if I were dying." To this he responds, with his old intellectual vanity, that he knows already. By this point, the reason is truly unimportant. She will never tell him, not because it is such a secret, but because she has already moved beyond dissection of emotions to action: she is leaving him.

Godard spoke uncharitably about Alberto Moravia's *The Ghost at Noon*, the novel he adapted for *Contempt*, calling it "a nice, vulgar read for a train journey." In fact, he took a good deal of the psychology, characters and plot line from Moravia—a decent storyteller, now neglected, who was once regarded as a major European writer. Perhaps Godard's un-generosity toward Moravia reflects an embarrassment at this debt, or a knee-jerk need to apologize to his avant-garde fans.

The exigencies of making a movie with a comparatively large budget and stars, based on a well-known writer's novel, limited the experimental-collage side of Godard and forced him to focus on getting across a linear narrative. In the process he was "freed" or "obliged" (depending on one's point of view) to draw more psychologically shaded, complex char-acters, whose emotional lives rested on overt causalities and motivations, more so than he had ever demonstrated before or since. Godard himself admitted that he considered Paul the first fully developed character he had gotten on film. Go-dardians regard *Contempt* as an anomaly, the master's most "orthodox" movie. The paradox is that it may also be his finest. *Pierrot le Fou* has more epic expansiveness, *Breathless* and *Masculin-Féminin* more cinematic invention, but in *Contempt* Godard was able to strike his deepest human chords.

If the film records the process of disenchantment, it is also a seductive bouquet of enthrallments: Bardot's beauty, primary colors, luxury objects, nature. *Contempt* marked the first time that Godard went beyond the *jolie-laide* poetry of cities and revealed his romantic, unironic love of landscapes. The cypresses on Prokosch's estate exquisitely frame Bardot and Piccoli. Capri sits in the Mediterranean like a jewel in a turquoise setting. The last word in the film is Lang's assistant director (played by Godard himself) calling out "Silence!" to the crew, after which the camera pans to a tranquilly static ocean. The serene classicism of sea and sky refutes the thrash-ings of men.

A personal note: Contempt shook me up a great deal when I saw it the first time, sitting next to my first wife, Carol, in a theater on 42nd Street. It seemed to deliver the news of the *fragility of marriage, to expose the fault lines that might be lying in wait for us. I overidentified with the insecure writer, played by Piccoli, who is torn between blusteringly asserting and passively abnegating possessive claims to his lovely wife's affections. I also found Carl Dreyer's Gertrud and Robert Musil's story "The Perfection of a Love" utterly revelatory at the same time, for much the same reasons. Of course I could not go into this in my article for the* New York Times; *but I did make a point of stressing the psychological underpinnings of the film, since Godardians tend to focus obsessively on the director's formalistic moves. As to my elevation of* Contempt *above Godard's other movies, this is certainly debatable: I was trying to tweak the orthodox scholarly approach with a perverse provocation. In the end, there is no need to rank* Contempt *above (or below) such masterworks as* Pierrot le Fou, Vivre Sa Vie, Masculin-Féminin, Breathless, Two or Three Things I Know About Her, Band Apart, etc.*

ANTONIONI'S *CRONACA*

What a shock that *Cronaca di un Amore (Story of a Love Affair)*, for which Michelangelo Antonioni fans have been waiting fifteen years to trace the rough origins of his style, should turn out to be one of his ripest, smoothest and most dramatically satisfying works. The director's first feature, made in 1950, is mature and self-possesssed: photographed in black and white with the richness of a chocolate cake, it also draws energy from a taut *film noir* plot, which Antonioni had the good grace (or beginner's insecurity) not to disdain.

Antonioni was thirty-nine when he directed *Cronaca*, so it can hardly be considered a youthful work. Before that he had been a film critic—of austere inclinations, one is told; a Marxist; an assistant director/screenwriter for Rossellini, Visconti and Marcel Carné; and the maker of a few short subjects, such as *N.U.*, a documentary on Milanese street sweepers. I have seen *N.U.* It is a lyrical tone poem, a little dry, but easy to look at, chiefly interesting for the way Antonioni's filming of city streets at daybreak, in long shot, conveys the melancholy beauty of near-empty sidewalks, much like an Atget photograph, and the futility of the workers' sweeping the gutters, trying to clean a city which is dirty by its very nature.

Already—whatever social message was intended—the streets steal the action from the mere humans.

In *Cronaca di un Amore*, the wet, rain-glistened streets, the municipal plazas, the blacktop highways outside the city, project an eerie pathos. Antonioni plays *flâneur* with the camera: watching and stopping, walking and following with unhasty, practiced eye the retreating figures in raincoats and the worn boulevards.

Antonioni told a reporter once that he discovered in making this first feature the "slow cut": he told the cinematographer to keep the camera running on the actor after he had completed the scene and walked off the set, returning to his private, everyday self. Yet even when the camera does not stay with the actor at shot's end, it often permits itself the luxury of another slow cut, by panning away to the surroundings, which seem to be waiting patiently for the actors to leave. Antonioni's appetite for photographing street scenes or landscapes or objects at rest (as in the end of *Eclipse*) reminds one in some respects of the great Japanese director Ozu. But the difference is more revealing. Ozu takes cutaway shots—separate inserts of a beaded-curtained hallway where the family is temporarily absent, or a lantern hanging in front of a restaurant—and makes them into self-enclosed still lifes, restoring the world to its peaceful, static mode of objecthood. Antonioni's tendency is to start with his characters and, in the same shot, pan away from them, so that the effect is of losing sight of them, or, more pointedly, rejecting them. Unable to take quite seriously the difficulties and sickly longings of his characters, the reality of their sufferings, his camera eye seems pulled as by a magnet across the road, where he is able to do what he likes best: look at the anonymous world.

This tension between following the protagonist or moving off into the background points ahead to what would be

Antonioni's never-resolved ambivalence toward telling a story. After seeing a later work like *The Passenger* (1975), where he seems so little invested in the slender story he sets out to tell, where his main characters are so thinly developed and where, conversely, so many of the most stunning moments occur precisely in that nonnarrative, meditational zone (like the great final sequence where the camera abandons Jack Nicholson for the hotel window), one has to wonder whether he might be better off dispensing with plot entirely. Flaubert used to have a fantasy of writing a novel that was "pure style." Yet plot brings out some of Antonioni's best gestures and efforts, it gives his reveries a spine. And some parts of plot suit him quite well: he can be strong in the setups. The first fifteen minutes of even the most flawed Antonioni film are invariably fascinating. He understands the idea of strangers meeting, of the *pickup*. Then a relationship ensues. Ordinary intimacy is his weak suit. He begins dragging his feet, looking around for something to release him from his narrative contract, as if to say: "Do I have to finish this? I'm a visual artist—what have I in common with all this operatic emotionalism?" His disdain for the principals begins to show. Soon enough the ending will come: an existential ending in which someone will be killed, commit suicide, walk out on a lover, or attempt a bleak gesture of reconciliation. If he can just hold out until then. . . .

In *Cronaca di un Amore*, he stays involved for an extremely long time: right up to the end. It is after all a *cronaca*, a story. Perhaps he even chose a strong narrative to lean on for his first film, imitating his master, Visconti, who also began with a *film noir, Ossessione*. Here, the story is set in motion by a millionaire industrialist who hires a detective agency to investigate his young, beautiful wife, Paola, because he knows very little about her past. The detective assigned to the case—squat, homely, Bogart's antipode—would rather go to a soccer match than chase the truth. The opening sequences show him carrying out the routine legwork of interviewing Paola's former teachers, neighbors and friends. Before we have even met the male and female leads, we spend an informative quarter hour nudging around postwar Italy—maids, priests, poor and well-off folk—via the device of the investigation. We learn that Paola had been one of a trio of girlfriends, all of whom were in love with the same man, Guido. One of the girls, who had been Guido's fiancée, died in an "accidental fall" down an open elevator shaft, while Guido and Paola were standing by. Shortly thereafter, Paola moved from her home town and met the wealthy industrialist whom she married.

The detective goes to interview the third girlfriend, now married, and her teacher-husband in their shabby, book-laden apartment. The husband is an intellectual who resents Paola's comfortable new life and equally resents down-and-out Guido, possibly because he suspects his own wife of retaining a lingering crush on him. When asked to describe Guido, the husband says, "He was a handsome young man— the kind I detest." As he is answering the detective's questions, his wife enters the room, unforgettably: with her short, severe haircut and black eyes speaking volumes of disappointment and bitterness, she moves like a panther inside the flat, silencing her husband's spiteful loquacity with her scorn. The detective realizes he is not going to get any further information out of this embittered pair and leaves. Though the couple is never seen onscreen again, it is worth noting how sharply etched they are: typical of Antonioni's adept handling of "throwaway" minor characters early in his career.

From this point the story picks up the former lovers, Paola and Guido, who are forced to meet in order to plan strategies against the investigation. In a tense, fragile reunion (aided by Giovanni Fusco's saxophone-drenched musical score), they drive to a deserted beach and sit on some concrete bleachers overlooking the sea, the morose expanse suggesting their uneasiness before a recollected, guilty past. Everything about their relationship seems over, exhausted. For a while the movie threatens only to hover around rueful memories. But slowly, almost against their will, their past passion is wrenched into the present tense.

Antonioni alternates scenes where horizontals predominate, like the moody beach rendezvous, with scenes of a vertical emphasis, like the claustrophobic, columnar shot where the couple runs from the detective up the marble staircase, only to find themselves confronted with the elevator shaft, emblem of their old guilt. From the beginning he shows his loyalty to long takes and to what André Bazin called the "continuity of space," ensuring that if a composition has been set up along a horizontal or vertical axis, it will only become more so as the shot progresses.

Paola and Guido lapse into the old habit of making love, now even more dangerous because of her spying husband and her visible social position. Milan becomes their only cover: the city's plazas and retail arcades, where they meet and walk incessantly, paradoxically offer them anonymity while never relaxing the threat of being spotted. Soon they are renting shabby hotel rooms for an afternoon, copulating with desperation, and Paola is trying to convince Guido to kill her husband so that they can "be free."

Someday a doctoral candidate will put forward a nice politico-historical explanation as to why audiences and filmmakers of the 1940s and '50s were so taken with this particular plot of the lonely, sexy wife who entices her proletarian lover to murder her husband for money—they never seem to be able just to run off together or get a divorce! *Cronaca di un Amore* belongs to the same husband-killing genre as *Double Indemnity*, *The Postman Always Rings Twice*, *Ossessione* and

Human Desire, at the crossroads where *film noir* and neorealism intersect. In the line of lusty actresses in half-slips, part bad girl, part waif (the queen was Gloria Grahame, who made a career of it), Lucia Bosé seems at first almost too modish, a beautiful fashion model type but a stilted actress. Yet her performance heats up and, in the end, overshadows everyone else's, so that what stays in the mind is Bosé's hot dark features, all the more hungry for breaking out of a composed, Italian *Vogue* mask.

Guido, played by Massimo Girotti, in a role similar to his lead in *Ossessione*, is first cousin to the prototype Glenn Ford used to play for Fritz Lang: a big-shouldered, dense, basically honest guy in over his head. Guido is also the first in Antonioni's interminable line of weak-willed, vain, reluctant men. He stations himself on the road at night to shoot Paola's husband, but (to his credit) cannot go through with it, and is saved further temptation to violence by the suicide which the husband commits farther down the road. The husband is thus out of the way, but Guido, disgusted with his role as potential murderer, and with his second involvement (a passive but guilty bystander: repetition-nightmare à la *Vertigo*) through the same woman in someone else's death, deserts Paola and leaves Milan forever.

Guido's distaste for the murder scheme is finally analogous to Antonioni's for the plot, as both men turn from the shrill Paola without much compassion. Lucia Bosé's tears in the last scene are like glass earring droplets; she stands there emoting like a soprano glimpsed through the binoculars' diminishing side. And so the least-felt, weakest part of the film turns out to be the ending. An Ophuls, a Nick Ray, a Minnelli might have graced Paola's heartbreak with some touching physical detail, but Antonioni lets her tears stand as punishment and makes them somehow ridiculous. A happy ending, perhaps, from Antonioni's standpoint, in that he thinks we should be alone.

Phillip Lopate

• • •

Cronaca di un Amore has in common with Antonioni's other early, black-and-white features *(La Signora senza Camelie, I Vinti, Le Amiche* and *Il Grido)* a gentle, sad, understated, modest tone, and a subtlety of perception that make them one of the most intriguing, internally consistent bodies of work in modern cinema—comparable, say, to Rossellini's films with Ingrid Bergman. *L'Avventura*, his masterpiece in many ways, was also his first international triumph: after it, a painful element of artistic self-seriousness entered the picture, side by side with his continuing brilliance. What makes these pre-*L'Avventura* works so fascinating and pleasing to me is not only their humble air (partly the result of underfinancing), but their richly layered social observation, which works perfectly with a deep-focus photographic style that layers the spatial planes. These early features are mellowed with what I might call *Pavesissimo*—that quality, inspired by the Turinese novelist Cesare Pavese, of bittersweet restlessness, disenchantment, moral concern, acerbic self-judgment and laconic aesthetic purity—which so influenced the Italian intelligentsia, Antonioni included, in the postwar era. Pavese, who was exiled by the Fascists and who committed suicide in 1950, came to symbolize integrity, social-democratic civility and weary truth-telling, in a period of shoddy accommodation. Antonioni later adapted one of Pavese's short novels, *Among Women Only*, into *Le Amiche*, but the novelist's influence can be detected in all these early films, through their patient exploration of social factors, friendship circles, family ties and urban psychology. At this point in his career, Antonioni was making consciously local films, putting to use his precise knowledge of the Italian class structure.

Cronaca is in fact a tragedy of social class, of a kind familiar to European audiences. A woman from a family of modest income is lifted into the upper classes by her beauty, but the sterility of that life bores her, she has no outlet for her emotions, dwells in the past, and takes (or retakes) someone from her previous milieu, an unemployed car salesman, as her lover. He, however, feels the new difference in their stations acutely. His first remark at their reunion—ironic, admiring—when she asks him if he finds her changed, is: "Yes. You have, I don't know—class!" She tries to equalize their social position by offering to share her money, insisting that love alone has value, and ultimately proposing murder, which will put them on the same ethical if not financial plane; but he continues to act as if he is loving above his station. And that social distance, more than even their guilt at having contemplated a crime, may finally be what prevents them from sharing a future.

Antonioni's interest in local mores and the material divisions of the social world was obviously still strong when he made this first feature. Later it would evaporate in the face of a jet-set rootlessness: the filmmaker would take up comfortable international residence in what Georg Lukács called "the Hotel Abyss." If we consider merely one aforementioned variable, his handling of minor characters, we see a striking difference between the director's sympathetic curiosity over the types who populate the edges of the story, from *Cronaca* to *L'Avventura* (*Le Amiche* is in fact a complex symphony of secondaries without a hero)—and the cartoonish characterizations of Swinging London in *Blow-Up*, or the painfully unknowledgeable portrayals of American youth in *Zabriskie Point*. *Red Desert*, *Blow-Up*, *Zabriskie Point* and *The Passenger* are all lovely to look at, and magnificent each in its way, but they put forth a more primitive worldview, the trendy-absurdist philosophy of an aging hippie, bored with intellect, longing to drop out, hungry for a newly innocent vision (see the "island" fantasy sequence in *Red Desert*), senescently fascinated with the Sexual Revolution of world youth. Compared to these, the Mizoguchian stoicism and worldly, disenchanted realism of the early features seem to me now like the more mature wisdom. So much for artistic progression.

While I wrote this is the late seventies, before the appearance of Antonioni's last three films, I doubt they would have altered my position. Perhaps I was being unfair to so great a filmmaker—certainly one of the major artists of this century—but I could not bring myself to take the genuflecting, don't-criticize-anything attitude of many who write about Antonioni, particularly academics handling his later period. Precisely because Antonioni had gotten to me first (see my essay in this book, "Anticipation of La Notte"), I was disappointed when he turned out not to be the world-historical philosopher/artist I needed him to be. I wanted him to stay middle-aged and disenchanted, representing a point ahead on the curve toward which I could aspire, and was embarrassed when he started fawning on youth—my own generation—whom I knew from close experience had nothing to teach him. At the same time, I fell head over heels in love with the look of fifties black-and-white movies. I think even now I tend to overrate obscure b&w films from this period just because I like something about the lighting, the film stock, the artifacts and the cinematic grammar of that time. So it was inevitable that the archivist in me would come to prefer the pleasureable rarities of early Antonioni to his more available color films—though he is certainly a great colorist.

DIARY OF A COUNTRY PRIEST:

Films as Spiritual Life

> *It is the flattest and dullest parts that have in the end the most life.*
>   —Robert Bresson

The earliest film I remember was *The Spanish Main*, made shortly after World War II had ended. I must have been all of three or four—which is to say, too young to offer the auteurist apology I would now, that the wonderful romantic director Frank Borzage was simply misused in a swashbuckler. I remember a good deal of blushing orange-pink, the color of so many movies by the time a print got to our local theater. But what irritated me were the love scenes, especially the long clinch at the end, when the hero held Maureen O'Hara in his puffy sleeves. "Cut out the mushy stuff!" I yelled.

What children want from movies is very simple: a chair smashed over the gunman's head, a battle with a giant scorpion. They get restless through the early development scenes that give background information, the tender glances, the landscapes. But then a knife is hurled through the air and they are back into it. The kinetic at its most basic captivates them.

This was the initial charm and promise of the medium, as

a somewhat astonished Georg Lukács reflected in 1913 after a visit to the motion picture emporium:

> The pieces of furniture keep moving in the room of a drunkard, his bed flies out of his room with him lying in it and they fly over the town. Balls some people wanted to use playing skittles revolt against their "users" and pursue them uphill and downhill. . . . The "movie" can become fantastic in a purely mechanical manner . . . the characters only have movements but no soul of their own, and what happens to them is simply an event that has nothing to do with fate. . . . Man has lost his soul, but he has won his body in exchange; his magnitude and poetry lie in the way he overcomes physical obstacles with his strength or skill, while the comedy lies in his losing to them.

What Lukács could not have predicted was that, side by side with this fantastic cinema of movement, would develop a cinema of interiority, slowness, contemplation. Certain directors of the so-called transcendental style, like Dreyer, Bresson, Ozu, Mizoguchi, Rossellini, Antonioni, Hou Hsiao-Hsien, would not be content until they had revealed the fateful motions of their characters' souls on film.

I remember the first time I saw such a movie, in college: Robert Bresson's *Diary of a Country Priest*. The picture follows the misfortunes of a young priest, alienated from his worldly and cynical parishioners, who undermines his health in a quest for divine communion by eating nothing but bread soaked in wine. At the end he dies, attaining grace on his deathbed. Bresson frustrates conventional expectations of entertainment by denying the audience melodrama, spectacle, or comic diversion, offering instead an alternation of tense theological discussions and scenes of the priest alone, trapped by landscape or interiors in psychic solitary confinement. No doubt I identified, in my seventeen-year-old self-pity, with the hero's poetic heartache. But what affected me so strongly at the time was something else.

There was a solitary chapel scene, ending in one of those strange short dolly shots that Bresson was so fond of, a movement of almost clumsy longing toward the priest at the altar, as though the camera itself were taking communion. Suddenly I had the impression that the film had stopped, or, rather, that time had stopped. All forward motion was arrested, and I was staring into "eternity." Now, I am not the kind of person readily given to mystical experiences, but at that moment I had a sensation of delicious temporal freedom. What I "saw" was not a presence, exactly, but a prolongation, a dilation, as though I might step into the image and walk around it at my leisure.

I'm sure most people have at one time or another experienced such a moment of stasis. If you stay up working all night and then go for a walk in the deserted streets at dawn and look at, say, a traffic light, you may fixate with wonderment on the everyday object, in an illumination half-caused by giddy exhaustion. Recently, while watching *Diary of a Country Priest* on videotape, I confess I kept dozing off, which made me wonder whether that first celluloid experience of eternity was nothing more than the catnap of a tired student faced with a slow, demanding movie. But no, this is taking demystification too far. Bresson's austere technique had more likely slowed down all my bodily and mental processes, so that I was ready to receive a whiff of the transcendent.

In Paul Schrader's *Transcendental Style in Film,* he accounts for this phenomenon by arguing from the bare, sparse means of Bresson's direction, which eschews drama and audience empathy: "Stasis, of course, is the final example of sparse means. The image simply stops. . . . When the image stops, the viewer keeps going, moving deeper and deeper, one might say, *into* the image. This is the 'miracle' of sacred art."

All I know is that I was fascinated with the still, hushed, lugubrious, unadrenalated world of *Diary*. I kept noticing how the characters gravitated toward windows: could not the panes' transparency be a metaphor for the border between substance and immateriality? "Your film's beauty," wrote Bresson to himself in *Notes on Cinematography*, "will not be in the images (postcardism) but in the ineffable that they will emanate." Perversely, it seemed, he was struggling to express the invisible, the ineffable, through the most visually concrete and literal of media. Yet perhaps this is less of a paradox than it might at first appear; perhaps there is something in the very nature of film, whose images live or die by projected beams of light, that courts the invisible, the otherworldly. The climax of Murnau's *Nosferatu*, where the vampire, standing before the window, is "dissolved" by the rays of morning light, must derive some of its iconic power from self-reflexive commentary on the medium itself.

I noticed at the time that Bresson was also very fond of doors—in much the same way that Cocteau used mirrors in *Orpheus*, as conductors from one world to another. *Pickpocket*, Bresson's greatest film, has a multitude of scenes of a door opening, followed by a brief, tense dialogue between well-meaning visitor and protagonist (the pickpocket), and ending with the frustrated visitor's exit through the same door. This closed-door motif suggests both the pickpocket's stubbornness, his refusal of grace, and the doors of spiritual perception, which (Bresson seems to be saying) are always close by, inviting us to embrace salvation. Bresson's world tends to be claustrophobic, encompassing a space from the door to the window and back, as though telling us how little maneuvering room there is between grace and damnation. Curious how such a chilly idea, which would be appalling to me as a precept to follow in daily life, could prove so attractive when expressed in cinematic form. But part of its attraction was precisely that it seemed an intensification, a self-conscious foregrounding of problems of cinematic form.

A director must make a decision about how to slice up space, where to put the camera. Jean Renoir generously composes the frame so that it spills toward the sides, suggesting an interesting, fecund world awaiting us just beyond the screen, coterminous with the action, if momentarily off-camera; a Bresson composition draws inward, implodes, abstractly denies truck with daily life, cuts off all exits. In many scenes of *Diary*, the priest, let into a parishioner's house, encounters almost immediately a painful interview in which his own values are attacked, ridiculed, tempted. There is no room for small talk; every conversation leads directly to the heart of the matter: sin, suicide, perversity, redemption, grace.

I wonder why this forbidding Jansenist work so deeply moved me. I think it had something to do with the movie's offer of silence ("Build your film on white, on silence and on stillness," wrote Bresson) and, with it, an implicit offer of greater mental freedom. A film like *Diary of a Country Priest* was not constantly dinning reaction cues into me. With the surrounding darkness acting as a relaxant, its stream of composed images induced a harmony that cleansed and calmed my brain; the plot may have been ultimately tragic, but it brought me into a quieter space of serene resignation through the measured unfurling of a story of human suffering.

I could say a good deal more about Bresson's *Diary*, but, first of all, the film has already been picked clean by scholars and academics, and, second of all, rather than fall into the prolixities of scene-by-scene analysis, I want to concentrate on the challenge at hand: to explain how this one movie

changed my life.* It did so by putting me in contact with a
habit of mind that I may as well call spiritual, and a mental
process suspiciously like meditation.

The monks in Fra Angelico's order were each assigned a
cell with a painting on which to meditate. It may sound far-
fetched to speak of watching a movie as a meditative discipline, given the passivity of the spectator compared with the
rigors of Zen or monastic sitting; but parallels do exist. There
is a familiar type of meditation called one-pointedness, which
focuses the meditator's attention through the repetition of a
single sound or mental image. Yet another meditation practice encourages the sitter to let thoughts fall freely and dis-
orientedly, without anchoring them to any one point. The
films of Mizoguchi, say, seem to me a fusion of these two
methods: by their even, level presentation of one sort of trouble after another, they focus the viewer's mind on a single
point of truth, the Buddhist doctrine of suffering; and by
their extreme cinematographic fluidity, they arouse a state
akin to free fall.

At first I used to resist my mind's wandering during such
films, thinking I was wasting the price of admission. But just
as in Buddhist meditation one is instructed not to brush aside
the petty or silly thoughts that rise up, since these "distractions" are precisely the material of the meditation, so I began
to allow my movie-watching mind to yield more freely to daily
preoccupations, cares, memories that arose from some image
association. Sometimes I might be lost to a personal mental
thread for several minutes before returning with full attention
to the events onscreen; but when I did come back, it was with
a refreshed consciousness, a deeper level of feeling. What *Diary of a Country Priest* taught me was that certain kinds of
movies—those with austere aesthetic means; an unhurried,

---

*This essay was originally published in an anthology entitled *The Movie That
Changed My Life*, edited by David Rosenberg.

deliberate pace; tonal consistency; a penchant for long shots as opposed to close-ups; an attention to backgrounds and milieu; a mature acceptance of suffering as fate—allowed me more room for meditation. And I began to seek out other examples.

In various films by Ozu, Mizoguchi, Naruse, there will be a scene early on where the main characters are fiddling around in the house and someone comes by, a neighbor or the postman (the traditional Japanese domestic architecture, with its sliding shoji, is particularly good at capturing this interpenetration of inside and outside); a kimono-clad figure moves sluggishly through the darkened interior to answer, some sort of polite conversation follows; and throughout this business, one is not unpleasantly aware of an odd aural hollowness, like the mechanical thud-thud of the camera that used to characterize all films just after sound came in; and it isn't clear what the point of the scene is, except maybe to establish the ground of dailiness; and at such junctures I often start to daydream, to fantasize about a movie without any plot, just these shuttlings and patient, quiet moments that I like so much. Ah, yes, the lure of pure quotidian plotlessness for a writer like myself, who has trouble making up plots. But then I always remember that what gives these scenes their poignant edge is our knowledge that some plot is about to take hold, so that their very lack of tension engenders suspense: when will all this daily flux coalesce into a single dramatic conflict? Without the catastrophe to come, we probably would not experience so refreshingly these narrative backwaters; just as without the established, calm, spiritual ground of dailiness, we would not feel so keenly the ensuing betrayals, suicide pacts and sublimely orchestrated disenchantments.

I tried to take from these calm cinematic moments—to

convince myself I believed in—a sense of the sacredness of everyday life. I even piously titled my second poetry collection *The Daily Round*. I wanted the security, the solace of a constant, enduring order underneath things—without having to pay the price through ecstasy or transcendence. My desire had something to do with finding an inner harmony in the arrangement of backgrounds and foregrounds as I came across them in real life; an effort, part spiritual, part aesthetic, to graft an order I had learned through movies onto reality. How it originally came about was this way: watching a film, I would sometimes find myself transfixed by the objects in the background. I remember a scene in Max Ophuls's *Letter from an Unknown Woman*, when the heroine is ironing in the kitchen, and suddenly I became invaded by the skillets and homely kitchenware behind her. For several moments I began to dream about the life of these objects, which had become inexplicably more important to me than Joan Fontaine.

Certain directors convey a respect for rooms and landscapes at rest, for the world that surrounds the drama of the characters and will survive it long after these struggles are over. Ozu frequently used static cutaway shots of hallways, beaded curtains in restaurants—passageways made for routine human traffic, which are momentarily devoid of people. Bresson wrote: "One single mystery of persons and objects." And: "Make the objects look as if they want to be there. . . . The persons and objects in your film *must walk at the same pace, as companions.*" Antonioni also engaged in a tactful spying on objects, keeping his camera running long after the characters had quit the frame. Why these motionless transitions, I thought, if not as a way of asserting some constant and eternal order under the messy flux of accident, transience, unhappiness?

I tried, as I said, to apply this way of seeing to my own daily life outside movie theaters. I waited on objects to catch what Bresson calls their "phosphorescence." In general, these exercises left me feeling pretty pretentious. Just as there are people whom dogs and children don't seem to trust, so objects did not open up to me, beyond a polite, stiff acquaintance. They kept their dignified distance; I kept mine.

Once, I took Kay, a woman I had been dating for several years while steadfastly refusing to marry, to see Dreyer's *Ordet*. It has been as hard for me to surrender spiritually as conjugally; I have long since become the kind of skeptic who gets embarrassed for someone when he or she starts talking about astrology, out-of-body experiences, past lives or karma. I don't say I'm right, just that I'm rendered uncomfortable by such terms. And if the exotic vocabulary of Eastern religions makes me uneasy, the closer-to-home terminology of Christ the King and Christianity makes me doubly so—perhaps for no reason other than that I'm an American Jew. In any case, there we were at the Carnegie Hall Cinema, Kay (who is Presbyterian) and I; we had just seen the magnificent final sequence, in which Dreyer "photographs" a resurrection: the mentally disturbed Johannes, invoking Jesus Christ, raises Inger from the dead—which is shown not by any optical trick, mind you, but simply by filming the event head-on, unadorned. One moment the woman is lying in her bed; the next moment she sits up and kisses her husband. I don't know which moved me more, Dreyer's own seeming faith in miracles, his cinematic restraint, or the audacity of his challenge to the audience to believe or disbelieve as we saw fit. The lights went up, and, just as I was wiping away a tear, Kay punched me. "You see, you can take it in films, but you can't take it in life!" she said.

Sometimes I think I am especially inclined to the spiritual, and that is why I resist it so. At other times this seems nothing but a conceit on my part. You cannot claim credit for possessing a trait you have run away from all your life. This does not prevent me from secretly hoping that spirituality has somehow sneaked in the back door when I wasn't looking, or was miraculously earned, like coupons, through my "solitary struggles" as a writer. (It would not be the first time that making poetry or art was confused with spiritual discipline.)

Every once in a blue moon I go to religious services or read the Bible—hoping that this time it will have a deeper effect on me than merely satisfying some anthropological curiosity. I do not, by and large, perform good works; I do not pray, except in desperation. I have never pursued a regular meditative practice, or even meditated under a learned person's guidance (though I have many friends and relatives who described the experience for me). No, the truth is I probably have a very weak (though still alive) spiritual drive, which I exercise for the most part in movie theaters.

It is, I suppose, a truism that the cinema is the secular temple of modern life. A movie house is like a chapel, where one is alone with one's soul. Film intrinsically avows an afterlife by creating immortals, stars. In its fixing of transient moments with permanence, it bestows on even the silliest comic farce an air of fatalism and eternity. All well and good. What I want to know is: Did I purposely seek out the spiritual in movies in order to create a *cordon sanitaire*, to keep it from spilling into the other facets of my life?

Films have been a way for me to aspire to the spiritual, without taking it altogether seriously. *Diary of a Country Priest* may have helped shape my sense of beauty, but I notice that as a writer I have never striven for Bressonian purity. I am too gabby; such austerity is beyond me. In fact, when I encounter Bresson on the page, in interviews and in his writings, he sometimes seems to me insufferable. Even some of his films, especially the later ones like *The Devil, Probably,* and *Lancelot du Lac,* have passages that strike me as moronically solemn. And, as I am not the first to observe, there is often something mechanical in plots of Bresson, along with those of other modern Catholic storytellers—Graham Greene, Mauriac, Bernanos (who supplied the novel on which *Diary of a Country Priest* is based)—that stacks the deck in favor of sin, perverse willfulness and despair, the better to draw grace out of the pile later on. I think even as a college student I suspected this, but the very air of contrivance, which alluded to theological principles I ill understood, filled me with uncertainty and awe.

Another reason why I did not build more on the glimpses of spiritual illumination I received in movies occurs to me belatedly: all the films I was attracted to were either Christian* or Buddhist. I could not travel very far along this path without becoming disloyal to Judaism. Though I haven't been a particularly observant Jew, I retain an attachment to that identity; put bluntly, it would horrify me to convert to another faith. What, then, of Jewish models? Was there no Jewish transcendental cinema? I think not, partly because modern American Judaism doesn't appear to be very big on transcendence. There may be transcendental currents in the Old Testament, the Kabbalah or Kafka, but Judaism doesn't seem to me to put forward a particular theology of transcendence. Catholicism asserts that death can bring redemption and an afterlife, but it is unclear whether Judaism even believes in an afterlife. In my experience of Judaism, there is only morality, guilt, expiation and satisfaction in this life. Catholicism insists on the centrality of a mystery. Bresson quotes Pascal: "They want to find the solution where all is enigma only." And in Bresson's own words: "Accustom the public to divining the whole of which they are only given a

---

*Even Buñuel, another early favorite whom I took to be antireligious by his parodies of the transcendent, seems, in films like *Nazarin, Viridiana, Simon of the Desert*, heavily shaped by a Catholic worldview. To turn something inside out is still to be dependent on it.

part. Make people diviners." This language of divination and mystery seems to me very far from the analytical, Talmudic, potentially skeptical methods of Jewish study; as it happens, it is with the latter that I have come to identify.

One of the most beautiful passages in motion pictures is the ending of Mizoguchi's *Ugetsu*, when the errant potter returns to his cottage after long travels and a 180-degree pan finds his old wife sitting there, preparing him a meal. He falls asleep happy, only to wake up the next morning and learn from neighbors that his wife is dead: the woman who had tended him the night before was a ghost. The 180-degree movement had inscribed the loss all the more deeply through its play on absence and presence, invisibility and appearance. Such a noble presentation of the spirit life, common in Buddhist art, would be extremely rare in Jewish narratives, where ghosts are not often met.

If you were to think of a "Jewish cinema," names like the Marx Brothers, Woody Allen, Ernst Lubitsch, Jerry Lewis, Mel Brooks, Billy Wilder spring to mind—all skeptical mockers, ironists, wonderful clowns and secular sentimentalists. Yiddish films like *Green Fields* and *The Light Ahead* do have scenes of religious piety and custom, but even these celebrate the warmth and sorrows of a people rather than the spiritual quest of a lonely soul straining toward God. Whatever the virtues of Yiddish movies—humanity and humor in abundance—they are not aesthetically rigorous: indeed, it is the very muzziness of communal life that seems to constitute the core of their triumphant religious feeling.

As I look back, I realize that I needed to find something different, something I did not know how to locate in my watered-down Jewish background. I took to the "transcendental style" immediately; it was obviously the missing link in my aesthetic education. Movies introduced me to a constellation of ritual and spiritual emotion that I could willingly embrace so long as it was presented to me in the guise of cinematic expression, but not otherwise. At that point these appeals, these seductions, came into conflict with a competing spiritual claim, indefinitely put off but never quite abandoned: to become a good Jew, sometime before I die.

In writing an essay for an anthology called The Movie That Changed My Life, *I chose* Diary of a Country Priest *somewhat arbitrarily, out of the many dozens of movies that equally "changed" me, because it allowed me to reflect on the larger issue of spirituality and cinema. Since the piece appeared, I have been corrected numerous times by those learned in Judaica for making the statement that Judaism doesn't have "a particular ideology of transcendence." Being somewhat of an antitranscendentalist myself, I thought I was paying Judaism a compliment; but obviously I didn't know what I was talking about.*

FASSBINDER'S *DESPAIR*

September 1979, twenty years ago, at the height of my bachelor days.

I was at a party given for the German directors in the New York Film Festival; the Goethe House was filled with press agents, cultural attachés, distributors and freeloaders (like myself)—and I was talking to this bald-headed acquaintance of mine, Bruce, when a stunning blonde sauntered up and saucily hailed us, with Marlene Dietrich camaraderie: "*Junge, sind Sie Deutsche?*"

When we admitted we didn't speak the language, she translated, "Boys, are you German men?"—an odd, shivery question, in that we were both actually Jewish men. She had a model-chiseled face with an ambiguous, slightly cruel smile, the face of a beautiful betrayer, Marthe Keller in *Marathon Man* (I adore Marthe Keller), and her hips rotated boldly in a swishy black-purple skirt of pleated silk. So I strung together some chatter and she turned, more toward me than my friend, and asked (impertinently or flirtatiously, I was not sure which), "What are you doing here?"

"I'm here to celebrate the great German filmmaker Rainer Werner Fassbinder."

"Ah, yes, Fassbinder," she said with vague bitterness, as if she had completely forgotten that the party was being given largely in his honor. "I know him . . ." she said, even more vaguely. I wondered if she was an actress who had tried out unsuccessfully for a part in one of his films.

"Has he arrived yet?" I asked.

"Yah, sure," she said with the same air of contempt. And she pointed to a thicket of male backs surrounding the black-leather-jacketed, lardy figure, well known from his photographs, with scraggly beard and porcupine hair: his provokingly unwashed appearance a seeming incitement to those with a knack for turning frogs into princes.

I was tempted to go over there and pay my respects; but a fumbled blurting of sycophantic homage, met very possibly by rudeness on his part, would only muck up the pristine Fassbinder cosmos that existed in my head. Besides, I was more interested just then in my alluring conversant. "Forget Fassbinder; I just want to see his new film, *Despair*."

"Ya, *Despair*," she said, disappointedly.

"You're not interested in seeing it? It's supposed to be very good."

"I am but . . . I have not a bill. It was too late by the time I tried." Bruce wandered off, leaving the field to me. "Also, I hear they are very expensive."

Not so, but I allowed the error to stand. "I happen to have an extra ticket. Would you like to go with me?"

"Certainly!" Now she is all attention: she trains her green, huntress eyes on me. "You have an extra ticket? Perhaps you have two extra tickets."

"No, I'm sorry. Just one."

"I ask only because of my roommate. But—that doesn't matter. I would like very much to see it."

"Fine. When shall I pick you up? The film starts at nine o'clock."

"Eight-fifteen? Here is my address," she said, writing down on a cocktail napkin Gudrun something (I read upside down). Our names and phone numbers exchanged, we laughed, and suddenly had nothing further to say; each began to scan the room.

I now had a beautiful date for Saturday night. My bachelor strategy of buying pairs of tickets to the film festival was working. Fassbinder had always brought me romantic good luck: ever since his films had started appearing in the New York Film Festival, one or two each fall (taking over the position of fecund house-genius from Godard), they seemed to generate erotic as well as aesthetic rewards. Making out passionately in a taxicab after *Merchant of Four Seasons*; sleeping for the first time with someone new after *Fear Eats the Soul: Ali*; being taken back temporarily into an ex-girlfriend's good graces as a coda to *Fox and His Friends*.

It is a curious fact that, in the New York of the seventies, the films of this quintessentially gay director functioned as hot dates for straight couples.* Their aphrodisiac effect came, I suspect, from the coldness with which he portrayed sex. Especially sex between men and women. Think of the nude, adulterous Irm Hermann riding her prone lover in *Merchant of Four Seasons*, like a self-righteous *Hausfrau* performing with Lutheran grimness her duty to the sexual revolution. Fassbinder's couplings displayed none of the mistiness found in commercial movies' sex scenes, but rather, a bold, brutal pleasure-taking, less sentimental even than pornography, because pornography has its own sentimentality (the achievement of orgasm), whereas Fassbinder disdained to record this final tenderness. One of his early titles, *Love Is Colder Than*

---

*I realize that Ingrid Caven has insisted, in the pages of *Cahiers du Cinéma*, that Fassbinder was bisexual, but I still maintain that his was largely a gay aesthetic: the camp treatment of melodrama, the stylization of women's romantic emotion, the emphasis placed on cruising and tricks, etc.

Death, expressed his (peculiarly liberating) denial of the humanistic pretensions of love. I cherished his intransigent pessimism and his ruthless division between love and sexual appetite. He was like Bresson: one of the strict ones.

I had already suspected on our first meeting that Gudrun was false, coldhearted and probably unable to appreciate my best qualities. I expected little to come of our date, yet I was excited enough for the chance to pursue her. Was this longing for beautiful women to be explained by simple immaturity, insecurity or unimaginative consumerism on my part? Ought I to chalk it up to a film aesthete's saturation with the impossible dreams and erotic ideals the screen insidiously provided? Or perhaps this desire for beautiful women requires no excuse at all.

At the time, I kept picturing Gudrun's roommate as a redhead—seeing them as two sexy continental actresses sharing a New York apartment. Fantasies, fantasies and more fantasies. Yet I also had my doubts; I even imagined arriving and finding nobody home. Maybe that was why I got to her posh address—she lived in a thin, tasty town house on the Upper East Side—ten minutes early.

The door opened on several people scurrying and scraping their chairs. A small dinner party of Europeans, at the grapes, cheese and espresso stage. My evening date was clearing off the dishes from the table: it looked like the bones of a pork roast.

"So sorry, we have nothing to offer you!" said Gudrun with a dazzling smile. "It is all gone." She introduced me quickly to her company as they headed out the door, and to her roommate, Emil, a curly-haired, handsome fellow in a turtleneck. He shook my hand affably, thinking nothing of loaning his woman to me for the evening. Such *savoir-faire.*

Gudrun had gone to fetch a jacket, leaving me alone with her beau.

"So you like modern German cinema?" he asked me with feigned astonishment.

"Some of it, yes."

"But Fassbinder you like? I think I prefer Geistermacher and Schlöndorff, *The Tin Drum*."

"Schlöndorff has made some good films," I agreed.

"What do all you Americans see in Fassbinder? In Germany the public hates him."

Just then, Gudrun returned and stared at us both suspiciously. There was something strained, older-looking about her tonight. I began to justify my liking for Fassbinder: first, formally (his economy of means, his rigorous camera style, his expressive framing and color sense, his sly, deliberate tempo), then thematically. All Fassbinder movies, I said, no matter where they start, end up illustrating that life is cruel, humiliating and disappointing. In this way they were like Ozu or Naruse films, they gave no false consolation. And they were "religious" in the Buñuelian sense that every scene conveyed an underlying sense of sin.

I may as well have been speaking Chinese as far as Emil was concerned. Meanwhile, Gudrun pounced, "Say why you think that!" like a Prussian schoolmaster demanding, Define your terms, and when I did, then, "Ya, I see," reluctantly impressed, but as though sniffing out potentially stale, coffeehouse ideologies with her sharp, chiseled nose.

"Are you a film critic?" Emil asked, as though only this could explain my taking movies so seriously.

"No, but I am a writer. What do *you* do?" I asked, shifting the spotlight off myself.

He pretended not to hear the question, and said something in German to Gudrun. She replied curtly. The second time I asked (I was curious!), he told me with disinclination that he ran a business in New Jersey. What kind of business? I inquired. Repairing stock cars, he muttered. I saw nothing shameful in that: it helped pay for this duplex, which, with a white staircase connecting one floor to the other, had the kind of charm a New Yorker would kill for, and that a foreigner of a certain class seemed to luck into effortlessly. I congratulated him on the find. He said it was not as expensive as it looked: the landlord was an eccentric, who liked them, so he gave them a bargain. "We even get to use his roof garden, which has *Astroturf*." Though he said the word with the annoyingly slumming affection which hip Germans (like Wenders) have for American *Kitsch*, there was something about this Emil I could not help liking: a square-jawed, basic innocence, perhaps.

He saw us to the door, and they again exchanged a few sentences in German. I imagined her saying, "I'll ditch this sucker by eleven-thirty and return to you, luv, so keep the bed warm," because his face lit up at the end.

In the taxi Gudrun told me she was writing a novel. It was to be all about America, from the viewpoint of a European woman. It would be called *The Money Farm* (what else?). "I don't know if the title sounds so good in English. In German it sounds just right to my ear. The story is about an intellectual woman living in America with a racing car driver. She does not understand him because he is not intellectual and so on. They start in New York and go to Las Vegas. It is written in short scenes. No chapters, just extra white space. Like in a film—oh, what is the word? In German we call it *Schnitt*."

"Cuts?"

"Yes," she said, surprised.

I told her I had recently published a novel. She asked me avidly how often I wrote, how many hours and pages a day, whether I made outlines. After each answer I gave, she became more insecure. She confessed she had never written a novel before and was probably not doing it right. I tried to reassure her that there was no "right way" to do a novel, each time one was in the dark. I sensed that she was both discounting my words and secretly holding on to them.

The taxi to Lincoln Center got us there ahead of time and in our seats waiting for the film to begin she told me her life story. She had been a sensitive child, had written poems from early on, had done a little modeling and acting but decided to become a journalist "for practical reasons," had married young and gotten divorced, had come to America to make big money but all she had gotten was the runaround. Now she wants to go back. But not until she finishes her novel. "I am at an age where I must make a success."

"How old are you?" I asked.

"Thirty-five."

"The same as me. That's not so old. Why must you have a success just now?"

"Because I am living in a country where I don't feel I belong. And my child is back in Germany. She is ten years old and I want to join her. But it's difficult, because of the father. . . . And I don't communicate well with Emil. And for many other reasons."

She looks unhappy, momentarily overwhelmed by her life. The lights dim. I would like to know how solid is this discontent with her boyfriend; but I don't dare allow myself to think of it as an invitation. At stage-front, Richard Roud, the festival director, introduces Fassbinder, who says a few words in sweet halting English, ending with the obligatory "I hope you will like the film."

In fact, *Despair* is awful.

So awful that I probably would have left in the middle, were I by myself. Moreover, it is the first time I have failed to be charmed by Fassbinder. Oh, I'd seen weaker Fassbinders before (*Chinese Roulette*, *Jailbait*, *Satan's Brew*, etc.), but each time there was the pleasure of watching a minor work by a major director, and enjoying the signature of his orderly style flowing through the chaotic, sloppy ruins. Indeed, some of my favorite Fassbinders were precisely the rawer or more plotless ones, when characters lurched around wasting time in an interesting way: *Beware of a Holy Whore*, *The Bitter Tears of Petra von Kant*, *In a Year of Thirteen Moons*. . . . The problem with *Despair* was that it did not feel, properly speaking, like a Fassbinder picture. It was a European Art Film, slickly shot, polished, with high production values—but no soul. Working from such seemingly highbrow material, a Tom Stoppard script adapted from a Nabokov novel, the director seemed lost, like a maître d' at a fancy restaurant, left with nothing to do but seat people. The first half of the movie was taken up with shooting the characters through lamps and glass partitions, against frosted glass walls, amid every Art Deco prop imaginable. John Grierson once remarked, à propos von Sternberg, that when a filmmaker deteriorates he becomes a photographer. In Fassbinder's case, the temptation was to become an art director.

One reason the film lacked the proper Fassbinder tone was that it was in English; perhaps I was being snobbish in missing the exotic distancing of the German tongue. Another reason was the fetishistically tony way its international star, Dirk Bogarde, was employed, in a congealed parody of Visconti's and Losey's earlier, sexually ambiguous use of that actor. It did not help matters that Bogarde was called upon to fake a Russian accent, nor made to writhe randily yet distastefully in elegant dressing gown over a plump, naked Andrea Ferreol, whose fleshy corpulence the director seemed to mock. So much dialogue in the early reels was taken up with the hero calling his wife "a stupid woman" and a "featherbrain," and she concurring with this judgment (while cuckolding him with her "cousin"), that it was hard not to scent misogyny. This time I felt alienated from Fassbinder's overall sensibility: he seemed to be portraying heterosexuality itself as a vulgar, tacky prejudice.

The secret of Fassbinder's dramatic power had always been the underground sympathy he showed for his otherwise messed-up characters; but this time there was no sympathy, only chilly mannerism. Bogarde plays a rich, jaded Russian, Herman Herman, who owns a chocolate factory. Neurotically detached from himself and his life, he meets a worker named Felix, who is broad-shouldered and endomorphic, but whom Herman deludedly believes is the spit-and-image of himself. As in Hitchcock's *Stranger on a Train*, the two men seem to merge identities, with homoerotic undertones. Herman kills Felix, and exchanges his clothing with the corpse, thinking he can assume the dead man's life as well. But of course, looking nothing like the victim, he is tracked down by the police, and the film ends with a Norman Bates–like voice-over monologue of the madman to the camera.

All this occurs against a rise-of-Nazism backdrop, which seems present more as costume opportunity—Weimar decadent chic—than serious political commentary. Amid the deadeningly cynical reversals, the only feeling of any kind seems reserved for the scenes between Bogarde's Herman and the proletarian Felix (Klaus Lowitsch). The plot, while admittedly clever, is also so far-fetched, so sterilely "playful," that Fassbinder cannot settle down to telling it; his camera, usually so patient, roams over the natty decor like a restless shopper. The film itself ends up a box of (bitter) chocolates.

I cast about for some way to excuse my directorial idol. Perhaps it was the big budget: Fassbinder's vitality came out strongest when improvising on the cheap. Or was it the script?—that Stoppard was all too crafty, I never liked *Rosencrantz and Guildenstern Are Dead*, he'd tricked Fassbinder into playing his academic illusion-and-reality games, the way that other British playwright, David Mercer, had crippled poor

Resnais in *Providence*. Or maybe it was excessive reverence for Nabokov's text: Fassbinder's crude power matched up poorly with the subtle, devious Russian master.* And surely Bogarde's arched-eyebrow performance deserved some blame; fine actor though he was, he needed sitting on. But in the end, the fault rested with Fassbinder. I wondered if he had exhausted the personal in his previous year's masterpiece, *In a Year of Thirteen Moons*—gone so far in the direction of honesty that he could only retreat to this smoothly mannerist, armored style.

When we stood up, Gudrun slipped her cinnamon tweed jacket over her tapioca satin blouse. I notice that a) she is very beautiful, with that remarkable golden hair; and b) her cheeks look puffy. Could she have been so moved by that tripe?

"What did you think?" I ask.

"Well—I am afraid to say, not very good!"

"A total mess. Fassbinder's worst," I declare. We are relieved to agree. As we leave the theater, I ask self-consciously, "Would you like to go somewhere for a drink?"

"Yes, why not?" she answers, but somberly; she seems preoccupied, reabsorbed in her problems. She tells me she must fly tomorrow to Las Vegas to research the novel and write an article on American gambling for a German magazine. "This editor is a total swine."

We walk a block or two to O'Neals, and just as we are about to go inside, she stops at the revolving doors, as if trying to remember something.

"I must go home because my teeth are hurting. I have

---

*Years later I read David Thomson's tough appraisal: "*Despair* was his most lavish picture and the expense only showed a mind far more trite than that of Nabokov. *Despair* is one of the most dreadful spectacles of bull filmmaking being humiliated by literature's droll veronicas." (*A Biographical Dictionary of Film*) had root canal today, and it still feels very sore. Did you ever have root canal?"

"No," I say, "but it must be painful." I put her in a yellow taxi, telling her to have a good time in Las Vegas, and walk home thinking, Root canal—that's a new one.

"Root canal" seemed to put the perfect sardonic cap on this romantic misadventure. I regarded it purely as an alibi, and she as a "cheat," escaping her social obligations to have a drink with me (the prolongation of my erotic fantasy); though I now wonder if her teeth were actually in pain, which would explain her puffy cheeks. In retrospect, I see that I had set myself up for disappointment: by bribing her with the ticket, I made it almost impossible to accept that she was interested in me, and I thrust her into the role of the heartless coquette who would leave me at the door of the saloon. I can hardly believe I was so naïve as not to guess that her "roommate" was a man. Beautiful women rarely live alone. Perhaps I did have a premonition, but simply needed to play out the farce. When I met Emil, his rugged handsomeness clicked in my mind as the physically appropriate counterpart for the exquisite Gudrun. I was getting my comeuppance for thinking I could make off with this lovely starlet type I had no business to covet. Back to your kennel.

Which shows how far we are willing to stretch reality to fit our need for rejection. The irony was that Gudrun was not a starlet, after all, but another struggling writer, eager for craft advice, who—far from dismissing me as a clumsy nerd—perhaps even looked up to me. Neither was she that clichéd "cold German" I had wanted her to be (as a *frisson* to my New York Jewish soul), but someone with a mountain of problems, who seemed trapped, baffled by life, going round and round in place. It was I who showed a measure of coldness by my inadequate, or uneven, sympathy. True, I had been touched by the frankness of her despair; yet, once I realized that my chances of sleeping with her were nil, I was happy to dismiss her as something between a misdirected opportunist and a loser. More precisely, I saw her as the prototype of an insecure glamorous woman who is utterly bored with her looks but has traded on them all her life, so that she doesn't know how to substitute patience and discipline for the shortcuts they have given her.

And yet, I had listened eagerly enough. My mother had trained me from childhood on to listen to a woman's troubles. Gudrun remarked that she thought it odd to be telling so many personal things so shortly after meeting me, but to me it was perfectly natural: I had slipped into the Oedipal situation, complete with larger virile man in the background whom she complained did not understand her. I had become the "son" paralyzed between pressing his suit and loyally defending his father. In the end, I had listened to Gudrun with the same engrossment I might have felt while watching one of Fassbinder's films about women in crisis, such as *Fear of Fear*, in which a gaunt, elegant blonde becomes increasingly isolated and anxious. Life is the continuation of film by other means.

As it happened, I was given a second chance to take her seriously as a human being, when—marring the perfection of the "root canal" vignette—Gudrun phoned me, after her return from Las Vegas. She had greatly enjoyed our last conversation, she said, and called just to chat. She may also have been indirectly looking for a way out of her life with Emil, but this I will never know; I was not that encouraging and failed to arrange another meeting with her. It struck me at the time that she was lonely for a writing guru or a brotherly confidant, neither of which role I wanted to play with her. You see, I was in the market strictly for a lover.

• • •

And what about Fassbinder? *Despair* proved to be a turning point in my appreciation of him. Though I never reneged on my passion for his earlier movies, it was one of those films that jolted me out of a particular *auteur* worship. With Antonioni, the disenchantment had been *Zabriskie Point*, with Fellini, *Juliet of the Spirits*, with Kurosawa, *Red Beard*, with Truffaut, *Stolen Kisses*: these were works that exposed some smug, rancid or intellectually shallow side of their maker's personality, to an extent that it was no longer possible for me to look forward to their future productions with uncritical faith.

After *Despair,* Fassbinder went on to make a few decent movies, like *Lola* and *Veronika Voss*, but for the most part, I felt, his juices had dried up. *Berlin Alexanderplatz*, that supposed summit of Fassbinderist art, actually seems to me flat and indifferently realized, a TV miniseries directed by the yard. He appeared to have lost his way, partly thanks to drugs, by the time he died of an overdose. Of course, such hindsight can never be trusted: had he lived, he may well have got a second wind and turned out even riper, more mature masterpieces.

Indeed, I believe that the cinema has never properly recovered from the untimely deaths of its last two great visionaries, Fassbinder and Tarkovsky. Perhaps because we have never properly grieved them—allowed ourselves fully to feel the emptiness their passing left on the world's screens—we cinephiles stumble on, mumbling and complaining and hoping and exaggerating our enthusiasms, in the perplexing, splintered and mostly numb terrain which is contemporary film.

"We have lost our greasy wild boar," Werner Herzog said after Fassbinder's death. Hearing his words, I felt a pang of loss myself; and I wished I had bothered to introduce myself to the leather-jacketed maestro that evening at the Goethe House.

FILMS AND FILM-MAKERS

THE OPERATIC REALISM OF
LUCHINO VISCONTI

Rocco and His Brothers is the kind of film you either embrace as one of the most powerful moviegoing experiences
ever, or dismiss as corny and overwrought. I saw it when it
opened in 1961, and I have to say it changed my life. The
three-hour epic of five Southern Italian brothers and their
mother who migrate to Milan, driven by economic hope, only
to encounter tragedy and the family's destruction through
the perversity of goodness (that Dostoevskian theme), was as
close as I could imagine to a novel on film. Having seen it
many times since, it still seems so. The depth of characterization captured in three extraordinary performances by Alain
Delon, Renato Salvatori and Annie Girardot, the piercing
black and white photography by the great Giuseppe Rotunno,
the ever-intelligent screenwriting by Suso Cecchi D'Amico,
the haunting score by Nino Rota, and above all, the warm,
commanding direction of Luchino Visconti, cast a spell over
me that I have never shaken off. Yet I understand when someone tells me the film left him or her cold—because Visconti
and *Rocco* are not for everyone.

Perhaps more than any other giant of world cinema,
Luchino Visconti occupies an uneasy critical niche. He does
not fit tidily into the pat formal lineages by which cinema his-

tory gets divided. He is usually credited as one of the founders of Italian neorealism (along with Rossellini and De Sica), but his love of melodrama, of grand passions spilling from overflowing canvases, turned him into a walking oxymoron of operatic realism, bisexuality, extravagant restraint. Politically progressive, celebrating in many of his greatest films the vitality of the working class, he was also the supreme elegiast of his own aristocratic world—exemplifying, as it were, that truism that patricians often feel more compatible with the poor than the middle class. Caricatured as the "red Count," accused of "voting Left and living Right" because of his taste for caviar and gloved servants, Visconti was a defiant individualist, a handsome man of royal, seductive presence, a magnet for controversy—and always a bit out of sync with his times, which may explain why he has gone in and out of style so often.

Now, twenty years after his death, he is back in fashion: starting November 21, the Museum of Modern Art, in connection with Ente Cinema and the Centro Sperimentale of the Cinematografia/Cineteca Nationale, Rome, is presenting the first complete Visconti retrospective in the United States, with restored prints of all fourteen features and four shorts, including rarities (such as the 1945 documentary *Days of Glory*) never seen here. For a filmmaking career that spanned thirty-five years, it is a fairly tight body of work. This is partly because Visconti divided his energies between the theater, opera and film (only Orson Welles had a similar impact on three media), and partly because, being a man of independent means, he did not have to accept commercial assignments. For better or worse, every film that bore his signature was a personal artistic project he wanted to make.

Luchino Visconti, born in 1906, came from one of the oldest, most noble families in Milan. His grandfather, the Duke of Modrone, had heavily supported the La Scala opera house; his father was a cultivated playboy, who arranged private theatricals in the palazzo, usually starring his mother, a talented amateur actress and musician who was the daughter of a millionaire industrialist. Luchino early showed a propensity for staging plays at home, bossing his siblings and friends into taking part. His parents had an open marriage, with infidelities on both sides (like many of the wedded characters who would later appear in his films); but they were ultimately too incompatible and separated. Luchino adored his mother, and was leery of his father, who sent him to cavalry school for discipline. The young man fell in love with horses, and spent ten years racing and raising them—he was well on his way to becoming a playboy himself.

It was not until his thirties, when he went to Paris in the 1930s, that he fell in with an artistic crowd. Two of his lovers, the fashion designer Coco Chanel and the photographer Horst Horst, completed his aesthetic education. Chanel introduced him to the great French filmmaker Jean Renoir, who took him on as third assistant director for *A Day in the Country*. From Renoir he learned not only the rudiments of filmmaking, but an appreciation for a humanistic cinema bursting with vitality, focusing on ordinary people, using natural locations and uninterrupted, deep focus shots. The crowd around Renoir were all supporters of the social-democratic Popular Front, and Visconti, who had earlier dabbled in Fascism, quickly switched leftward, maintaining allegiance to Italian Communism for the rest of his life.

Renoir, who was quite fond of Visconti (they were to have collaborated on a film of *La Tosca*), passed along to him a script based on James M. Cain's *The Postman Always Rings Twice*, about a drifter and a woman who kill her husband. It was this story Visconti decided to film as his first feature, using his own private funds for financing. Hard-boiled American fiction had a vogue among Italian anti-Fascists at the time; and simply by choosing such a pessimistic story, Visconti could register a veiled protest against the gung-ho state propaganda and frothy "white telephone" movies that were the staple of Mussolini's film industry. *Ossessione (Obsession)*, made in 1942, has often been credited as the first neorealist movie, because of its hardscrabble look and focus on the have-nots. But, to the degree that Italian neorealism was a specific response to a historical moment (the end of the war and its aftermath), it would probably be more accurate to say *Ossessione* was pre-neorealist. In fact, it had more in common with the sensual fatalism of French poetic realist films made by Renoir, Julien Duvivier and Marcel Carné. And, though it shares many *film noir* plot elements with the two American versions of Cain's *The Postman Always Rings Twice*, its pace is more leisurely, unspooling at two hours and fifteen minutes. Some of the best scenes are digressive, unhurried, like the singing contest in the café or the moody road cutaways. And, unlike the Hollywood *film noir* versions, Visconti's is less violent (the murder occurs offscreen) and gravitates toward a surprisingly tender place, as the guilty couple (memorably played by Massimo Girotti and Clara Calamai) modulate from lust to revulsion to a more committed, grown-up love. The third pole of the "triangle" is not the husband but a free-spirited, homosexual vagabond named the Spaniard, who tempts the drifter with his Whitmanesque vision of the open road. The scene where the Spaniard contemplates the sleeping back of the protagonist has an adult lyricism that goes far beyond what we usually expect from this genre.

By all accounts, Visconti was an authoritative maestro from his first day of shooting; he never had to be told where to place the camera or how to coach the actors. *Ossessione* is as good a first feature as has ever been made. It ran into problems with first the Italian censors and then the American distribution companies (Visconti had never bothered to secure film rights for Cain's novel). As he cast about for a project that would more directly express his growing political commitment, he gave money to the Resistance and hid partisans in his house—actions which eventually led to his being arrested by the Gestapo, imprisoned in a toilet and beaten up. Visconti's anti-Fascist credentials, in short, were probably better than those of any other neorealist director by the time the war ended. He went way out on a limb with his next opus, a three-hour semidocumentary, *La Terra Trema (The Earth Trembles,* 1948), loosely inspired by Verga's novel *I Maravoglia,* about impoverished Sicilian fishermen and their struggle to improve their lot. The film daringly refused to sentimentalize the chances for hope or economic reform, which did not promote its commercial possibilities. Nor did it help sell tickets that the fishermen (he used the population of Aci Trezza as his "actors") spoke a dialect even the average Italian could not fathom. But of course Visconti was not governed by box office considerations: he wanted to make a cinematically beautiful agitprop statement, on the order of those other quixotic films about the People, Eisenstein's *Que Viva Mexico* or Orson Welles's *It's All True.* And again he succeeded, with a unique, moving, sweeping if at times tedious epic, magnificently photographed. One reviewer noted that the fishermen came out looking like Renaissance princes, while the great French critic André Bazin spoke of the "refined theatrical sense of Visconti, who makes compositions of the most down-to-earth reality as if they were scenes from an opera or a classical tragedy."

Truly, Visconti was a man of the theater. In the fifties he turned his attention to innovative stage productions of plays by Tennessee Williams, Arthur Miller and Shakespeare, whipping the undisciplined Italian actors (and audiences) into shape. A lifelong devotee of classical music, he also began directing a series of legendary opera productions, most memorably those with Maria Callas, whose acting ability and stage presence he did much to develop. To the staging of theater and opera he brought an understated fluency learned from making movies, just as he continued to inform his film direction with an operatic vision.

To say that Visconti's films are operatic should not be read as disparaging. What he took from his knowledge of opera was a lyrical ability to make you feel continuity—the overall arch of the story; a disposition to present the narrative in duets, trios, even solos; and a patient accumulation of affect until it burst like an aria released with volcanic force. Visconti was unafraid of oversized emotion; his willingness to go for the big emotional payoff onscreen is brave and, for the most part, effective. If he courted melodrama, he averted the cruder sentimentalities of the form by carefully preparing for climaxes with psychological shading.

Another carryover from opera, some might argue, is the diva-ish presentation of the suffering woman who wreaks havoc. This figure occurs in *Ossessione*, *Bellissima*, *Sandra* and, especially, *Senso*. In the 1954 *Senso*, Alida Valli, as a highborn Venetian woman who enters into a degrading affair with a younger, narcissistic Austrian officer (played by Farley Granger), brings a hysterical conviction to the role. To those who, at the time, accused Visconti of "betraying" neorealism by making such a sumptuous period film of grand emotions, the director replied that he *was* being realistic because there are people who are genuinely melodramatic. Now we can better appreciate the thematic continuity of destructive passion from *Ossessione* to *Senso*: how much in common the bedraggled Giovanna or the harassed Countess have, despite their different class status. Toward the end, when the Countess visits her lover, whose freedom from the army she has paid for with funds stolen from the partisans, only to find him shacked up with a prostitute, she must experience a protracted humiliation (Farley Granger at his most sneering) very similar to what Giovanna experienced, in *Ossessione*, coming upon Gino with another woman.

Senso is one of Visconti's greatest achievements: a

densely layered story set in the Garibaldi period of Italian na-
tionalism, as much about the bitter lessons of history (idealism yielding to maintenance of the status quo) as it is about
erotic passion. Indeed, nineteenth-century history was a passion of Visconti's, and he became a stickler for accurate detail.
When male extras showed up wearing black top hats in the
opening opera scene, Visconti blew up at his long-suffering
costume designer, Piero Tosi, exclaiming that any ignoramus
knew in those days they wore gray top hats to the opera. "If
you had read Stendhal or Balzac with more attention, you
would have known!" Like Erich von Stroheim, who splurged
on details, like the royal guardsmen's underwear, in order to
engender the aura of authenticity, Visconti could go overboard spending on flowers or building churches as sets. But,
like Stroheim, there was method behind his mania: he constructed narratives out of the dogged massing of physical fact,
detail by detail, until the past took on a Balzackian material
solidity.

Nowhere does this weight of accurately observed detail
more triumphantly bear fruit than in Visconti's other masterpiece set in the Risorgimento period, *The Leopard*. Based on
di Lampedusa's lush, memorable novel, and anchored by Burt
Lancaster's wonderful performance as the Sicilian nobleman
who witnesses philosophically the transfer of power from his
own aristocratic class to a grasping set of opportunistic *par-
venus*, *The Leopard* is a mellow and melancholy feast. Visconti
the Marxist is fully aware of the need for the old order to disappear; Visconti the patrician conservative cannot help but
imbue it with heroism and dignity. Pauline Kael, who called
the full version of the film "intelligent and rapturous," noted
that "in the concluding hour, at the Ponteleone Ball—certainly the finest hour of film that Visconti ever shot (and the
most influential, as *The Godfather* and *The Deer Hunter* testify)—it all comes together. . . . Throughout this sequence, in
which the Prince relives his life, experiences regret, and ac-

cepts the dying of his class and his own death, we feel we're inside the mind of the Leopard saying farewell to life." The ball is a tour de force, as the camera glides from room to room—a vindication of Visconti's practice of taking his time and letting a scene settle in.

It is precisely because Visconti made such long movies, however, that his work was so often mutilated by distributors and producers. *The Leopard*'s initial American release was not only egregiously dubbed, but hacked to pieces: the shorter version, paradoxically, felt overlong, as Andrew Sarris noted, "because the meaningful links are severed and the plot dribbles out in all directions." Visconti, who had already seen *Ossessione*, *Senso*, and *Rocco* suffer at the hands of censors and distribution companies, disowned the American *Leopard*, crying out: "It is our destiny to be always in the hands of assassins. . . . We work for months and months to create material that is then torn to shreds by ravening dogs."

The Leopard marked a moment of classical equilibrium between Visconti's objective, dispassionate interest in the world and his need to express the more intense personal aspects of his character. Afterward—perhaps buoyed by the international prestige received from *The Leopard*—he entered a phase that was more subjectively, and, it must be said, self-indulgently, expressive of his inner demons and family scars. Not that the family unit hadn't always been a basic preoccupation for the filmmaker. As Visconti eloquently put it: "Maybe for reasons of my own, maybe because it is within the family that there still exist these last unique taboos, the moral and social prohibitions, the last impossible loves—in any case, the family nucleus seems to me very important. All our way of living, of being, of loving, derives from there, from the inheritance we carry with us, from the happiness or unhappiness of our childhood. Each of us is the product of the smallest social cell, before being the product of society—often an unchangeable product, or capable of modification only with great difficulty. So the family represents a kind of fate or destiny, impossible to elude."

Starting with *Sandra*, he began to tackle more directly the idea of the Inescapable Family as a breeding ground for incest, homosexuality, political perversion and genetic karma. Though it has breathtaking scenes of black-and-white visuals (here, as elsewhere, Visconti approaches more than any other modern director the silent film poetry of Murnau and Stroheim), we come away much more convinced of the carnal beauty of Claudia Cardinale and Jean Sorel, who play brother and sister, than the murky, unresolved mess which passes for *Sandra's* plot.

Visconti, a Lombard proud of his cultural ties to Austria and Germany, then went through an overblown Teutonic phase, trying to promote in the process his actor-companion Helmut Berger. The so-called German trilogy—*Death in Venice*, *The Damned* and *Ludwig*—was an inspiration to Fassbinder, if no one else, in its overly self-conscious decadence. As his biographer, Gaia Servadio, observed, "He adopted realism when decadence was the accepted line and he moved to decadence when realism was." *Death in Venice* seems to me, like Visconti's other claustrophobic, overliterary adaptation of that period, *The Stranger*, purely and simply a mistake. In filming the Mann novella, his psychic energies seemed to have been most engaged with re-creating Silvana Mangano as a dead ringer for his own mother. Otherwise it is surprisingly inert. *The Damned* has its champions, but I have never been able to get beyond its treatment of Nazism as spectacle, which comes dangerously close to that attitude Susan Sontag characterized as "Fascinating Fascism." Yet no Visconti film is badly made, and even the three-hour *Ludwig*, dioramic and becalmed as it may be, is not without its loopy grandeur.

Because Visconti's five masterworks—*Ossessione*, *La Terra Trema*, *Senso*, *Rocco and His Brothers* and *The Leop-*

ard—all belong in the early part of his filmmaking career, there is a tendency to view the later years simplistically as one long decline. Actually, Visconti finished up with two excellent pictures: the brittle, intelligent *Conversation Piece*, again starring Burt Lancaster and Silvana Mangano as Visconti's parental figures, with Helmut Berger as representative of the younger generation (a film much better in the Italian-language version than the original American-dubbed release), and *The Innocent*, with Laura Antonelli and Giancarlo Giannini, a sensually compelling and hypnotically twisted tale based on the D'Annunzio novel. If nothing else, the wallpaper and drapes in *The Innocent* are worth memorizing: we may never see such historically informed, gorgeous art direction in a *fin de siècle* picture again. Not to be overlooked are some earlier minor gems in Visconti's oeuvre: *Bellissima*, that wry, bustling Visconti comedy about movie mania, gifted by the unstoppable Anna Magnani as the stage mother; *White Nights*, an eerie fairy tale set in an abstract city (obviously studio-built), with Marcello Mastroianni and Maria Schell, which gracefully reimagines the Dostoevsky novella in modern terms; and *The Job*, a segment from the compilation film *Boccaccio '70*, with a delicious Romy Schneider performance as a wife getting revenge on her playboy husband.

Visconti, who was well read and venerated Mann and Proust, ran out of time before he could film his two dream projects: *Buddenbrooks* and *Remembrance of Things Past*. (He had gone so far as to cast the Proust, but negotiations fell through.) His nicotine habit of eighty cigarettes a day eventually took its toll, as did other abuses of his once superbly athletic physique; he suffered a stroke, and was forced to direct in the end from a wheelchair.

There is a funny anecdote, characteristic of the maestro at the height of his powers, when he tried to go backstage after an opera to see Callas. Prevented by the usher, Visconti yelled at him: "Don't you know who I am?" "Yes," replied the man, "and I know that you are going to die, just the same as I am." Visconti retorted: "You, yes, me, no!" He often laughed afterward at this story and what it said about himself. In the end, of course, the usher proved right: Visconti passed away in 1976, but not before leaving a body of filmic work whose nobility and vitality will, I think, ensure its survival.

Like many film directors, only more so, Visconti worshiped physical beauty. In the most barren rock pile in Sicily, he could not help but frame a stunning landscape worthy of Mantegna. The Northern Italian masters of the Renaissance (Titian, Veronese) hovered over his imagination. He captured Claudia Cardinale's face with voluptuous ferocity in *Sandra*, caressed Laura Antonelli's naked curves in *The Innocent*. When his camera's gaze rested on a handsome man, be it Massimo Girotti stripped to a sleeveless undershirt in *Ossessione* or Alain Delon in the shower in *Rocco*, you could feel the homoerotic interest steaming off the lens. He loved talented performers and he was a great director of actors, and his grasp of staging a scene, of entrances and exits, could not have been bettered. Possessing all the refined taste in the world, he knew how to decorate and light a shot so that it glowed but did not crow. Still, he was as much a humanist as a mannerist, as *Rocco and His Brothers* amply demonstrates.

As this piece was commissioned for the Sunday Arts and Leisure section of the New York Times, I could not expatiate on some of my more personal responses to Visconti's work. While writing it, I found myself almost sickened by the burden of trying to do justice to this fascinating, complicated oeuvre in 1600 words (only a book would suffice), while at the same time wondering why I was so drawn to Visconti's movies in the first place, since usually I am much less attracted to mannerist, operatic narrative. Perhaps I was hooked by the importance he accorded family drama. Certainly, much also had to do with the formative impact that Rocco and His Brothers *had had on me as a teenager. It was playing at a large Times Square theater (the Rivoli, no?), with prices higher than normal, and there was even an intermission in the middle—all of which made the experience seem more an "event." (The same treatment had been successful in launching* La Dolce Vita: *a reserved ticket policy at a theater usually showing Broadway plays.) Anyhow, I went to see* Rocco *with my older brother, Lenny, which in itself was significant, since so much of the drama revolves around sibling jealousy—a familiar theme in our household. I come from a large family, quite poor—the emotional terrain of* Rocco *was, in short, spookily familiar. There had been intense competition among the Lopate siblings, not least emanating from me: I gloated at doing better scholastically than my older brother, but I was also physically frightened of him, since he'd beaten me up when we were younger—not regularly, but enough to make the point. As the prototypical Good Boy, I identified with the younger, saintlier—and more "chosen"—Rocco, just as I had identified with Alyosha in* The Brothers Karamazov *(which served, by the way, as one of the sources for the Visconti film). So we watched spellbound, Lenny and I, as Simone beat the shit out of Rocco. In the intermission, Lenny blurted out a family secret which our mother had confided to him some time earlier. Under the pressure of the Visconti movie, he could no longer hold it in. I sat through the second half enthralled with the movie, and shattered by the secret which I was now burdened with—which I am not at liberty to tell here. (Years later, when approached by David Rosenberg to contribute to his anthology* The Movie That Changed My Life, *I immediately thought of* Rocco and His Brothers, *but decided in the end that a personal essay on the subject would be too explosive, and so switched to Bresson's* Diary of a Country Priest.)

Now, when I think of Rocco, *what strikes me most is its glamorous sheen. Even its scenes of poverty, like the one when all the brothers shovel snow, seemed tinged from the beginning with glamour: perhaps because the family's straitened circumstances when they arrive in the big city did not strike me as so downtrodden or unfamiliar (my family was living at the time in a Brooklyn slum), I focused instead on the allure of Milan: the train station, the night scenes, the pavement's reflections in rain and snow, the Duomo, even the bleak public housing. Part of it was because everything European looked romantic to me then, and part of it was Visconti's intention: never had a city's grubby face been rendered as lustrously. One would have to go back to Borzage's Seventh Heaven or Street Angel to find ordinary, naked-bulb poverty so spiritualized.*

Though the film purported to be about the scars of economic immiseration, visually I received another, undercover message: it was about the aura, and with it the power, that gets transferred from face to face, person to person—first alighting on Simone (Renato Salvatori), then passing to the beautiful, soiled Nadia (Annie Girardot), then coming to rest definitively on Rocco, the innocent, the champ (Alain Delon). It is not so much that Simone beats up Rocco, as that Salvatori thrashes Delon, so resentful is the displaced actor for having to relinquish center stage. Rocco is Visconti's paean to the star system, with Delon as Garbo. And the cinematographer Giuseppe Rotunno is Lee Garmes to both Delon and Milan equally.

The way other people worship movie stars, I worship cities. Those stirrings of urban romance which I would come to feel more and more, I first became aware of in adolescence, while looking at Visconti's Milan, or Godard's Paris, or Buñuel's Mexico City.

Later, there was an aura around all of Visconti's movies, largely because they were so impossible to see. One would read, and drool over, descriptions of Senso, Ossessione, Bellissima, White Nights. *When the mangled American version of* The Leopard *opened, I was deeply disappointed; the film seemed random, pointless. Decades later I would see the restored, full-length version and feel it belonged on my Ten Best list.*

Ossessione *seemed even more unattainable, a Holy Grail of*

cinema—until one day, in the early seventies, when I was visiting my friend Tom Luddy in San Francisco, he casually remarked that the Pacific Film Archives, which he had run, had a 16mm print of Ossessione. I was welcome to take it home and look at it anytime. Trembling, I carried it back that night to my friend Herbert Kohl's house, where I was staying, and projected it against a sheet hanging on the wall. The ritual air of the screening was accentuated by my having to change each reel by hand, which I did so lovingly and laboriously, with ten-minute breaks between reels; Herb, his children and his wife Judy had long gone to sleep by the time I finished projecting it, for myself alone. When it ended, I could not tell if I was in a dusty town in Italy in the mid-forties or in Berkeley, California, the only one awake in a suburban house. Seeing Ossessione against that wrinkled bedsheet hung on a bumpy wall remains one of my most cherished movie experiences.

THE WORLD ACCORDING TO MAKAVEJEV

Dušan Makavejev's films are sly, earthy, intellectual, invigorating and provocative. A true anarchist, he takes audiences on a cinematic joyride, unleashing mayhem, exciting fantasies of pleasure, then showing with a jolt the price that ride exacts. Once, in an interview with me, he spoke mischievously about substituting Stalin for Lenin in a political montage sequence, saying "this is like when children discover that this is not grandma, but the wolf." In a sense, "Grandma, what big teeth you have!" might be the subtitle of his entire *oeuvre*.

A psychology student at the University of Belgrade, Yugoslavia, who also wrote film criticism, Makavejev by his own admission wanted to make political films like Eisenstein and Godard. "But," he told me, "I wanted to do it with *soul*. To do it with feeling, to do it with humor, and to do it so that you can *touch* it."

Makavejev comes across in person as a man with vitality and a salivating appetite for life. What is most remarkable is his ability to project his own powerful body-rhythms onto the screen, which is no mean feat given the fragmented processes and interruptions in feature filmmaking. He often jettisons a script on the set, improvising something entirely new in response to the environment he is shooting in; to this extent, he remains a semidocumentarian (a skill he learned during his short-subjects apprenticeship). His gut sensitivity to ordinary materials as metaphors and props also has something in common with the Eastern European avant-garde theater of Grotowski and Kantor.

Makavejev's first two features, *Man Is Not a Bird* (1966) and *Love Affair: The Story of the Switchboard Operator* (1967), are extraordinary tragicomedies charting the collision between the quest for sexual joy and the needs of the state. Filmed in a freewheeling, gritty style, in wide-screen black and white, they express Makavejev's conviction that any political solution must take into consideration the body's happiness. His satiric handling of the solemnities and pedantries of Yugoslavian socialism somehow got past the censors. His third feature, *Innocence Unprotected* (1971), combined fiction, documentary and found footage in a loving tribute to the pioneers of Yugoslavian cinema. As would happen more and more, his fascination with history provided a jumping-off point for his imagination. With his next film, *W.R.: Mysteries of the Organism* (1974), Makavejev would vault onto the world stage, crossing continents and historical epochs in an effort to make a grand synthesis of what he knew and didn't know.

Makavejev must be seen as both an international artist and an intensely Yugoslavian one. Just as Milan Kundera asserts that the Eastern European writer has a unique position as a witness to history, by virtue of being ground between the two superpowers, so Makavejev's viewpoint makes capital of his status as a wonder-struck skeptic from a nonpowerful country.

W.R. pointed toward a new, freer era in filmmaking. With all its shortcomings, it was a courageous, fertile model. Cutting across documentary, fantasy, agitprop and camp, side-stepping the entrapments ready to leap out from any of those forms, it kept chugging along leaving hundreds of loose ends for analytical viewers to get tangled in, and somehow made it all the way home by assertive energy and timeliness. For Makavejev had fastened on the problem of the hour: the relations between sexuality and political change.

Wilhelm Reich had asked, in *The Mass Psychology of Fascism*, why do the masses, instead of allying with an antiauthoritarian Left which would objectively seem to serve their best interests, turn to the bosses and the Fascists? Reich's conclusion was that most men are made to feel sexually afraid, ashamed of their drives, and once this fear is anchored biologically it is easy for the ruling class to manipulate public opinion. Man is sexually sick: no revolution that really hopes to change things can be built until the sickness is treated. (After emigrating to the United States, Reich of course went off the deep end with his belief in the orgone box as a way of accumulating sexual energy, and was ultimately tried for selling these "bogus" boxes and sent to Lewisburg Penitentiary, a sad ending for a great clinician and thinker.)

Using Reich and the story of his persecution by the U.S. government as a starting point, Makavejev went around shooting footage of the psychiatrist's colleagues, the American countryside, body therapy groups, phallic plaster-casters, transvestites and other experimenters in sexual liberation. The film became a tool of scientific research: open-ended, probing, tolerant (at least initially), proceeding from an appetite for fact, the shape emerging organically from the gathered materials. Perhaps it was no accident that the only other movie shown at the New York Film Festival in 1974 that seemed to effect a similar breakthrough was Marcel Ophuls's *The Sorrow and the Pity*, another historico-sociological research that fanned outward to encounter and embrace the human condition. It was a moment that seemed to demand of filmmakers that they not only be storytellers but sociologists, psychologists, economists, historians, and give audiences some fresh information along with catharsis.

Makavejev was at the front lines of this new cinema, performing amazing interdisciplinary juggling acts—appropriate for an artist from Yugoslavia, which was itself a juggling act between Russia and the West. But if W.R. was strong in conveying information, it was less satisfying in its analysis and interpretation. We learn, for instance, that Reich did an about-face on Communism and voted for Eisenhower, without finding out if this was merely a private change of heart or had implications for Reichian therapy. We see some distressing footage of patients screaming and going through convulsions while therapists look on, and never find out if this is what Reich had in mind (it wasn't) nor what Makavejev himself thinks of it. The director's noncommittal stance toward some of the new therapeutic or political expressions he presents onscreen can be read as an ambivalence, or as tolerance for a raw, prerevolutionary transitional phase. True, we all live with radio noise and the Fugs and mind-bending sexual static, but we have a right to have the contradictions more clearly spelled out than Makavejev seems willing or able to do.

The clearest analysis emerges, interestingly enough, in the dramatized, fictional scenes, where positions and ideologies are dramatized with Brechtian conciseness, for instance Milena's haranguing, demagogic speech on the balcony, which has an erotic effect on her listeners. Perhaps Makavejev felt more sure of making points with actors and a script under his control, and on native Yugoslav soil. Perhaps it is foolish to try to approach a film like this as a logical entity. At its best the movie soars, like the scene when the car drives through the forest and Reich's voice speculates on whether he is a creature from another planet, or the transcendent duet between the woman's severed head and her killer, the Russian champion skater, who stumbles through the snow reciting

Mayakovski. Makavejev the documentarist and dialectical montagist gives way to Makavejev the poet, a director who knows how to burst into song. Maybe you must pick your way through a lot of impurities to get to those moments, but then, as Pablo Neruda decreed: "Those who shun the 'bad taste' of things will fall on their faces in the snow."

After W.R., which encountered problems with the censors, Makavejev was disinvited from making films in Yugoslavia. Undaunted, he began *Sweet Movie*—if anything, a more radical, flamboyant and provocative work (in one sequence, people in a commune eat feces; in another, there is a suggested seduction of children)—shot in Canada and Europe. This was also a collage-movie—an uneasy cross between cinema verité, *Dallas*, travelogue, pornography, fairy tale and lyrical ballad. Such structures demand a great film editor; and, in any case, Makavejev's cinematic style has usually derived less from the complexity of individual shots than from his brilliant contrapuntal juxtapositions.

Sweet Movie puts you through a seminar on revolutionary hope and despair. Though Makavejev has often parodied the scientific lecture, in truth he is something of a pedagogue. "To see a Makavejev film," noted David Thomson in *A Biographical Dictionary of Film*, "is as close to a stimulating educational experience as the cinema has come. The 'stories' of his films are models, pulled this way and that until the flexibility of shape itself becomes the center of attention."

For all its exuberance, *Sweet Movie* has the *triste* undertone of a work by a homeless artist. Makavejev had gone so far out on a limb with it, commercially speaking, that he had to scramble back to a safer place or lose all hope of future financing. His next commission took him to Scandinavia, where he made *Montenegro* with a mixture of stars and unknowns. Susan Anspach played a disenchanted, rich American housewife-mother, neglected by her stuffed-shirt Swedish husband (Erland Josephson, the eternal husband of Ingmar

Bergman movies). She starts engaging in acts of sabotage, like preparing wiener schnitzel for the family and then eating it all herself, which prompts her husband to call in a (very fishy) psychiatrist.

All this sets up the real adventure: Anspach allows herself to be carried off by a pack of Yugoslavian guest-workers, who congregate in a seedy nightclub run by one of them, the Zani-Bar. Entranced and appalled by their earthiness, she watches, shell-shocked, in her mink as the men crack heads over her—"a real lady." Next thing we know, she is waiting on tables, taking a young lover and doing a musical number. "And now, direct from USA, Suzie Nashville!" barks the proprietor, holding a ridiculous photo-lamp in her face for lighting while she obliges with a wobbly but charming "Gimme a Little Kiss, Will Ya, Hon?"

Here, at the Zani-Bar, Makavejev is in his anarchic, improvisational element: he has a field day with this low-class immigrant nightclub. From the horny, greasy proprietor to the pig roasting in the middle of the dance floor, the screen images burst with fecund detail. Capping it all off is a comically touching erotic dance by a waif who first appears layered in bulky outfits like Heidi, but who is transformed for the night into a "sex goddess."

The problem with *Montenegro* is the framing material: the satire of Swedish suburban life is one-dimensional, the husband and the psychiatrist are too obviously figures of ridicule, and Makavejev's camera eye grows listless scanning the lifeless bourgeois décor. Without a collage structure to fall back on, the film comes dangerously close to a simplistic clash between national stereotypes: "cold, orderly" Swedes versus "chaotic, down-home" Yugoslavs, with the American wife alone able to bridge these extremes. Susan Anspach's warm, natural performance unifies the picture—though paradoxically, she conveys too much intelligence and inner balance for us to credit her character's final gruesome deeds.

Then again, *Montenegro* is intended as a wicked fairy tale, not a work of realism.

Makavejev's imagination has always had something of a childlike—or childish—quality. His leering approach to sex, like many Eastern European males, suggests the wish fulfillment of a naughty boy lifting up a woman's skirts. A true nonauthoritarian, he loves disorder. The Reichian equation he draws throughout his work between political and sexual repression would sometimes have him appear a libidinous Pied Piper. Yet, the scenes of orgiastic release in his films are usually followed by (punished by?) murder of one kind or another. Is there a secret puritan inside this satyr-filmmaker, or is Makavejev trying to tell us that, in our present politically screwed-up, anxious state, the liberation of our instincts is only a mocking dream, and those who try to throw off their social conditioning may discover darker forces released in them? As in Grimm's fairy tales, gratifications of desire often lead to a cruel surprise: Grandma baring her teeth.

Since I wrote this appreciation, in 1982, Makavejev has made only three movies, all pretty lame: The Coca Cola Kid, Manifesto *and* Gorillas Kiss at Dawn. *The reasons for his decline, I think, may be traced primarily to two breakdowns: Yugoslavia (which might have welcomed him back from his peregrinations if it had managed to hold together) and what used to be called, in the sixties, "the Movement." In retrospect, Makavejev seems more and more a figure of the sixties, who, by main strength and determination, was able to drag some of that wayward energy into the seventies. But by the eighties, it was all too apparent that the politics of world revolution had evaporated; and Makavejev, who had positioned himself as the conscience and clown, the Holy Fool, of the coming liberation, had nothing to kibbitz any longer. He was a refugee from a country and a movement neither of which existed. In the interim, he has* gracefully supported himself as a roving teacher at various film schools, while trying to mount the next project. He freely admits that his gentle mocking style does not seem suited to grapple with the enormous brutality that tore apart his native land.

I knew Makavejev in the seventies and eighties—was his friend, in fact, and watched him go through some frustrating experiences in Europe and Hollywood. Paris, which had hailed him as a genius until he relocated there, then treated him, he told me, "like just another French filmmaker competing for a job." Lured to Los Angeles by the vague promises of this or that producer, he sat around hotel rooms waiting for them to call him, or to return his calls. Meanwhile, the dominant film aesthetic evolved away from Makavejev's experiment—though I have no doubt that his best films will continue to inspire those future filmmakers with the eyes to see.

FOURTEEN KOANS BY A LEVITE
ON SCORSESE'S *THE LAST TEMPTATION*
OF CHRIST

1. PREFACE: WHAT IS TRUTH?

The first time I saw Martin Scorsese's *The Last Temptation of Christ* I thought it was an impressive, ambitious, noble and powerful film with a slow middle section. The second time around I thought it was silly and forced, and didn't believe a minute of it. Must the truth lie in between?

2. APOLOGIA

There is no point in writing a straight review of *The Last Temptation of Christ*. Everything has already been said; the movie has been picked clean by intelligent daily and weekly reviewers. All that remains for me, the laggard bimonthly film critic, are scraps, digressions, asides.

3. THE CONTROVERSY

In the brouhaha over the film, both sides have engaged in ritualistic oratory: the Fundamentalists have seized the situation as a fund-raising opportunity and a distraction from the Bakker and Swaggart scandals; the liberals have had a self-righteous field day, patting themselves on the back for defending free artistic expression. Naturally I throw in my lot with the liberals, but after listening to their elitist mocking of the other side as cretinous Flannery O'Connor characters, I begin to get perverse twinges of contrariety. For instance, a colleague of mine was ridiculing the Fundamentalists' logic, which asserts that they don't need to see the movie to know it is bad for them, just as they don't need to take cocaine to know it will harm them. "As if seeing a movie were the same as taking drugs," sneered my colleague. But, in fact, to a Fundamentalist Christian it might seem that the media are a kind of drug capturing the minds of the young and filling them with immoral images. Furthermore, every intelligent person makes conscious decisions to avoid certain experiences based on knowledge of his or her tastes and values. In short, the Fundamentalists' argument does not seem as internally illogical as the liberals make it out to be.

On the other hand, I am at a loss to know what to make of the Fundamentalists' claim that the true, "historical Jesus" has been distorted. What historical Jesus are they talking about?

4. THE GREATEST STORY EVER TOLD

I may as well admit that the Jesus story has always made me uneasy. I am bothered by the endless privileging of one man's bodily anguish when so many millions have suffered at least as much. There are Jews who have the capacity and imagination to be deeply moved by the figure of Jesus on a moral or mythic level, but I seem to be unable to join them in this empathetic adventure. The fact that the Jesus story is so anti-Semitic—or has been misconstrued toward that end throughout Christian history, to the detriment of the Jewish population—may be part of the problem, but not all of it. For even without considering the Inquisitional violence which, like a Jungian shadow, seems inextricably tied to the doctrine of Christian meekness, I am put off by the whole idea of perfect human goodness. How can I sympathize with a man totally without sin? Jesus seems too humorless and solemn—already too goyish. The story has beautiful language, yes; wisdom, yes; but no comic spark. Perhaps this fact is more the fault of later iconography than of the Jesus of the Gospels. Still, it is the iconography that we must live with, all that self-satisfied moaning over one lucky victim. I think I understand that he (He?) is supposed to stand for all human suffering, but the idea that this guy's death has somehow redeemed the whole world, on whatever symbolic or literal terms you care to take it, makes no sense to me. The world is unredeemed, *n'est-ce pas?*

Given this old grudge against the story, I tend to like those passages in *Last Temptation* that stray farthest from the Gospels. In particular, I like the tension of the first part, where Jesus is trying to resist the onus of godhead; I admire his honest insistence that fear is his essential nature: "My mother and father are fear." Nevertheless, as soon as he accepts his destiny as the Christ—for reasons never made entirely clear—and begins to deliver sermons and make miracles, I lose all interest. It's like going down a checklist—water into wine, dead into living, expulsion of the money changers. Giotto and Nick Ray did it better.

5. QUESTIONS OF GENRE

The biblical epic is characterized by spectacle and excess. A much maligned genre, due any minute for scholarly up-grading, its main virtues lie in the areas of art direction, costumes, special effects, and *mise-en-scène*. Where else can you find those shamelessly entertaining long shots teeming with masses of background extras scurrying over architectural fantasias—whole cities, on a scale demanded previously only by pharaohs and tyrants—composed of endless plaster, like world's-fair pavilions redolent with temporary grandeur?

The biblical epic's vision of the Past as readily available to the art director's imagination, in mix-and-match forms, necessarily rests on questionable universalist, ahistorical assumptions, which downplay the influence of specific conditions, in honor of the cliché that people have always been the same. The biblical epic tends toward a flattened psychology: its huge expenses have necessitated attracting mass audiences and orienting them quickly to stereotyped narrative patterns, while the distractions of lavish sets, special effects, and tumult hinder subtle character development.

Silent biblical epics at least had the advantage of being unfettered by dialogue, except for an occasional intertitle. Sound epics encountered the further problem of developing a dialogue style that could be spoken naturally and yet seem sufficiently elevated to escape contemporary anachronism. This problem led to all sorts of quasi-Shakespearean and Shavian locutions (and put a premium on British actors). Critics of the biblical epic have been quick to poke fun at the acting, which often ran the gamut from wooden to hammy; a babel of international accents delivering lines in togas or Roman armor further eroded credibility.

Nevertheless, biblical epics were widely successful in the period after World War II and throughout the fifties. The world war itself had been a vast staging of gruesome spectacle, accustoming the public to movements of armies and matériel, and the new wide-screen technologies cried out for historical panoramas. The postwar era also saw America in a victorious mood, looking about for earlier models of chosen peoples that would justify its new hegemonic destiny.

Finally, the Bible offered a feast of narratives that combined sin and piety (David and Bathsheba, Salome, Sodom and Gomorrah, etc.). As one critic noted about DeMille's *Samson and Delilah* (1949): "Its huge popularity demonstrated once again that the Bible is the picture-maker's best friend, a never-failing source of spectacle, sex and sadism that no censor could dare to suppress and no movie-goer could afford to miss." But with the softening of censorship in the sixties, it no longer was necessary to add religion to one's sex and sadism. The public's taste "sophisticated" away from the biblical epic, which had acquired the odor of hokum.

With *Last Temptation*, Scorsese does everything in his power to evade the passé aspects of the biblical epic—its Taj Mahal tackiness, its costumed pomp, its scrolled or intoned preambles, its inflated language, its lack of psychology, its imperialistic presumptions. But in ducking that genre's clichés, he falls headlong into the arms of another: the "metamorphosis" or "alien possession" movie. Originally a horror/sci-fi staple in the radioactive-anxious fifties (*The Incredible Shrinking Man, The Fly*), the "metamorphosis" genre was renovated in the late seventies and eighties, most elegantly by David Cronenberg (*They Came from Within, Rabid, Scanners, The Brood, The Fly* remake) and Ridley Scott (*Alien*), to reflect a new set of technological and ecological anxieties. Most recently, this horror film idea of being invaded by a foreign body or persona has migrated into comedy (*All of Me, Eighteen Again*, etc.), as the crossing of genders or generations in the same body is exploited for "hilarious" confusion. I have no doubt that some future doctoral student will write a thesis arguing how this dybbuk fad was the result of a) demographic shifts in the work force; b) AIDS and the corresponding need to believe that the soul is eternal; c) the greenhouse effect; d) the temporary halting of the space program, which channeled fantasies of travel from interplanetary to intercorporeal. . . . While Scorsese may have changed the script from demonic to divine possession, his hero is often made to writhe on the ground from unwelcome alien implosions. *The Last Temptation* is less biblical epic than horror movie.

6. THE SOURCE

The Nikos Kazantzakis novel on which the movie is based is overwrought, Raskolnikovian-feverish, good for adolescents searching for Big Answers. Supposedly, Barbara Hershey, the actress who would later be cast as Mary Magdalene, gave a copy to Scorsese years ago, and ever since then he had been dreaming of making a film of it. (This is the same Barbara Hershey who not long before giving this gift had changed her name to Barbara Seagull in a fit of creature-identification.) Many of the problems and hyperventilating tendencies of the film can be traced directly to the Kazantzakis novel. Scorsese has struggled stalwartly with its pseudo-Nietzschean mysteries and general portentousness. My advice is that in the future he think twice about accepting any books from Barbara Hershey.

7. THE SCREENPLAY

Paul Schrader adapted Kazantzakis's novel into screenplay form. Later, some revisions were made by Scorsese and writer Jay Cocks, but, according to Schrader (*New York Times*, Sept. 1, 1988): "That first script, with the exception of two scenes, is exactly, scene for scene, the movie that's on the screen." Schrader has been criticized for flattening the eloquent speech of the Gospels into stammering Americanese. In principle, if one grants that the story is important enough to retell in any number of garbs and variations in order to make it more relevant for our times, then Schrader's adaptation seems perfectly legitimate. Indeed, often it achieves a touching simplicity. (Judas: "Do you love mankind?" Jesus: "I see men and I feel sorry for them, that's all.") Still, Schrader may have gone too far in depriving Jesus of any rhetorical powers, reducing his capacity to clumsy plain speech.

Schrader once wrote a book called *Transcendental Style in Film*, which focused on such great filmmakers as Ozu, Dreyer, Rossellini and Bresson. The transcendental style was developed, according to Schrader, "to express the Holy": it is characterized by an austere, formalist rigor; a deep respect for objects and light; and a reflective pace and silence-gathering, indwelling calm, often in the face of narratives about intense suffering. Schrader himself has directed seven feature films, which, while fascinating, generally suffer from an unresolved tension between his transcendental-cinema formal leanings and his penchant for sensationalist content.

In the same *Times* interview, it is reported that Schrader had a clause in his *Last Temptation* contract that would have given him the next shot at directing the film in the event that Scorsese did not direct it. One suspects Schrader's version would have had a more distanced, stylized, "transcendental cinema" air—and probably would have been better for it.

8. THE STYLE

In *Last Temptation*, Scorsese alternates between tense psychological close-ups and overhead shots (suggesting fate or heaven's point of view). For movement he resorts to rough handheld tracks, lurching right into the middle of knots of people and grabbing onto their torsos. It is a hot style intended to keep the pressure up, but there is very little allowance for perspective, or detachment. The film, in fact, does not feel spiritual at all in the transcendental-cinema sense, but only in the way of an unrelenting agon, Jacob wrestling with the angel. In *Raging Bull*, Scorsese reveled in the opportunity for physical action, but here his problem is different: he must render cinematic an interior, religious conflict; and his tendency is to physicalize too much, to sweat blood, to make Jesus fall to the ground like an epileptic.

The style is at once punched-up and tentative. Scorsese seems to be casting about restlessly throughout the film for a technique to suit his intended masterpiece. There are echoes of Pasolini's *Gospel According to St. Matthew* (of which more later). A horizon shot of Christ and his disciples advancing toward us dissolves into a much larger flock, the music swells, and suddenly we are in a Sergio Leone spaghetti western. At times a minimalist, Straubian vocabulary is invoked. The casting-out-of-devils sequence is choreographed like the Living Theater; the wrapped mummies seem like something out of Robert Wilson's experimental pieces. Painting references also abound: the lion advancing into the circle is pure Henri Rousseau; the taunting of Christ is slo-mo Brueghel.

Scorsese has always been an eclectic director, changing his visual style to suit the project: from the ragged neorealism of *Mean Streets* to the elegant long takes and tracking shots of *New York, New York*, to the furious montage of *Raging Bull*, to the cool classicism of *The Color of Money*. He does not have a "signature" shot or a consistent cinematic vocabulary. Not that this is necessarily bad, but it should be kept in mind when people speak of Scorsese's "style"; I think they mean more his edgy intensity and recurring themes. In *Last Temptation*, he films many of the dialogue scenes in the boringly standard American studio Ping-Pong of close-up/reaction shot/close-up/close-up, while improvising one new shtick after another for the visual transition sequences. These devices leave an impression of gratuitous invention—perhaps a futile, last-ditch defense on Scorsese's part against the intractability of the Kazantzakis/Gospels material, which seems persistently on the verge of crushing his spirit.

In the actual "last temptation" sequence, when Christ imagines himself getting off the cross and leading a normal life, Scorsese changes his style yet again—fittingly this time,

I think. Suddenly the camera pulls back and we no longer see Christ in anguished close-ups, but in flowing long shots. It is as though we were inside Christ's dream, and in a dream one tends to see oneself objectified, full-figure. Meanwhile the landscape has turned temperate, lushly wooded, and the light is more benign. Many observers have complained that this fantasy sequence is overlong, but I found it a welcome relief. The editing slows down and catches its breath. The change of pace is analogous to that lovely sequence in Scorsese's *After Hours*, when the headlong chase comes to rest in a deserted disco for a slow dance to Peggy Lee's "Is That All There Is?"

Emotionality remains both the strength and limitation of Scorsese's approach. Keen on pushing the audience through a visceral experience, he leaps from climax to climax, sometimes losing the point of the story in the process. So *Taxi Driver* tries to bludgeon its way through the muddled loose ends of Travis's character with a storm of gunfire, while *New York, New York*, after seeming to want to chart the path of a relationship, dissolves into a set of production numbers. *Last Temptation* is no different: It picks up stray nail filings of Hebrew politics, theological contradictions and psychological conflicts without resolving them in a thoughtful, intellectually responsible manner. Along the way, however, Scorsese manages to create some stunning images: the sunlit loft in which David Bowie (the Roman administrator) questions Willem Dafoe, the burning of Jerusalem sequence near the end and Jesus taking his dripping heart out and offering it to his disciples.

9. MY FAVORITE SCENE

My favorite scene in the movie is the one in which Jesus visits the brothel of Mary Magdalene. It is intoxicated filmmaking, a largely silent scene in which Jesus, first pulled almost against his will to her house, sits in her outer room with the other waiting clients, watching Magdalene make love to one customer after another. We see her through a veiled curtain, sweating under the weight of men of all colors and touching them tenderly or consolingly. At one point, a coal-black man indicates to Jesus that it is his turn next (such politeness!), and Jesus morosely declines. The light changes, the hours pass, night comes on and at last Jesus is the only one left. The actual dialogue that follows, between Jesus and Magdalene, is less interesting—overly dramatic, shrill—but the memory of that hypnotic, hallucinogenic passage lingers tantalizingly: if only more of the film had been that way.

Kazantzakis has Jesus sitting in Magdalene's outer courtyard, in front of her closed door. Scorsese, by upping the ante so that Jesus must witness Magdalene's carnal acts directly, shows that he is not just the innocent adapter of Kazantzakis, but intentionally provocative—a bit of a "bad boy." If the Fundamentalists keep harping on this brothel scene and the later one of Jesus copulating with Magdalene, it is partly because Scorsese has planted the image of Barbara Hershey's naked, painted body in the viewer's mind far more graphically than that of the crucifixion.

10. COUSIN PASOLINI, FATHER ROSSELLINI

"Peering in the glass of vision, contemporary poets confront their too-recent giant precursors staring back at them, inducing a profound anxiety that hides itself, but cannot be evaded totally." (Harold Bloom, A *Map of Misreading*, 1975.) Pasolini's *The Gospel According to St. Matthew* (1964) is Scorsese's immediate precursor, and Scorsese seems much influenced by the earlier film's North African setting, slightly demented Jesus and stark *cinema povera* quality. (It is questionable how much *Last Temptation*'s stylized reductions are a product of aesthetic intention or of making a virtue of necessity; even at a slashed budget of six million dollars, however, the film still has the polished look of a Hollywood studio picture, compared to the Pasolini film, which is sandpaper-rough.) In return for this penury, the Pasolini film retains the infinite richness of the Gospel language, while Scorsese's features the comparatively impoverished Schrader dialogue. The Pasolini version also displays a much more effortless access to the culture of the New Testament and the imagery of Italian Renaissance painting; it is the difference perhaps between growing up Italian and growing up Italian-American.

Pasolini's *Gospel*, beautiful and severe as it is, already suffers from a faux-naïf air that we might attribute, with Bloom, to its "belatedness." The musical score (Bach, Blind Willie Johnson, *Kol Nidre*, African chants) tips off the fact that it is a pastiche. Visually, it practically plagiarizes from (or is a tribute to) Dreyer's technique of facial close-ups in *Passion of Joan of Arc* and the sacred-figures-in-craggy-landscape look of Rossellini's *Little Flowers of St. Francis*.

In considering Scorsese's precursors one must look past Pasolini to Rossellini, the last confident classicist and synthesist in the Renaissance mode. Rossellini's educational history series, which occupied him for the last fifteen years of his life, included a three-part *Acts of the Apostles* and concluded with a film about Jesus, *The Messiah*. (*The Messiah*, Rossellini's last film, was never released in this country, but rumor has it that Scorsese himself is trying to arrange for new prints and distribution.) Given Scorsese's longtime passion for Rossellini (which included marrying his daughter, Isabella—though one would not have to be a Rossellini fan to do that), my guess is that *Last Temptation* is as much an act of piety to Rossellini the Father as to Jesus the Son.

11. ORIENTALISM

Last Temptation is steeped in a background of Islamic details: the women all have Berber markings, the instruments are Berber, the wedding is Arabic. There are frequent cutaway shots of gnarled, turbaned *fellaheen,* as though Scorsese could not resist lending a semidocumentary air to his tale: since we're shooting in Morocco, why not a bit of local color? Of course, the fact that there were no Arabs at the time of Christ poses a problem. Peter Gabriel's minimalist musical score has many hints of Middle Eastern dirge; meanwhile, elements of Hebraic culture are few and far between (as are Jewish actors). Why is this? Is it some sort of subterranean gesture of support for the Palestinians' political struggle, or a sense that the ancient, the unchanging and the eternal are better represented by weathered contemporary Arabic faces than Jewish ones? I see a species here of what Edward Said has diagnosed as "Orientalism"—the tendency of Westerners to romanticize the Arabic Middle East as exotic and static.

12. A BUDDY MOVIE

Much of the warmth in *Last Temptation* comes from the relationship between Jesus and Judas, which is central to the film. In part because Harvey Keitel is such a pungent, over-the-top actor, in part because his character is written to be so much more articulate and steady than the disturbed, mutating Jesus, Judas becomes the audience's representative. We sympathize with Judas's nationalist efforts to free his people—to the extent that he seems at times the secret, real hero of the film. When Judas demands, "Could *you* betray your Master?" and Jesus answers, "No, that's why God gave me the easier job: to be crucified," we are inclined to agree. This Judas does seem the stronger of the two, temperamentally: Jesus frequently expresses his dependence on him. "Judas, I'm afraid; stay with me," he says, and Judas spends the night cradling him in his arms. These campfire scenes between the two, beautifully lit, have the air of something out of *Viva Za-*

pata, or a buddy movie. Jesus and Judas are Butch Cassidy and the Sundance Kid, getting the jitters the night before a bank robbery.

13. THE STAR

Willem Dafoe plays Jesus like a sixties dropout carpenter from Taos on a spiritual quest. Dafoe is a compelling, gifted actor, trained in experimental theater, and he does as well as anyone could with the physical aspects of the role. According to the press, Scorsese cast him not on the basis of his (slightly sappy) saintly performance in *Platoon*, but only after seeing him in William Friedkin's *To Live and Die in L.A.*, where he played a demonic gang leader. Oddly enough, Dafoe spun a much more mysteriously spiritual aura around himself while playing a villain in *To Live and Die in L.A.* (which, by the way, is one of the best, and most underrated, American films of the 1980s), than he was able to do in *Last Temptation*. Friedkin filmed him in long shot, emphasizing his impenetrable scowl, waxy complexion and Amerindian cheekbones at a discreet distance, whereas Scorsese was all over him in close-up, trying to crawl into his head; and this X-ray treatment backfired with such a remote, spooky actor, who would probably do better playing Frankenstein than Jesus.

In any case, Dafoe brought to both roles a purified air of dedication to Higher Powers, combined with an almost-menacing self-disgust. In *Last Temptation*, his most convincing scenes lie in the first third of the movie, when this Jesus still hates himself. But as soon as Dafoe is called upon to represent the Jesus whose doubts have disappeared, who speechifies and performs miracles, he seems embarrassed, projecting a shrinking pariah loneliness—the opposite of charisma. It is impossible to understand why crowds are following this platitudinous mumbler.

14. TWO ENDINGS

Scorsese shows a penchant for multiple endings. *The King of Comedy,* brilliant in other respects, had one too many endings tacked on. In *Last Temptation,* Scorsese is legitimately able to indulge this tendency: Christ gets down off the cross and lives a normal life; Christ gets back on the cross and sacrifices himself for the sins of the world. He handles it so well that the audience roots for both alternatives in turn. This double-jointed narrative approach does, however, raise in my mind a theological question: If Jesus has already enjoyed a normal full life, including the pleasures of the flesh, *even if only in his imagination*—remember, we have already seen how detailed and somatic that imagination is— can he be said to be sacrificing quite so much in going back to the cross? Hasn't he, as much as the audience, had his cake and eaten it too?

Straight film criticism becomes boring, after a while. I relished the opportunity given me by Tikkun, *a liberal Jewish bimonthly, to try a more playful, "formatted" approach. I had no intention in mind beyond being cheeky. Martin Scorsese continues to fascinate me. I know no other filmmaker of his manifest genius and skill who has failed to make an overall great movie. Others might argue that* Mean Streets *or* Raging Bull *qualify as great; I would say they are very good. Parts of* New York, New York, After Hours, King of Comedy, Goodfellas *are wonderful; you could maybe make an anthology of peak Scorsese sequences and have a great film, something like* That's Entertainment, Marty!

Curiously, his undervalued Kundun *may come closest to being a masterpiece. It has a consistent, harmonious and intransigent approach; it doesn't give an inch; if you accept it on its terms, it's a one-of-a-kind sublime experience. Interesting to compare* Kundun *to* The Last Temptation of Christ, *since in both Scorsese stretched himself to encounter an alien culture. He overexoticized and hystericized the Middle East, whereas he was able to enter calmly into the Tibetan milieu, its rituals and sorrows.*

TRUFFAUT'S *THE WOMAN NEXT DOOR*

The Woman Next Door, at the Greenway III, is François Truffaut's most substantial and intriguing film in years. I say this
as one who was not a fan of *The Last Metro*, that self-satisfied
and calculated confection, nor of the overly cute *Small
Change*, nor the vacant *The Man Who Loved Women*. These
films suffered from a conventional, sterile and canned visual
manner, while their scripts all too coyly and single-mindedly
labored to charm. Now we see the other side of the crowd-
pleaser in Truffaut's latest, *The Woman Next Door*. Though it
unfolds as smoothly as the others, it *is* a more difficult film,
perverse in what it chooses to leave out as well as in what it
chooses to tell us.

The movie begins and ends with a framing device: our
narrator, Madame Jouve, a middle-aged woman, is sitting in
front of a tennis court. "If you think I am a tennis pro, you are
all wrong," she says, mildly laughing at herself and us. The
camera pulls back to show her standing painfully and walking
with a stiff metal leg brace. This is Truffaut's painful way of
forewarning us that things may not be what they at first appear.

She is going to tell us a story, she explains, and onto her
face is superimposed an overhead shot of an ambulance mak-

ing its way through the well-ordered streets of a small provincial city (Grenoble). The ambulance alerts us that something is wrong. At the same time the narrator's placid manner reassures us (falsely) that it is nothing too terrible.

Truffaut takes pains to lull us into an early sense of tranquillity as we are introduced to a nice, blond couple, Bernard and Arlette Coudray. Bernard (Gérard Depardieu) is a boating engineer, at first glance a doltish but stable type. His wife (Michele Baumgartner) is pleasant and sweet; they have a child. The couple discovers that the house next door has finally been rented and learn that their new neighbors, the Bouchards, also have a son. They go over to meet their neighbors for the first time, and that is when Bernard sees—da dum!—the woman next door.

As it turns out, he had been in love with this very woman eight years before, and she had driven him nearly crazy when she broke off their affair. Bernard is still carrying a grudge. Mathilde Bouchard phones him to explain it was an accident that her husband rented the house next to his; had she known, she would certainly have insisted against it, but since there is nothing to do now about this awkward situation, can't they behave at least "neighborly" toward each other? Bernard continues to snub her.

Then she runs into him by accident at a supermarket, and they succeed in conversing amicably, even with a certain rueful nostalgia. He kisses her; she faints. Not long afterward, Bernard and Mathilde are meeting in a hotel room routinely set aside for assignations. They talk of the past: what went wrong? You were selfish, she says; you didn't believe in love. And you, says Bernard, were a pain, insecure, needy. . . . But now, as they gaze at each other, proud of the self-possessed, mature adults they have become, they will do it right this time.

So their love affair continues on two levels: discussions of the way they were, which has left a living hurt in both; and continuation in the present where they are doomed to repeat the same mistakes and patterns. At first this is not at all obvious. We have some trouble believing that the solid Bernard was ever a "manic-depressive," or that the wonderfully sympathetic, intelligent Mathilde could ever have been a drag. But slowly the adolescent loss of control begins to emerge from underneath their stability, and we see how fragile a thing maturity is.

Bernard's problem (though never stated as such) seems to be that he loves Mathilde more now that she is no longer a potential millstone, now that she keeps him at a distance because she belongs to another. At the same time he seems compelled to try to conquer that reserve and possess more of her. Mathilde's problem is that, when she surrenders to her love for Bernard, she loses her boundaries of self. Overwhelmed by him, she begins to hate herself. She was able to keep her equilibrium and self-esteem with her husband—but without the romantic intensity.

The French have an expression for this sort of thing—*amour fou*, which connotes crazy, obsessive, self-destructive passion. It's an old story, but what is fresh about this film is the psychology of these two characters, and the chemistry of these two actors.

Gérard Depardieu, France's biggest male star, is a peculiar matinee idol to begin with. Beefy, hulking, stolid (you would have to go back to Emil Jannings to find so broad-shouldered a male lead), he has neither the tough-guy sparkle of Jean Gabin nor the pretty-boy looks of Alain Delon. His pasty face at first looks perfectly ordinary, a sullen jaw and stubborn forehead not promising much in the way of intelligence. But Depardieu's genius as an actor is precisely in knowing how long to hold back, to establish the quality of latency. By the time you have gotten around to trusting his character as phlegmatically dependable if not very interesting, he brings up the character's restlessness, insight, malice, instability, romantic playfulness, physical grace (surprising in such a big man). The women in the audience seem to love that slow-starting, long-lasting fire. His resourceful portrayal of Bernard sympathetically resolves the contradictions in that character: hotheaded, coldly reasonable, concerned, egotistic, baffled.

But Depardieu's main job here is to partner unselfishly, as in a ballet *pas de deux*, the real star of the show. *The Woman Next Door*'s success finally comes down to the beguiling, emotionally loaded performance of Fanny Ardant as Mathilde. She is beautiful, of course, with a wild Arabian or Spanish cast to her dark features. But there is an earthy, acutely responsive quality to her looks that makes her somehow not a professional beauty. Ardant is above all sensitive, her deep eyes expressive of intelligence or pain or laughter or desire—a desire not to hurt anyone, as well. In that sense, she is not at all a *femme fatale*—or let us say, she represents a new variation. Ardant's Mathilde is not the kind of woman one would kill for—simply because she would not allow it.

The tragedy of Bernard and Mathilde is that they are both good, well-intending people who don't understand why this madness is happening to them. Truffaut knows the psychology of such relationships: the noble renunciations, the backsliding, the attempts to turn the insane itch into a "friendship." What is it that keeps driving these two together, against all sense? Sexual attraction, certainly, but also unresolved anger and an appetite they share for the dramatics that ordinary family life doesn't seem to satisfy.

Eventually, Mathilde decides to move away. She and her husband have a goodbye lawn party, a model of suburban propriety and decency. (All along, the movie exploits the tension between the ritualized pleasantness of middle-class life, which smooths away any conflicts, and the heedless disorder of the lovers' passion.) Mathilde is on good behavior along with everyone and, posing with Bernard for a photo, whispers, "See? We can be friends, after all." Bernard is having none of it. He throws a tantrum of possessiveness in front of the guests, and their misery spreads to their mates.

There are still many twists to go in this film, which is composed of fairly short scenes, each one patiently taking a different temperature reading. The last, adagio movement is handled with great subtlety and discretion. True, some of the narrative solutions have too much of the script doctor's craft about them, as when Mathilde overhears the discussion of a case similar to hers, and it sends her over the edge. Truffaut and his co-scriptwriter, Suzanne Schiffman, have gotten so "literary" lately that their foreshadowings and distributed hints can be a bit overprecise. And Truffaut's interest in Jamesian storytelling, with its control, delay and suppression of information, can sometimes produce an unwanted side effect of lack of vitality or just plain *air*.

For instance, we get very little sense of a world around the principals. Grenoble is reduced to a tennis club, a pair of adjoining houses, a shabby-genteel hotel and Bernard's boatyard, all tightly cropped. Perhaps this cramped focus is a fair price to pay for a well-thought-out script, whose every detail connects logically with every other.

Still, Truffaut's current visual style is a little too self-composed and neutral. The camera setups do the job but lack inevitability, and in following characters through rooms or outdoors there is neither rigor nor those surprising, felicitous grace notes that lovers of film as a visual medium hope for. This is a strange charge to level against a director whose early works, like Shoot the Piano Player, Jules and Jim and The Four Hundred Blows dazzled the film world with their rich kinetic imagination. I can understand Truffaut wanting to leave all that showy cinematic stuff behind as his "youthful" manner, and exchange it for an even-handed, unobtrusive style more befitting middle age; but there need be no contradiction between calm detachment and formal brilliance, as films by Mizoguchi or Hitchcock can attest. Nevertheless, by placing Fanny Ardant in the center of things and recording her moody force with few distractions, Truffaut has gone far toward satisfying our appetite for the visually arresting.

DAVID LYNCH'S *WILD AT HEART*

David Lynch has become a fashion phenomenon, the man of the hour, one of those litmus-test artists whom the cult adores while skeptics wonder what the fuss is about. While all of his films *look* great, with enough visual panache to supply a dozen directors, they're also juvenile at times, repetitious and emotionally unresolved. (The exception is *The Elephant Man*, his most controlled and affecting film, which Lynch cultists dismiss as a contract job.) Just as *Dune* can be seen as a twisted *Star Wars*, so Lynch seems, however naughty, a member of the Spielberg/Lucas club: the same boys' stories of mythic quest, morally cartoonish characters, popcorn Saturday-matinee spectacle. *Blue Velvet* was a breakthrough, no doubt: rough and ravishing, even if the naïve rite-of-passage mythology marred it for me. *Twin Peaks* struck me as a prolonged tease: beautiful surfaces, hollow at the center, with little bonbons of eccentricity thrown to the fans.

Part of Lynch's new popularity is that audiences can read his shtick and feel complicity—smiling at his placement of plot conventions in smirky quotation marks. The question is whether mannerisms alone constitute a style, or better, a "vision"; and, even if his do, whether having a vision is enough to make mature films that will last.

Whatever its merits, Lynch's new movie, *Wild at Heart*, hasn't much to say to adults. It is the apotheosis of movie-as-joyride, a tendency that invaded American filmmaking, for better or worse, in the 1970s. Lynch piles on heat, sensation: the virtue is, you never know what's coming next; the drawback is, you may not care. Roller coasters get monotonous.

Lynch is experimenting here with melodramatic textures, borrowing from *Dynasty*-type soaps, cooking up potboiler "family secrets" and diabolical rites—none of which is particularly shocking. His characters quote pop culture (Elvis, *The Wizard of Oz*) to rope in the audience quickly, or to show that our mental lives are the sum of media inputs. The film dares you not to find all this pop detritus and trashy luridness fun. I didn't, but felt like a spoilsport: there's a certain populist bullying operating here. The plot sends a pair of country-and-western lovers, Sailor (played Elvistically by Nicolas Cage) and Lula (Laura Dern), down the highway, pursued by Lula's wicked mother, Marietta (Diane Ladd), and her hired hit men. It's the frisky young innocents, trying to follow their yellow brick road, versus the corrupt older generation.

Much has been made of Lynch's exploration of the dark side of the American psyche, the nastiness crawling just below the surface of small-town U.S.A. Why this should seem such a revelatory idea is beyond me. Perhaps what *is* novel is Lynch's enclosing American wholesomeness and random violence in the same embrace. (I get the feeling that the real threat to Lynch's patriotic piety is not anything as apple pie as evil, but big-city intellectuals with pluralistic values, like the obnoxious autopsist from "back east" in *Twin Peaks*.) In any case, while *Blue Velvet* managed to hit an anxious nerve by flirting with the night world, the menace in *Wild at Heart* is all bogeyman stuff. Willem Dafoe, try as he might, is not as scary as Dennis Hopper; and more important, since Sailor's and Lula's love for each other is never in doubt, all the impediments and psychopaths in their way come across as mere nuisances.

Painters love Lynch. His compositions are exquisite, the frame divided into stylized pools of shadow and light. Then there is his signature color sense, that brownish-blue acidic palette that seems to derive most from art photographers like William Eggleston and Cindy Sherman. In *Wild at Heart*, however, his inclination to create memorable autonomous images sometimes leads him off in a static, uncinematic direction. Like Fellini, Lynch is too uncritically fond of the Absurd, and cannot resist showing off his collection of miscellaneous grotesqueries: his close-up of flies buzzing on vomit, his obese topless dancers, his rich man on the can surrounded by harem girls. There's no discrimination between true perversity and silliness. Of course, Lynch might say that this silliness is intentional, that he wants a polyphony of moods from the transcendent to the inane. The trouble is, the moods get jumbled. Miraculously adaptable as the Angelo Badalamenti score is, too much stress is placed on music to key the change of emotions. The ear adjusts, but not always the heart.

One thing that gave *Blue Velvet* an eerie edge was its daring slowness, its willingness to space out—like the Dean Stockwell party where the plot drifts away and we simply watch the spook carnival unfold. *Wild at Heart* has much shorter, choppier scenes, and less vivid places: I wonder if Lynch's television work, with its episodic hopping about, has not had an adverse effect on his cinematic rhythms.

That the film took the grand prize at Cannes is a tribute to David Lynch's audaciously strong directorial personality. But for all his attempts to juice up his material, *Wild at Heart* is finally a coyly sweet, slight romantic ballad. By once again straddling the line between naïve and disingenuous, Lynch provokes a shiver of fashionableness but does not go very deep.

KENJI MIZOGUCHI

His approach was called, by Parker Tyler, "tragic realism"; he called himself "a director of atmosphere." He demanded of his screenwriter a script so real it would capture the body odor of his characters, while providing some of the most haunted, poetic visuals in movie history.

Who is the greatest Japanese director? Yasujiro Ozu and Akira Kurosawa each have their champions; but I concur with Jean-Luc Godard's opinion that Kenji Mizoguchi was "the greatest of Japanese film-makers. Or, quite simply, one of the greatest film-makers." Kurosawa himself felt that way: "Of all Japanese directors I have the greatest respect for him." Others, like Robin Wood, went even further: "If the cinema has yet produced a Shakespeare, its Shakespeare is Mizoguchi. . . . There are no more beautiful compositions anywhere in the cinema."

Alas, the object of these encomia—one of the major artists of the twentieth century—still draws a blank from most educated Americans. "Miz Gucci?" misheard a friend, thinking I was referring to a new line of accessories. Rather than waste time bemoaning this lapse, I would simply urge it be rectified by rushing to the Film Forum and catching the upcoming Mizoguchi retrospective, which runs from September 20 to October 24. (The same package of twenty-six films, curated by James Quandt at Cinematheque Ontario and the Japan Foundation, Tokyo, will be touring twelve cities in North America.) The chance to see fourteen of these Mizoguchis in new 35mm prints, including his supreme masterpieces (*Ugetsu, The Life of Oharu, The Story of the Last Chrysanthemum*) and his other masterworks (*Osaka Elegy, Sisters of the Gion, A Story from Chikamatsu, Sansho the Bailiff, A Geisha, Street of Shame*), ought to make movie-lovers drool. Those who get the Mizoguchi bug should also check out his fascinating, rarely seen minor works, such as *Miss Oyu, The Woman in the Rumor, My Love Has Been Burning*, and *Utamaro and His Five Women*.

As some of these titles indicate, Mizoguchi was primarily concerned with stories about women's struggles. Because of the compassion shown his heroines, he was often considered in Japan and abroad a champion of women's rights. ("No director in the history of the cinema has so completely identified with the point of view of the woman," wrote Andrew Sarris.) But the question has become a thorny one: feminist film critics Joan Mellen and Audie Bock have read his relentless attention to the sufferings of women as disguised sadism, while viewing his stoicism as politically conservative. On the other hand, Keiko Macdonald, a Japanese film scholar, in her book on Mizoguchi, says that the American "feminist perspective unintentionally slights the subtle cultural contexts Mizoguchi's women inhabit." She grants he may have ambivalence toward women, but concludes approvingly: "Mizoguchi's vision of women's struggle offers no comfortable answers."

In the final analysis, I think it scarcely matters whether we call Mizoguchi a proto-feminist or find sexist strains in him (what men has none?). The point is that he was fascinated with women: with the way they turned their necks, moved across a room, expressed their ideas or released emotion. The women in Mizoguchi films tend to be strong, passionate and complex; the men, spineless egotists.

Mizoguchi himself told an interviewer that "women have always been treated like slaves," a statement that expresses both sympathy and fatalism. He once gave a typically gruff explanation for how he became a "specialist" in women's stories: "While I was working for Nikkatsu, the company already had Murata Minoru making films which featured a hero so, for balance, they made me do films featuring a heroine. As a result I've always approached man-woman problems from the woman's viewpoint. Also, I'm a man who is short-tempered and quarrelsome, so when I work with men there's always the possibility of a fight. But I can't very well slug an actress. I've never yet punched Kinuyo Tanaka!" he added with a laugh, referring to the great actress who was his frequent leading lady.

After World War II, Mizoguchi did make a number of explicitly feminist films (*The Victory of Women*, *Sumako the Actress* and *My Love Has Been Burning*) which were greenlighted by the American Occupation censors partly because of their democratizing message. For all their ardor, they are not his most convincing work: the clumsy agitprop in these films has been taken as evidence of Mizoguchi's uneasiness with intellectual, activist heroines.

He seemed on much firmer ground in the geisha milieu.

Mizoguchi was obsessed with the theme of prostitution, a fact that again may be interpreted in opposite ways: as proof that he wanted to degrade women, or as evidence that he saw the pressures faced by the geisha/prostitute as dramatically emblematic of women's oppressed condition in Japanese society. The truth is that Mizoguchi's own erotic experience was almost entirely with geishas and dance hall hostesses; hence, he knew this world intimately enough to bring it vividly alive onscreen, time and again. In Mizoguchi's demimonde, everyone is always selling herself out: the question is when, to whom and at what price? Perhaps Mizoguchi identified with the geisha's need to find a decent "patron" because of his own painful quest for a studio that would not force on him excessive compromises.

Curiously, the one aspect of women's psychology into which Mizoguchi entered most deeply was their mistrust of men. The younger geisha in his *Sisters of the Gion* who denounces males for using women as their playthings, and flaunts her right to deceive them in turn; the jilted beauty in *Utamaro and His Five Women* who, to defend the sanctity of love, stabs to death her faithless lover and his mistress—these flare-ups of violent animosity and resentment have a convincing tone that suggests Mizoguchi knew something about the problem firsthand. In fact, he was once seriously slashed with a razor by a jealous call girl. After that incident, the director seems to have changed. "He began to adopt the obsessive search for perfection for which he would become famous," note Dudley and Paul Andrew, "and he became fixated on stories of women who, behind the delicate masks of their faces, repress tremendous emotion and hostility."

Certainly, something must have altered in Mizoguchi to turn him from a skilled, stylish studio director, with over fifty films (many of them quickies) to his credit, into a demanding, personal *auteur*. Part of it was his move from Tokyo, after the Great Earthquake, to the Kansai region of Kyoto and Osaka, where he encountered a more colorful, earthy dialect and female type. Too, he was approaching forty: Mizoguchi always maintained that a younger director knew nothing of life. "I didn't begin portraying humanity accurately until *Osaka Elegy* and *Sisters of the Gion*," he later said, referring to the harsh, contemporary slices of life by which he virtually invented neorealist filmmaking in Japan.

What makes these two 1936 features shocking even today is their intransigent bitterness. The young woman who has sold her body to her boss in order to save her father from prison, only to reap the ingratitude and disapproval of her family, is seen in the last shot walking along a bridge, face set in rebellion (or is it despair?). She has come to the end of her rope; nothing is offered audiences to soften the blow. *Sisters of the Gion* ends with a young geisha, injured after having been thrown from a car by an ex-customer, delivering a diatribe against men, as Mizoguchi's camera watches from across the hospital room.

It was in these breakthrough pictures that Mizoguchi honed his signature style: the "one scene/one shot" approach of filming an entire sequence in a single cut. If properly done, uninterrupted sequences could release, in his words, a "hypnotic power"; the actors' performances could achieve a "psychological weight or density . . . different in a continuous one-cut scene than in a scene chopped into cuts and crosscuts."

When his camera moved—and Mizoguchi loved to track, crane or pan, the better to avoid cutting—it would remain a certain distance from the action. "I hate close-ups," he said. He preferred to have audiences work harder in selecting for themselves the salient detail, or get his actors to convey through body language the meaning that another director might reinforce with close-ups. Paradoxically, Mizoguchi was attracted to scenes of extreme pathos or conflict—to anything intensely emotional—but he would film these moments in a purposely dispassionate manner. Often a potentially melodramatic scene would play more movingly, of course, by dint of his restraint.

Beyond questions of technique, a consistent philosophical or spiritual worldview was being asserted, which encouraged the unblinking contemplation of human suffering, in order to arrive at a consolatory acceptance.

It is a wonder how Mizoguchi's relentless prescription of this "bitter pill" about the unhappiness of human existence manages to feel so calming and satisfying. Is it that his disciplined style achieves the catharsis of classical tragedy? Or perhaps we viewers are put under a spell that approximates the liberating, emptying-out effects of Buddhist detachment. (Mizoguchi was an intermittently practicing Buddhist: once, while staring at a stone Buddha in a garden during a rainstorm, he told his crew: "That's what I want.") In the celebrated endings of *Ugetsu* and *Sansho the Bailiff*, the camera pulls away from the protagonists to situate them in a larger, more forgiving cosmos, like the tiny human figures in classical Japanese landscape painting.

The most radical use of the "one scene/one cut" approach occurred in Mizoguchi's 1939 masterpiece *The Story of the Last Chrysanthemum*. The story is set in the Meiji era (1868–1912), a Westernizing, gaslit period of the recent past which Mizoguchi (born in 1898) had known as a boy, and was especially fond of re-creating onscreen. Here we are plunged into a backstage world: the adopted son of a great Kabuki actor is being given choice parts and groomed to take over the family troupe. The son is flattered and pampered on all sides, but the fact is he is not very good. Other actors gossip about his lack of talent. Only one young woman, a nurse in the family, will tell him the truth. An amazingly choreographed ten-minute tracking shot across marshy lots keeps pace with their first, halting conversation—interrupted by a wind-chimes seller and a crying baby—in which he is both stunned and grateful to her for telling him what he knows deep down is the case.

The rest of the movie, which shows the nurse's sacrifices to help her lover learn his craft in grubby touring shows, only to die alone in the hour of his triumph, unfolds with calm, inexorable rigor, via a set of dazzling sequence shots thick with period detail.

The altruistic heroine of *Last Chrysanthemum* embodies a typical Mizoguchian theme: that (shallow) man can only be redeemed through the sacrifices of (deeper) woman. As with many recurrent Mizoguchi motifs, its roots appear to be autobiographical. In childhood, Mizoguchi witnessed his father, an impoverished carpenter, ill-treat his beloved mother, and sell off Kenji's older sister to a geisha house. This older sister, who was quite fond of Kenji, supported him for years when he was trying to get started; she herself was lucky enough to find a wealthy, aristocratic patron who took her as his mistress. (Later in life, Mizoguchi tried to repay the debt by supporting his older sister when her patron's fortunes declined.)

Not all Mizoguchi's heroines are the self-sacrificing type. Many echo the geisha in *Sisters of the Gion* who says: "Obligation? I hate that word." Yet even the ones who profess selfishness often get caught up, despite themselves, in a sacrificial dynamic. Mizoguchi's movies chart the conflict in Japanese society between traditional values and the modern drive for individual gratification. He documents the people— usually women—who continue to honor the old morality of mutual obligation, sacrifice, conscience, while those around them look out for Number One.

Another characteristic Mizoguchi theme, which first surfaced in *The Story of the Last Chrysanthemum*, was the slow, uncertain development of artistic craft. From his film about the great printmaker Utamaro to Genjuro the potter in *Ugetsu*, to his many theater-actor protagonists, Mizoguchi explored the relationship between artistry and popularity. No doubt he felt some identification with these studies of an artist from the lower classes, working in a democratic, popular medium, who develops exquisite tastes. Certainly it is a quintessential tension in Mizoguchi that he brings an aristocratic sense of refinement to often rather seedy, tawdry surroundings.

"A man like myself is always tempted by the climate of beauty," Mizoguchi once said. He had originally studied to be a Western-style painter. He also read widely in literature, and was a habitual moviegoer (King Vidor and Josef von Sternberg were two of his favorite foreign directors). When he began making pictures, however, there were few models in Japanese film for obsessive devotion to cinematic craft. Mizoguchi's increasing dissatisfaction with mediocrity led to legendary, demanding behavior: he kept a urinal on the set so that he would not have to go to the toilet and break concentration; he cut down a dozen telephone poles on location because they marred the composition; he had a whole house moved when he disliked its effect on the perspective, only to change his mind and move it back; he rehearsed a scene with an uninspiring actress seven hundred times. If he was severe on others, he drove himself even harder. His screenwriter, Yoshikata Yoda, reported how enraged Mizoguchi would get at his own limitations. Once, when they were out drinking, Mizoguchi said, "Yoda, this man they call Mizoguchi is nothing but an idiot." He pounded his head against the tatami mat, ranting, "Idiot! Idiot! Idiot!"

The loyal, cheerfully masochistic Yoda—submissive as "a reptile," by his own admission—was Mizoguchi's alter ego and perhaps his sole confidant; he joined the director on *Osaka Elegy* in the thirties and stayed with him to the last. Mizoguchi regarded the screenplay as crucial to a film's success. He usually demanded three drafts, the first two as different as possible from each other, the third an amalgam of the previous versions' best elements. This was Mizoguchi's way of getting a script to "thicken." The notes he sent his screenwriter were terse, cryptic suggestions, often warning against cliché. "Create some dramatic 'cubism,'" he wrote Yoda, for instance. Another response captures in two sentences the contradictory sides of Mizoguchi's temperament, the irritable and the Zenlike: "If you don't give me something striking here, what's the use of having a scriptwriter? Think quietly and calmly."

It was part of Mizoguchi's perfectionism to demand only the most historically genuine props for his period films. He would send his assistants on missions to Japanese museums to wheedle loans of costumes, old currency, lanterns, armor. (Mizoguchi's feeling for the past was comparable to John Ford's; and when he died, it was said, as with Ford, that the national past had lost its most authentic interpreter.) His frequent collaborator, the art director Hiroshi Mizutani, deserves considerable credit for these accurate set designs. Trusting the decor's authenticity also enabled Mizoguchi to employ his long-shot, long-take approach, which tied his characters all the more tightly to their environments.

There is a profoundly intuitive connection between Mizoguchi's flowing camera style and Japanese architecture. "For instance," notes Keiko Macdonald, "he relies heavily upon the sliding door partitions which can be easily opened and closed, the long corridor connecting many rooms, and the white shoji door which can display an individual's action in silhouette," as well as the porous continuum between Japanese interiors and the natural world outside.

Mizoguchi drew on the aesthetic of classical Japanese scroll paintings by letting his camera mimic them in so-called "scroll shots," which peered over rooftops and ducked into rooms. He was also a devotee of Bunraku and Kabuki theater, and occasionally borrowed their stylized traditions for effect (as in the deliciously evocative sound track of *A Story from Chikamatsu*). Nevertheless, it would be a mistake to overstress the exotic, "quintessentially Japanese" side of Mizoguchi. For one thing, his narratives are universally accessible, because of his characters' well-observed psychology; for another, the singularity of his genius is demeaned by seeing it merely as culturally exotic. The Japanese themselves, though respecting him, were often mystified by and critical of Mizoguchi's movies; and he had trouble finding financing for one of his greatest masterpieces, *The Life of Oharu*. It took his European triumph in the fifties, when he won awards an unprecedented three years in a row (for *The Life of Oharu, Ugetsu* and *Sansho the Bailiff*) at the Venice Film Festival, to get the Japanese public to start venerating him.

The thirties and the fifties were Mizoguchi's great periods. He went through a slump during the forties, in part because the war years wreaked havoc with the Japanese film industry, in part because Mizoguchi's obsessions were private, and he felt adrift in the face of militaristic patriotism and world catastrophe. Called upon to do his patriotic part with the umpteenth version of Japan's national myth, *The Loyal 47 Ronin*, he made a dry, stately version that was so long and expensive it bankrupted the studio; worse, it didn't even have any swordplay!

During these years his personal life was also a shambles: his wife, an ex-prostitute whom he had met in a dance hall, and whom, for all her shrewishness, he depended on as his anchor, went insane and had to be committed to a mental hospital for the rest of her life. Her mental condition was diagnosed as induced by syphilis: congenital, in one version (which would exonerate Mizoguchi), given her by him, in another (which would further explain his guilt toward women). In 1948, while researching his hard-hitting *Women of the Night*, he visited a hospital for diseased prostitutes and broke down in front of them, apologizing on behalf of all men, including himself, for their plight. Mizoguchi also took his wife's sister into his house as his common-law wife, and helped support her two children.

Following Japan's defeat in 1945, unions were established throughout the film industry, as part of the American Occupation's democratizing effort; and the tyrannical Mizoguchi found himself elected union chairman of Shochiko's Kyoto Studio. As Kyoko Hirano tells it in her fine book, *Mr. Smith Goes to Tokyo*, he "appalled his fellow union members by making a speech saying 'I am now your union chairman, and therefore I will give you orders.'" Somehow this did not go over well. He resigned from the post, saying in any case he could not have supported a strike against film production.

The movies Mizoguchi made in the fifties had a broader sweep, and a more philosophical humanism, than his quirky thirties masterworks. They also increased the density of Fate brought to bear on characters. *The Life of Oharu*, for instance, opens with the heroine already old, seen from the back, lurching toward the other streetwalker crones, then flashes back to Oharu as a well-bred young woman at court, who errs by falling in love with a servant; then follows her from one disaster to the next, until she ends up (more fortunate than we had expected) a wandering nun with a begging bowl. *Sansho the Bailiff* moves forward inexorably in a straight line; but from the opening scenes, there is never any doubt that we are in for a story of epic grief.

Mizoguchi's experience of the war years seems to have made him more appreciative of the larger historical forces buffeting his characters; and this chaos of forced migrations and pillagings enriches the backgrounds of many of his fifties period films, giving them their "Shakespearean" sweep.

The fifties work is also warmer, less astringent, as is evident from *Gion Festival Music* (aka *A Geisha*), the marvelous remake he did of *Sisters of the Gion*. In the original, the emphasis had been on the bitter, aggressive younger geisha. In the later film, the focus shifts to the older geisha, who protects the younger apprentice a little longer from the sordid life lying in store, by taking a patron she dislikes. "I'll be your patron," she says to the young girl, only half-jokingly. In a world where love for men is so often counterfeited, these acts of womanly solidarity convey an authentic tenderness.

In the fifties, Mizoguchi also signaled his ambition to work on a larger canvas by adapting the literary texts of classic Japanese writers, such as Saikaku and Chikamatsu. His competitiveness had been revived by the shock of seeing another Japanese film, Kurosawa's *Rashomon*, take first prize at Venice in 1951. Mizoguchi was irritated that a comparative neophyte had beaten him to international honors. He resolved to make great films that the whole world would honor, and even cut out drinking as part of his new regimen.

Noel Burch, in his provocative book *To the Distant Observer*, argues that Mizoguchi smoothed out his uniquely Japanese syntax for foreign consumption in the fifties. Burch prefers the thirties work, seeing the celebrated movies of the fifties as a betrayal. I disagree. Granted, some of the late fifties films Mizoguchi made when he was in poor health, such as *The Empress Yang Kwei Fei* and *New Tales of the Taira Clan*, do have an inflated, decorative character. But the fifties were overall a period of enormous maturity and growth for Mizoguchi, and there is nothing wrong with smoothness when it results in a film like *Ugetsu*, which is as close to cinematic perfection as we may ever encounter.

In the fifties, Mizoguchi became the patron saint of the French New Wave critic-filmmakers, who saw in the consistency of his style and themes a vindication of their auteurist position, and in his fluid *mise en scène* an ideal demonstration of their preferred, deep-focus aesthetics.

Without doubt, Mizoguchi's visuals anticipated widescreen movies. Though the images in his later films became increasingly ravishing (thanks in part to his brilliant cinematographer, Kazuo Miyagawa), they were never pictorially static. What is so amazing about Mizoguchi's compositional sense is that, having set up a shot as formally exact and lovely as a Japanese print, he would then have his camera move across a very large space, at every point reestablishing an image of freshness and precision. He could get the composition to "hold" even as it kept metamorphosing—just as he could maintain a dynamic between an onrushing plot filled with troubles and an eternal quiet underneath.

Mizoguchi's great gift was to be able to *think* through his camera. Its circlings, hesitations and forays gave shape to his desires, his longing to unmask a reality he knew in advance was opaque. As Max Ophuls loved his tracks, Mizoguchi adored his crane, and would sometimes hold up shooting for days until it was delivered. "More than a symbol of power, the crane was for him a means of adjusting to the action before him," wrote Dudley and Paul Andrew. "He would glide fluidly amongst his actors and across the set, trying to penetrate the atmosphere of his fiction. These crane movements were the gestures of his personal pen, at the same time disciplined and instinctive."

Sometimes form and content came together with exquisite tact, as in the famous "paradise" scene in *Ugetsu*, where the potter Genjuro discovers the pleasures of the flesh with Lady Wakasa (played by the alluring Machiko Kyo). The enchantress and the potter are seen disporting in the rock pool; then the camera pans away from them, into the landscape of stream and field, only to pick them up (after a quick dissolve) at a later point, enjoying a picnic, as if time and space were collapsed in a continuous circle of delight. The dreamlike hide-and-seek game she teases him with acquires a more ominous meaning later, when he discovers he has been chasing and making love to a ghost.

An even more poignant passage occurs toward the end of *Ugetsu*, when the errant potter returns to his cottage after Odyssean travels and looks in every corner, the camera panning with him; he goes out, comes in again and finds his wife sitting there, preparing him a meal. He falls asleep happy, only to wake up the next morning and learn from neighbors that his wife is dead: the woman who had been tending him the night before, darning his clothes while he slept, was her ghost. We suddenly remember back to that 180-degree camera movement, searching the cottage interior, which had encapsulated loss by its play on absence and presence, invisibility and appearance.

Cinema may always, in the last analysis, be about absence and presence; but Mizoguchi gets us to feel this acutely. If *Ugetsu* is his one explicit "ghost story," all of his work has an apparitional aspect. One way to think about the melancholy and detached perspective of Mizoguchi's filmic viewpoint is that it is that of a ghost, who has already passed over to the other side of the river, from where he views with mournful calm the thrashings of mortals.

Critics who write about Mizoguchi are often reduced to such rhapsodizing, cop-out adjectives as "sublime," "transcendent," "ineffable"—which evade with mystical praise the precise, gritty nature of his accomplishment. On the other hand, "sublime" may in fact be the operative term, if we use the recent definition provided by French thinker Jean-François Lyotard: "An inevitable sadness coming from the inconsistency of all things, it is also the exaltation of thought passing beyond the limits of what can be presented."

Though suffering ill health in his last years, Mizoguchi continued to work feverishly. His very last movie, *Red Light District* (luridly retitled *Street of Shame* here), was as lean and powerfully entertaining as anything he ever shot. This sardonic ensemble piece about a postwar brothel marked something of a return to the (disenchanted) style of his thirties contemporary movies, and was so effective in its deglamorizing portrayal of the "pleasure quarters" that it led to the Japanese government outlawing prostitution a year after its release. By that time Mizoguchi himself was dead, at age fifty-eight. One wonders with what bemused ambivalence he might have greeted the news of this reform, hastened by his own artistry.

After his death, his rival and admirer Kurosawa was moved to say: "With the death of Mizoguchi, Japanese film lost its truest creator." He was right.

THE LEGACY OF JOHN CASSAVETES

John Cassavetes's reputation as a director has undergone a remarkable transformation since his death in 1989. An embattled maverick, once viewed as an amateurish hobbyist who brokered self-indulgent improvisations by his actor-friends, he has come to be seen, especially abroad, as one of the three or four major American filmmakers of the last thirty years. Books are written about him, retrospectives devoted to him, young directors from Budapest to Brooklyn imitate his passionate, infuriating dramas.

Somewhere the ghost of John Cassavetes must be chuckling. Six of his movies are about to be revived by Miramax at the Paris Theater, setting the stage for the opening of *She's So Lovely*, based on a Cassavetes script which his son, Nick, has directed. This convergence of a miniretrospective and a generational "collaboration" across mortal lines gives us a perfect opportunity to assess Cassavetes's legacy. How solid was his achievement? And how readily does it transfer to the present cinematic moment?

Cassavetes began, of course, as an actor, a broodingly handsome, riveting one who specialized in suave villainy (*Rosemary's Baby, The Fury*). Like Orson Welles, he often took acting jobs to pay for his filmmaking habit. His first directorial work, *Shadows*, is an irresistibly jazzy, black-and-white encapsulation of downbeat New York, circa 1960. This free-form, interracial drama made everyone young want to go out and make a movie. The success of *Shadows* landed Cassavetes a Hollywood contract for two studio pictures *(Too Late Blues, A Child Is Waiting)* which, while creditable, convinced him he should never again direct a film he didn't write or couldn't control. His next projects, *Faces* (1963) and *Husbands* (1970), took him over seven years to make, and both wore an aggressively raw, rough texture, as if to distance himself as much as possible from Hollywood's dream-machine smoothness.

Perhaps because of *Shadow*'s genesis in acting workshop exercises, all later Cassavetes films were saddled with the mistaken label of "improvs," though each was in fact carefully scripted by him. One of the revelations in revisiting such later Cassavetes masterworks as *Woman Under the Influence, The Killing of a Chinese Bookie* or *Opening Night* today is that they are much more tightly structured and narratively propulsive than they seemed when first premiered. It may be that Cassavetes worked through some of his need for meandering, amoebic scenes in the two sixties projects, *Faces* and *Husbands*. Both of those explorations went pretty far in forcing intensity from everyday discontent—sometimes crossing over into the very coarseness they decried. The "angry prophet" side of Cassavetes was not above rubbing viewers' noses in what he saw as the shoddier aspects of American materialism and pleasure pursuit.

Faces, the better of the two, keeps broadening and deepening as it goes, until we can't escape acknowledging the pain of the unhappy couple and the satellites they attract on their way to marital collapse. Particularly memorable is a scene in which Seymour Cassel, playing a male hustler, is set upon by an older woman while trying to flirt with Lynn Carlin, the polite, depressed wife. *Husbands*, which charted the adventures of three stags on the loose, is a field day for the directors' "rat pack," Ben Gazzara, Peter Falk and Cassavetes himself. While some critics saw its hysterical laughter and male boorishness as grating, the director stressed in interviews his desire to expose "the bustling, bravura ego" and "the meaninglessness of men's lives," and welcomed audiences' irritation.

Unquestionably, Cassavetes's is an actor's cinema. Ben Gazzara, who considered his work on *Husbands* the most creative experience of his life, described the director's drive to break down the little tricks a performer develops, and crack open a scene until it yielded a deeper truth. "He created an atmosphere in which the actor can do no wrong . . . can make a fool of himself, can go to the limits of absurdity. John wouldn't allow the camera to bend the actor, but the other way around: the actor bends the camera. The actor gives emotional flow. . . . John was not afraid of shooting film. He would shoot it, shoot it, shoot it, until something remarkable happened."

In Cassavetes's own words, "the camera is the slave to the actor." He disdained an obsession with photographic technique: "I feel like vomiting when a director says to me, 'I got the most gorgeous shot today.' " What mattered, he insisted, was putting feeling onscreen. To do this, Cassavetes (and his loyal cinematographer, Al Ruban) favored a hand-held camera style which would stay close to actors' faces, lurch between their bodies like a boxing referee breaking up a clinch, then fall backward, making for decentered, discomfiting, ever-restless compositions.

One reason why it took film critics (myself included) so long to appreciate Cassavetes's virtuosity as a filmmaker was that he broke with the perspectives and deep-focus framing of classical *mise en scène*. He did so because he wanted to convey a sense of the world as always in flux, and of human nature as chronically unsettled, up for grabs. Alcohol, a recurring motif in Cassavetes's films (and life), and mental illness helped to destabilize the characters further, and plunge them into that open-ended "lostness" that was so central to his vision.

"I'm lost by life," Cassavetes told an interviewer. Lots of artists say they don't want to know what they're doing, but Cassavetes meant it. "You have to fight sophistication. . . . You have to fight knowing, because once you know something, it's hard to be open and creative." These prescriptions betray an anti-intellectual bias; and indeed, the relative absence of calm reflection in his characters becomes a limitation, forcing them into hysteria. On the other hand, his strong suits were intuition and an emotional sympathy for disordered souls, which allowed him to reach other truths.

Nowhere was this tolerance for troubled psyches more evident than in A Woman Under the Influence. Gena Rowlands, Cassavetes's wife and frequent muse, gave an immortal performance as Mabel, the disturbed wife of a construction worker, Nick (Peter Falk). What makes her various tics and eccentricities so baffling is that they flow from her desire to do right by everyone. In refusing to judge Mabel's inappropriate behavior, Cassavetes risked romanticizing insanity; but he clearly believed, as he said, that "we're all crazy." What interested him in Mabel's "craziness" was the challenge it presented to the family ecosystem. Her husband Nick is particularly torn, one moment defending her with macho pride, the next betraying her to the medical powers or shaming her in public.

Humiliation is one of the two constants in Cassavetes's universe; the other is love. (His last personal film was aptly titled Love Streams.) Often the only way that love can occur, however, is by one character miraculously forgiving the other for a previous humiliation. Cassavetes's insistence that love exists should not be taken as a sunny affirmation on his part: he still saw the main unresolved problem in life as "how to love, and where to put your love. . . . I have a one-track mind. That's all that I'm interested in—love. And the lack of it. When it stops."

Certainly love stops prematurely in *The Killing of a Chinese Bookie*, a bleak, unusually taut thriller starring Ben Gazzara as the owner of a strip joint. Cassavetes admired certain of the veteran directors he acted for, such as Don Siegel (in *The Killers*) and Robert Aldrich (in *The Dirty Dozen*), and *The Killing of a Chinese Bookie* was his own flirtation with a genre picture. It may also be a disguised autobiographical testament, with Gazzara as a stand-in for the artist who has run out of money and luck.

She's So Lovely, which Cassavetes began writing shortly after *A Woman Under the Influence* and *The Killing of a Chinese Bookie*, brings together many of the filmmaker's pet motifs: drinking, going crazy, the temporariness of life's roles, the reasonings of the heart. Its scenario favors sudden shifts, time-jumps, marginal outsiders. Even little touches (like offering beer to a child) or the word "delovelies" echo other Cassavetes scripts.

At best, *She's So Lovely* gives us the chance to encounter this intriguing, heretofore lost Cassavetes script—and to fantasize how the Master might have executed it. Nick Cassavetes is nothing if not filial: his first feature was a vehicle for his mother, Gena Rowlands (the rather squishy but polished *Unhook the Stars*), and *She's So Lovely* is even more visually poised, though its style seems shaped more by generation than genes. Where John Cassavetes shied away from violence and nudity, Nick Cassavetes is more modishly brutal and sentimental. His bag of techniques—a lyrical, noirish style that includes slow-motion, music video romantic montages, an emphatic score and a helicopter shot for uplift at the end— streamlines the ambiguously conflicted relationship of the two leads into more of a true-love fairy tale. Cassavetes Sr. also insisted on hope in movies (his favorite director was

Frank Capra); but the voyage was rougher, making the optimism more deserved. At the end of *She's So Lovely*, what we mostly feel is the numbness that attends a commercially cinematic "ride."

As in any Cassavetes script, *She's So Lovely* offers actors parts that are full of bravura possibilities. The trio of Sean Penn, Robin Penn Wright and John Travolta jumps into the pool and splashes madly around. The result is a lot of acting: good, bad, over- and under-. Is it a generational matter, too, that Penn and Wright come across more as whiny, victimized waifs than as self-destructive adults? Only Travolta captures the rich dividedness of John Cassavetes's tortured leads.

Given the obsessive, go-for-broke process by which Cassavetes made his movies, it would seem hard to recapture their inner spirit, however faithful the adaptation. Yet his oddball narratives and characters continue to tantalize other filmmakers: Sidney Lumet has just signed to do a remake of Cassavetes's *Gloria* with Sharon Stone, and Nick Cassavetes is rewriting *The Killing of a Chinese Bookie*. While it could prove a dead end to try to imitate Cassavetes stylistically, his more lasting influence on American independent films may well be the example of his toughness and determination to make personal films. This is certainly what Martin Scorsese, perhaps the best we have today, took from Cassavetes. When Scorsese showed him a rough cut of *Boxcar Bertha*, Cassavetes told him he had just wasted a whole year of his life, and he should only film something that he "was dying to make." Scorsese heeded his advice, dusted off and rewrote a script he cared about, and shot what turned out to be *Mean Streets*.

Cassavetes had this to say about his stubbornness. "You can fail in films because you don't have the talent, or you have too much humility, or you lack ferociousness. I'm a gangster. If I want something, I'll grab it. . . . I think I probably have the philosophy of a poor man. You know, like maybe I'd steal the pennies off a dead man's eyes."

A TASTE FOR NARUSE

Posthumously—in fact, fifteen years after his death—Mikio Naruse is being presented to the American public as "a master of the Japanese cinema." A retrospective of his work has just toured nine cities, with the Museum of Modern Art in New York repeating the package because, according to Adrienne Mancia of MOMA's Film Department, they "have never received such enthusiastic mail for a series before." Naruse certainly has his champions and fanatical devotees (myself among them), but after you get past the first nine hundred or so film buffs, it becomes a harder sell. For one thing, Naruse does not come to us with a ready-made, international festival reputation like Fellini or Truffaut; and since he was never blessed with that sort of publicity buildup during his lifetime, he is unlikely to get it now. A painter or poet who dies unknown may leave a life's work which skyrockets in value and popularity, but this has never happened to a filmmaker.

With Naruse there are other problems of receptivity, because his work is so quiet and, to audiences primed on improbable victories, downbeat. Even sophisticated viewers may remain skeptical after seeing only one Naruse film: "Okay, but what's so special about this?" The material, dealing as it does with women's suffering, seems vaguely soap-operaish; the production values are B-picture; and the visual style is handsome but not dazzling. Compared to the other three undisputed giants of Japanese cinema, Mizoguchi with his majestic flowing-scroll tracking shots, Ozu with his static tatami camera setups, Kurosawa with his bravura action editing, Naruse seems to lack an immediately identifiable, "arty" trademark. He stays close to the grammar of mainstream illusionist narratives perfected in Hollywood, lots of dialogue sequences with reverse angles—handled, however, with masterly nuance. His visual artistry is rather hard to put into words, though we shall give it a try later. Kurosawa described the effect of Naruse's movies on him: "a flow of shots that looks calm and ordinary at first glance, reveals itself to be like a deep river with a quiet surface disguising a fast-raging current underneath."

Repeated visits to Naruse films draws one into a strangely singular, self-contained world, like a favorite drab restaurant one keeps returning to, reassuringly melancholy at nightfall. Naruse's forlorn flavor of existence can become addictive. In order to acquire the taste, however, the viewer may need to surrender his or her speeding mental processes to a far less hurried, subtler movement. The effort pays off: if Naruse's films are invariably about disappointment, he himself does not disappoint—no more than does Chekhov, an artist he greatly resembles in stimulating our appetite for larger and more bitter doses of truth.

One of the charms of Naruse's art is its earned pessimism. It takes for granted that life is unhappy; therefore, we can relax in the possession of sadness, acquiesce from the start to the fate of disenchantment, the only suspense being which details Naruse will use to bring it about. In American films and novels, it often takes the characters three-fourths of the plot to win through to the insight of unhappiness, whining and kicking all the way. We can see it as a trade-off: American art has a dynamism and energy generated by its optimism,

Japanese art a serenity and grace by its acceptance of the persistence of suffering. Naruse can even be playful about it, as when he shows two geisha in *Late Chrysanthemums* competing for who can sing the most unhappy drinking song, and one of them says crossly: "I *know* life is like that, already." It is expected knowledge, part of the culture. As Naruse himself put it: "From the youngest age, I have thought that the world we live in betrays us; the thought still remains with me."

Mikio Naruse remains something of a mystery man. All that we know in English comes to us from Anderson and Richie's pioneering book *The Japanese Film* and from Audie Bock's invaluable writings on the director. Naruse was born in 1905 and had a rather grim childhood, the youngest of three children of a poor embroiderer and his wife. A lifelong friend recalls that "the only thing the boy Mikio ever asked for from his family was a winter coat he saw in the window of a pawn shop. . . ." Naruse's father died when he was young and his mother shortly after; he was brought up by a "not overly affectionate elder sister and brother." Though he had a passion for literature, particularly fiction, and hoped to go to university, lack of money forced him to quit school. He got a job as a prop man at Shochiku Film Studios, and lived in a rented room near the studio. "The darkest period of my life," he admitted later.

The early days of Japanese film production offered opportunities for rapid advancement; Mizoguchi and Ozu apprenticed for only one year before being promoted to director. Typically, the unassuming Naruse spent ten years toiling as an assistant director before getting his chance. Even then, he was called on to make slapstick comedies with which he had little rapport. Still, they have a certain interest today: the earliest surviving, alternately titled *Flunky, Work Hard* or *Little Man, Do Your Best* (a world of difference between the two translations), shows a poor insurance salesman making a fool of himself and accepting any humiliation to compete for a rich man's clientele. Meanwhile, he ignores his son, who gets seriously injured. This pattern of slapstick taking a sudden tearjerker turn was very popular with Japanese audiences at the time. What seems surprising, as with some of Ozu's early silents, is the rather wild "show-off" style—quick cutting, weird camera angles, multiple dissolves—probably influenced by German expressionist films of the twenties, and so different from Naruse's later work. But we can already see the same interest in people at the end of their monetary rope, the same humanism, the same atmospheric accuracy and—heretical as this may sound—the same propensity for humor. Naruse buffs get so caught up talking about his famed pessimism that they lose sight of the many comic touches and amusing nuances of behavior in all his films. He always takes pleasure in the idiosyncrasies and one-track minds of his secondary characters, bringing vitality to the smallest bit parts. Even more—and here I am again tempted to cite Chekhov—the care with which the characters' illusions are set in place and then, at just the right moment, snatched away, produces a spasm rooted in comic techniques. So perhaps Naruse's long training in silent comedies contributed to his later, impeccable sense of timing in melodrama.

Nevertheless, he was eager to deal with a kind of material he felt temperamentally closer to, and so began his first efforts in the *shomin-geki* genre that was itself getting under way. Anderson and Richie define the *shomin-geki* as "drama about the common people. . . . Essentially a film about the proletarian or lower-middle-class, about the sometimes humorous, sometimes bitter relations within the family, about the struggle for existence, it is the kind of film many Japanese think of as being about 'you and me.' " I might add that it is also the kind of film which is heavier on character than plot, and allows for considerably more digressions and atmospheric touches than a typically Occidental film would permit. It is easy to see why the novelistically inclined Naruse was drawn to this meandering slice-of-life genre.

Naruse's life outside the studio certainly does not jibe with our usual glamorous image of film directors. "Although he was now a full-fledged director," Bock tells us, "until he left Shochiku in 1934 Naruse was earning less than 100 yen a month (almost $360), putting him in the class of studio employees who had to line up at the pay window and get cafeteria meal tickets. The very private, alcohol-loving Naruse, however, traded his meal tickets for cigarettes and went to eat at a cheap restaurant near the studio. Here he spent much time observing and conversing with the waitresses, one of whom fell in love with him. Naruse did not respond to her letters, and the unfortunate woman committed suicide, bringing the wrath of the film world upon the director for his 'cold heartlessness.' The incident may well have aggravated Naruse's already morose demeanor, for his life was exceedingly lonely—he always drank alone, at the same table, and conversations with these working women were his only social life. His mother had died in 1922, and his brother and sister had as little to do with him as possible; he rented a second-floor room from a family who did progressively worse in their sushi business, and every time they moved to poorer quarters, Naruse went along."

Meanwhile, though Ozu praised his work, the studio head of Shochiku seemed less enthralled. "Naruse, we don't need two Ozus," he told him, forcing him to leave for another studio. When we see their films side by side today, Naruse hardly seems a copycat. Certainly, there were similarities in the quietness of tone, in the preference for contemporary material (both stayed away from "period" pictures) and in the cinematic manner; increasingly Naruse was coming to rein in his camera and keep it relatively still and within doors.

On the other hand, Naruse showed people who were living much closer to the edge than Ozu did. Ozu's is more a gentle, middle-class world where manners are still respected and a rude word can cause a character to burst into tears. In the same situation a Naruse character might shrug or laugh in the other person's face. In Ozu, the "plot" often involves an exquisite dissection of ritualized politeness to reveal the characters' true emotions by film's end. Naruse's people make no bones about how they feel. When they want to wound, they get rough. When they want money or sex, they demand it openly. Perhaps the main difference is that Naruse is dealing mainly with the urban poor, where such time-consuming manners would be considered a luxury. The conditions under which these straitened families live, all packed together, getting on each other's nerves, promotes a style of interaction at once balder and refreshingly less formal than found in Ozu's decorous households.

Typically in a Naruse film, there is one character with a little more sensitivity and refinement, a sort of audience surrogate who can still wince at the coarseness and selfishness of those around her. Most Naruse families have at least two loafers and spongers; the family in *Lightning* is rather extreme in its slatternly, parasitic behavior—fun to watch, actually, as three half brothers and sisters (each from a different father) and their mother leech off one upright job-holding daughter. Lest we think this family has reached bottom, a beggar appears at the door (a typical Naruse touch); their casual dismissal of him barely interrupts the conversation, implying what a commonplace event this is.

Naruse may be the most materialist director in the history of cinema. It is remarkable how much of his dialogue is taken up with the collection and solicitation of money. When a new character enters the scene, his or her first words are apt to be: "I am here for the thirty-five yen you owe me." Naruse's movies are filled with characters who are landlords, moneylenders or bill-collecting merchants, on the one hand, and poor relatives, gigolos and ex-husbands looking for a handout, on the other. He chooses his heroines usually from the most vulnerable individuals in Japanese society: those outside the marital family relationship, single women or widows. As they struggle to keep their heads above water and, even more, to gain a measure of independence, to own their own laundry shop or bar or geisha house, they scramble to get loose of one creditor, only to find in their "rescuer" a new mortgage, a new master, a new indentured servitude. If the creditor is male, there may be an implied sexual obligation incurred as well.

Just as every Fassbinder film, for all his fecundity, turns out to be a demonstration of one form of exploitation or another, so all of Naruse's stories boil down to the problem of debts. Being obligated, as Ruth Benedict has pointed out in *The Chrysanthemum and the Sword,* is a powerful notion in the Japanese psyche, and for that reason Japanese people will sometimes take great pains to avoid the condition. Or, in Naruse's films, to rationalize it: "I have obligations to you," one geisha tells her boss, "but I also have reproaches." Family obligations are not so easily avoided, but that does not mean they need always be undertaken graciously. The beleaguered, otherwise sympathetic Keiko in *When a Woman Ascends the Stairs* helps her pathetic brother pay for his son's operation, but makes sure by her nasty manner that he will not soon bother her again. In a sense, Naruse can be seen as documenting a moment in Japanese social history when Westernization had weakened the nourishing core of the family support system, without, however, releasing the individual from its onerous economic obligations. We do not know what Naruse's political views were, if any. He shied away from making militaristic propaganda films in the early forties, just as he avoided Left-wing/democratic agitprop after the war. "Commitment" was not his style; but we learn more about the heavy weight of money on the world from him than from any other director.

In 1935 Naruse made one of his best films, *Wife, Be Like a Rose*, which was not only very popular in Japan, winning the Kinema Jumpo Award (equivalent to the Oscar), but which was the first Japanese talkie to play in New York. The *Variety* reviewer at the time admitted that the film was "completely without hokum" and that "Jap femmes are okay for looks," but predicted that it would "draw moderately well in a few arties.... Otherwise no dice." In any event *Wife, Be Like a Rose* was a more lighthearted project than usual for Naruse, touched by the ebullient lyricism of early sound films. Revolving around the efforts of a happily-in-love young woman to bring her estranged parents together so that all may be happy, the film is riveting for its portrayal of the girl's mother, a haiku poetess whose self-absorbed intellectual life poses a barrier for reconciliation with her laborer ex-husband. The story line (and the title) may appear antifeminist; but Naruse's sympathy for the strong-minded, independent and charmingly melancholy poet argues the reverse. We cannot help feeling a little relieved for her when she remains alone at the film's end, instead of being reconciled. Once again, Naruse shows compassion for solitariness, and implies the difficulty, if not impossibility, of marriage, in a comedy ostensibly defending that institution.

To his colleagues' surprise, the reclusive director pulled a major coup by winning the hand of his beautiful young star, the ingenue who had been so life-affirming in *Wife, Be Like a Rose*. Naturally, happiness was not so easily obtained for a man like Naruse. In fact he "went into a slump which lasted fifteen years and was the most serious any major director has ever experienced," according to Anderson and Richie. There is some debate among Naruseans as to whether his wife was at fault, or other factors. Those who argue the former point to all the portraits of shrewish, nagging wives in his later films. Those against say the wives in Naruse films always nagged. I myself do not see how we can blame the woman for making him unproductively miserable when misery had always been a creative spur to him before. The difficult war years, the foolish projects the studio foisted on him and his own creative fatigue may also have been at fault. In any case, coincidentally or not, when Naruse's marriage collapsed he moved into his old shabby rented rooms, returned to his sake bars—and entered upon his most fertile period as an artist.

It was in the decade from 1951 to 1960 that Naruse produced his greatest masterpieces, *Late Chrysanthemums*, *Floating Clouds* and *Flowing*, along with many very satisfying films, just below that standard, such as *Repast*, *Mother*, *Sound of the Mountain*, *Lightning*, *Older Brother*, *Younger Sister*, *Husband and Wife*, and *When a Woman Ascends the Stairs*. In a curious way, Naruse's melancholy temperament meshed perfectly with the postwar mood of malaise and defeat. At the same time, his cinematic style crystallized, becoming stripped of anything arbitrary or baroque. "The cinema of restraint," Richard Peña of the Film Center, Chicago, has called it: "In his fifties masterworks, Naruse's style is so austere that the slightest gesture—a look, a sudden camera movement, two or three rapid cuts—take on enormous significance."

Heretofore, due to his timidity or fatalism, he had made whatever pictures the studio asked of him. Now, however, he tried his hand at adapting a book by an author whose work he loved, Fumiko Hayashi (1904–51). "Probably Japan's most distinguished modern woman writer. . . . Born to hardship, she profoundly understood the lot of Tokyo's lower classes, and depicted them with an unobtrusively skillful realism and without a trace of sentimentality," the critic Martin Seymour-Smith wrote. Here was material Naruse felt comfortable with. Interestingly, Hayashi died in 1951, the very year that Naruse attempted his first film based on her work, *Repast*; they apparently never met, but the natural rapport between the disconsolate Naruse and the dead novelist led to one of the most successful collaborations in film history. He made six adaptations of Hayashi's work in all—*Repast*, *Lightning*, *Husband and Wife*, *Late Chrysanthemums*, *Floating Clouds*, and a final, beautiful tribute, Hayashi's autobiography, *A Wanderer's Notebook*. When he had adapted all that he could, he is reported to have lamented, " 'There's nothing left of Hayashi's any more, is there?' . . . as if he had truly lost a soul-mate." (Bock)

How is it that Naruse was able to enter so deeply into a woman's point of view? In light of recent feminist film criticism, what are we to make of this phenomenon in general of the male director who chooses again and again to tell a story through a woman's eyes? Naruse, Sirk, Mizoguchi, Cukor, Ophuls—are these men to be regarded as proto-feminists, or reinforcers of gender mythology, or both? There is of course the economic factor, that women constituted a large part of the moviegoing audience, in Japan as well as America, and that the so-called "weepies" or "three-hankie pictures" were made with their ticket-buying power in mind. J. Hoberman has astutely pointed out: "Like Douglas Sirk, Naruse suffered critically for being a maker of women's films (and incidentally a director of actresses at least on a par with Mizoguchi); like Sirk, as well, Naruse was able to use the melodramatic weepie—often at its most lurid—as a vehicle of social criticism." Too bad today's audiences feel so superior to this genre, and often laugh at the spectacle of intense suffering as though at a lapse in taste. One might ask to what extent this sophisticated giggling at the emotional "datedness" of women's films is our embarrassed confession of inadequacy before a once possible largeness of heart.

Of the two great Japanese directors who specialized in feminine psychology, Mizoguchi and Naruse, Mizoguchi is apt to seem the more borderline bathetic today, Naruse the more realistic. Both may have been working out their own guilt toward women in these empathetic portraits (Mizoguchi blamed himself for his wife's madness, after having given her a venereal disease; with Naruse, there was the waitress who committed suicide). Certainly, both selected women as a good vehicle for embodying the Buddhist doctrine of worldly suffering. Mizoguchi's heroines seem not only noble but at times verging on masochistic, like the title character in *The Life of Oharu*, who gets sold into prostitution and suffers the gamut of degradations on her road to transcendence. Naruse's women are apt to be more aggressive, falling a good deal short of the angelic. Naruse, in fact, was willing to go to audacious limits in risking an audience's sympathetic identification with a main character, preferring mixed types in the interests of psychological realism.

Many Naruse heroines work in bars and geisha houses, where they are wrongly taken for prostitutes and have to fend off men who prey on momentary weaknesses—compromising situations, in short, where their character and integrity will be tested to the limit. Audie Bock has written about Naruse's women: "A stubborn dedication to their own self-respect in the face of overwhelming crassness, vulgarity and exploitation . . . lends Naruse's heroines a distinctive nobility. They never allow themselves to be swallowed up in self-sacrifice to the extent that a Mizoguchi heroine like Oharu does; if they throw themselves away for a man, like Yukiko in Naruse's best-loved film in Japan, *Floating Clouds*, they do so with such a complete awareness that we cannot feel pity for them. Naruse heroines retain the dignity of evaluating their acts to the end. . . . It is with this self-awareness that Naruse prevents his heroines from being tragic and pathetic and makes them instead contrary and stubborn. They refuse to give up in the face of emotional blankness on the part of a lover or insurmountable financial obstacles to a secure life. . . . Unlike

Ozu's accepting protagonists or Mizoguchi's transcending heroines, Naruse's characters continue to question and to beat their heads against the wall."

The quintessential Naruse actress was Hideko Takamine, who had seventeen starring roles in the director's films, and who was certainly as important to Naruse's realization of his vision as Fumiko Hayashi. This beautiful woman has large, vulnerable, somewhat prideful eyes given to flashes of resistance and annoyance. It is interesting to contrast her with a seemingly more "classical" Japanese type, Setsuko Hara, the breathtaking "good girl" of many Ozu films like *Late Spring* (and whom Naruse also used). Hara never stops smiling as she resists whatever does not suit her; Takamine rebels from the start, but with a weariness which suggests she knows she may have to give in eventually. In what is probably her greatest performance, the biographical film about Fumiko Hayashi, *A Wanderer's Notebook* (also called *Her Lonely Lane*), Takamine even succeeds in making herself look homely, curling her mouth into a sarcastic grimace as she threads her way through Tokyo's literary bohemia, sloughing off insults and condescension or retaliating when it suits her, obstinately falling in love with the wrong men. In all of Takamine's Naruse roles, her face shows so abjectly when she is fond of a man that the object of her desires often starts taking her for granted right away. He would be wrong to think her easily gotten rid of, however, because a Takamine character in love can be quite a nuisance.

The perfect male partner for Takamine was Masayuki Mori, an actor Naruse used repeatedly, and who attained something like international renown as the enchanted potter in Mizoguchi's *Ugetsu*. This very intelligent actor was called upon to play something of a heel in both *Floating Clouds* and *When a Woman Ascends the Stairs*. If he were merely a cad he would have no interest for us. But one always gets the feeling with Mori—or the role he plays in Naruse's films—that a part of him does understand a woman's needs and would even like to go along with her program, if only he could believe love was not an illusion. As often as he turns away a woman, something in him expresses reluctant sympathy for her—and that is perhaps the hook. Mori's face, full of sharp angles, has shades of disdain, self-doubt, gentleness and cruelty—a Japanese James Mason, in a sense. Elegant-looking even when his character has fallen on hard times, as in *Floating Clouds*, the sardonic Mori is finally worn down by Takamine's love. It is she, the "rejected one," who, as is often the case with unrequited love, proves the stronger. When Mori finally breaks down at her deathbed, in one of the most moving (and uncharacteristically conclusive and tragic) endings in Naruse, we sense that a man like him can only feel love in the form of pity and remorse.

Naruse's is an actor-oriented cinema, where no exotic angles or camera devices are allowed to distract from full concentration on the human drama. Thus, it comes as somewhat of a surprise to learn that he rarely coached his actors. Hideko Takamine has left us a funny reminiscence of her experience with the director: "Mr. Naruse was more than merely reticent; he was a person whose refusal to talk was downright malicious. Even during the shooting of a picture, he would never say if something was good or bad, interesting or trite. He was a completely unresponsive director. I appeared in about twenty of his films, and yet there was never an instance in which he gave me any acting instructions. He never said anything, so it was always up to me to decide how to act on my own. . . . It was at the start of principal photography on the film . . . *Untamed* that I mustered all my courage and addressed a question to Mr. Naruse.

" 'How should I approach this role?'

" 'It'll be over before you know it.'

"This was all the answer I was to receive before he lapsed into his usual silence, and I was caught in my own trap. What a mean old man!"

And yet, Naruse's films are uncommonly well acted. It is said that the great Danish director Carl Dreyer generated a sort of energy field around him; more important than any verbal advice was the way he would walk over to an actor and touch him on the shoulder, and the actor would know instinctively the right quality to bring to the lines. So it may be that Naruse, through his own stoical, uncommunicative manner on the set, generated a force field that was so strong that the actors could not help but fall into the right, desperate mood, expressing what has been called his "vision of entrapment."

Naruse disliked breaking in new coworkers; if an actor understood instinctively what he wanted, he would use him or her over and over again. Of the stock company that Naruse built up over the years, first mention should be made of Daisuke Kato, the roly-poly secondary who seems to pop up in every Naruse film after 1952, almost like a good-luck charm. It was the unprepossessing Kato's lot to play a man who is obviously unattractive to the woman he desires, but who hangs around, hoping against hope that she will get desperate enough to settle for him. Another Naruse regular was Haruko Sugimura, whom Ozu fans will recognize as the comically meddlesome "Auntie," but whom Naruse brings out in more womanly leading roles, as the once seductive geisha in *Flowing*, or the ex-geisha turned moneylender in *Late Chrysanthemums*. It is something to see her counting money in the latter film, and sticking a wad efficiently into her kimono top. When her heart has been broken one last time by an old lover asking for money, she burns his photograph in a scene of chilling finality and accepts the platonic devotions of Daisuke Kato, who shares with her a passion for collecting rents.

Naruse made the key statement about his own aesthetics when he said about his characters: "If they move a little, they quickly hit the wall." This point applies not only to psychology and plot, but to the physical environment in which the characters interact. It is a tight set; we come to know these rooms, and the walls (those walls against which the characters keep beating their heads) are never far. Naruse's films largely take place in interiors, with a good deal of lush black-and-white shadow. Still, we are always aware of telltale background details which reveal the status of the characters' pocketbooks. Often we get a glimpse of the neighborhood, with its cheap tenements and noodle shops—usually a long shot of the street or alley where the characters dwell—shown once during the daytime, and once at night, with the lanterns glimmering in a smudgy moody darkness.

Okamoto, a director who apprenticed with Naruse, testified to his master's extreme reluctance to get bogged down in elaborate location shots, preferring small crews and cheap solutions. "For example, when we were scouting locations in the city, the cinematographer asked, 'Is this where you'd like to shoot?' and held his hands out wide to indicate the intersection of two broad, busy avenues. I began to tally up rough estimates in my head: fifty or sixty extras, five or six automobiles, ten traffic controllers would probably be needed. But then Mr. Naruse turned around in the opposite direction and squared his hands to indicate a narrow frame, 'Here will do.' It was the entrance to the subway. In this tight an area, we would only need two or three people to pass by the star, Hideko Takamine."

When we contrast this story with anecdotes about the imperious Mizoguchi demanding that a whole house be moved on the roadside to improve the background, or Ozu requiring that ceilings be built on all his sets, it is clear why studio chiefs came eventually to appreciate Naruse. He always brought his films in on time and even under budget. Audie Bock sees this unwillingness to ask for anything for himself as a "painful modesty" which held him back; and certainly, modesty is not a virtue we expect or reward in our modern artists.

Yet one may also view it as pride of another kind, equally stubborn at its root as Mizoguchi's demands. It is also the difference between the directorial style that sets out to create a universe, and the one that has an almost superstitiously spiritual respect for reality as it is: between Antonioni painting the trees purple, and Rossellini not moving so much as a boulder out of the way.

In spite of his dislike of location shooting, we often do get a sense of the city (usually Tokyo) in which Naruse's characters live—quickly and over their shoulders. The viewpoint has nothing touristic or documentary about it: it is that of the thoroughly acclimatized urbanite, who takes the metropolis more or less for granted, while hurrying through errands. In that respect the city is all the more convincingly and, as it were, lovingly portrayed: it does not have to be milked for "colorfulness."

One privileged location, used by Naruse so often it amounts to a signature, is the bridge or overpass. Here his protagonists repair, midway or two thirds through the story, to hash out their problems. These overpass sequences function as a kind of narrative resting point. The lyrical movement from confining interiors to open air, and the sudden elevation above the city, release an appetite for perspective, both physical and emotional. But the promenade often turns into a nervous pacing back and forth, reinforcing the awareness that there is no easy way out of the trap.

A case could be made for Naruse as a formalist on the level of Ozu and Mizoguchi, provided we begin to understand how his psychological genius translates into cinematic terms: as an art of discreet, subtle and *tactful* interventions. Each timing of a cut, each composition, each camera placement and movement of Naruse's reveals an absolutely reliable discretion and intelligence. Sometimes it is exquisite indeed, as when the heroine in *When a Woman Ascends the Stairs* reluctantly begins climbing the steps to her bar hostess job, and the camera tracks, for less than two seconds, a close-up of her feet. In *Floating Clouds* there is a haunting memory-sequence of Indochina, lit more brightly than the rest of the film and with a *Bolero*-like musical figure behind it, which depicts the couple's first sexual attraction (long since outgrown by the man, but not the woman). It functions as a denial of transience: once something is real in the past, it can never be dismissed. In this film Naruse also repeats a peculiar formal device every time the man and woman walk together. He tracks them in long shot, then moves the camera in for a closer, more languid tracking shot: this movement becomes the metaphor of the couple's true connection, in spite of the man's denial or the arguments of the moment.

Another example might be taken from *Late Chrysanthemums*, during a painful train station scene where an ex-geisha is seeing off her son, the one person she cares most about in the world, though he couldn't care less about her. The compositions have been very constrained, in line with the mood of loss and betrayal. But there is a sudden widening of the angle as a pair of new, young geisha pass by, and the middle-aged ex-geisha and her friend examine the girls' coiffure. On the one hand, it recalls the bitter shortness of a career based on fleshly beauty; on the other hand, the veterans seem to take some pride in their ability to evaluate the nuances of fashion. Then the camera pulls back farther still and we are given the whole train station, followed by three city views, until we end up on an overpass. The two faded ex-geisha are clopping along in their clogs, trying to remember the name of a new American movie sensation. "Marilyn Monroe!" one recalls with satisfaction, and the film ends as they continue walking with their backs to us. It is a singularly slight way to "resolve" such a somber movie—yet an ending perfectly in keeping with Naruse's sensibility, which fights shy of any resounding conclusions.

It has been said, by Audie Bock, that: "There are no

happy endings for Naruse, but there are incredibly enlight-
ened defeats." A beautiful sentence, and only partly true. Actually, there are cheerful notes struck in the very sweet, if
tentative, reconciliation between mother and daughter in
Lightning, the boyish somersaults in *The Whole Family Works*,
the young couple's happiness in *Wife, Be Like a Rose* and the
wife's return to her husband in *Repast*, leaning against his
shoulder in the train, embracing the role of wife in her mind,
like the bittersweet ending of Tolstoy's *Family Happiness*. Perhaps the most ambiguous and radical ending of Naruse's occurs in *Flowing*, a delicate, absorbing chamber work about the
decline of a geisha house. For the last several minutes the film
goes completely without dialogue, alternating shots of the
daughter practicing her sewing machine upstairs, the geisha
mother supervising her samisen pupils, the elderly maid going about her business—until one realizes with a shock that
this is it, the drama is not going to come to any point; we are
left with the image of life streaming or "flowing" through the
characters, the rooms, the evening, the river. It is a passage as
modern, as contrapuntally abstract, as Resnais's *Muriel*, or
the finale of Antonioni's *The Passenger*.

There is a tendency in Naruse criticism to interpret the
director's penchant for inconclusive endings, and his very es-
chewal of tragic denouement, as evidence of an even bleaker
pessimism. With this I cannot agree; nor can I go along with
assessments of Naruse as an archnihilist. For instance, Anderson and Richie state: "Naruse's view of the world, if one of the
most consistent, is also one of the least comforting. Mizoguchi may show us that in beauty lies salvation; . . . Ozu
may take away everything, but he at least leaves his people the
solace of each other's company. Naruse, however, believes
there is no escape. We are in a floating world which has no
meaning for us. If we are fortunate we die. If not, we must go
on and on." I do not see why the stoical endurance of
Naruse's characters is so bereft of meaning, nor what, if any-

thing, robs *them* of the solace of each other's company. How-ever, Bock also speaks of "the terrifying statement of all of Naruse's work," and, comparing him also to Mizoguchi and Ozu, calls him "the most withdrawn and the most clinical, and consequently, the one with the darkest view of life."

One needs to take with a grain of salt the contemporary critical tendency to validate a work of art by calling it "dark," "darker" or "darkest." Understandably, defenders of Naruse want to stake out a separate territory for him, but perhaps we do him a disservice by exaggerating his pessimism. In any case, is "pessimism" even the correct word, if all that we mean is a rejection of that sugarcoating of conventional cheerful-ness? Freud once said that he was trying to bring his patients from hysterical misery to ordinary unhappiness. Naruse's characters certainly know about ordinary unhappiness, but to the degree that they regularly fight clear of hysterical misery and hold on to a dazed integrity, finding momentary com-pensations, satisfactions and trade-offs along the way, I find his movies rather comforting—not to mention satisfying, in the way of all such poised, well-executed art.

The key to the restorative, consoling power of Naruse's films lies in their evenness. There is a sense of balance and peace that radiates from Naruse's own calm attitude that all these troubles have their rightful place in the world. It was this very even tempo which once made a studio head com-plain that he found Naruse's films "monotonous" and lacking dramatic highs and lows, just as it may have caused Noel Burch to say that "only such extreme films as Naruse's post-war *Mother* really achieve the 'void' " of "no dramatic conflict or underlying movement." Whether Burch means this as a compliment or an insult, it is simply untrue: that particular film depicts several family deaths, a romance, an expected proposal that is disappointed, the giving up of a child for adoption, the growing isolation of the widowed mother, and the teenage daughter's final wrenching, maturing insight that she will never understand what is going on in her mother's head. Perhaps what is meant by a "void" or absence of dramatic conflict refers simply to the quiet, methodical pace, and the equal weight given to everyday ordinary events and tragic ones.

Naruse was fond of first-person narrations, a device which suited his literary side and which brought a note of confiding warmth to many of his film narratives. In *Mother*, the teenage girl who narrates the movie, describing each family member, gets to her mother and says: "My mother prefers a small broom." It is a telling detail: the grandiosity of a large push-broom suits this self-contained, reserved, petite woman less than does getting down on her knees and bringing the dirt close to her in little arcs. One might see this as an analogue for the director's own technique—the small broom of Mikio Naruse.

He carried on until 1969, when he died of cancer. The last movie he made, *Scattered Clouds*, is one of his strangest and strongest. It is eerie to see how well his style worked inside the mode of the late sixties; how curiously modernist it looks in CinemaScope, with its cool, restrained colors and spare compositions; how suitable his theme was to the Age of Alienation, though it is only Naruse's old song: that people keep scheming to get a little of what they want in a world designed for unhappiness.

As Naruse himself told his apprentice Okamoto: "If you run from left to right and back again to suit the changing times, the results will be hollow. Look at me. I've been the same from before the war, through the war, up till now. What has changed has been fashion; sometimes it has coincided with my ideas, and sometimes it hasn't." Though most of the titles in the Naruse series are returning to Japan, a few hardy distributors like Audie Bock are preparing to rerelease several of his best. Let us hope that fashion is once again coming around to embrace Naruse's worthy films.

The traveling Mikio Naruse retrospective in 1984–85 was a revelation to me. For one thing, I was already over forty, with decades of cinephilic pokings behind me: I simply did not expect that such buried treasure—the uncovering of a major, major filmmaker with a prolific, hitherto unknown body of work— could still be made available. (It's like saying I didn't expect to fall in love again.) Actually, I had once seen a Naruse picture in my teens, When a Woman Ascends the Stairs, *as part of a pioneering Brandon package of Japanese films. At the time it seemed to me nothing special—which suggests either that Naruse is not a director for adolescents or that some filmmakers' greatness cannot be grasped by a single instance; you have to immerse yourself in their* oeuvre. *Now I adore* When a Woman Ascends the Stairs. *Defeat and I are on much closer terms.*

Naruse got under my skin; I wanted to make narrative art like his; and I ended up patterning my novel The Rug Merchant *after his luckless shopkeepers (as well as R. K. Narayan's heroes). One good thing about imitating obscure masters: nobody knows you're doing it. Sometimes I come across other dedicated Naruseans, such as the editor Robert Gottlieb or the writer Janet Malcolm: oddly enough, fellow Naruseans do not fall into each other's arms but are testy, as though irritated at meeting another keeper of the flame. One might almost suspect that Naruse's solitary spirit had passed into his fans.*

SIDNEY LUMET, OR THE NECESSITY
FOR COMPROMISE

What are we to make of Sidney Lumet? In his forty-year, forty-film career, the man has given us probably a greater number of decent, interesting movies—or interesting *parts* of movies—than any other working director. Whether we are talking about his peaks (*Long Day's Journey into Night, Dog Day Afternoon, Prince of the City*), his partial successes (*Bye Bye Braverman, Serpico, Running on Empty, Q & A, Just Tell Me What You Want*) or even his meretricious films, like *Network*, all have an absorbing, warm, *menschy* vitality. Yet he has rarely been accorded the cinephilic respect which even the esoteric André De Toth, say, receives. He has worked in a Hawksian variety of genres, and nourished as independent a producer-director name as Otto Preminger, without ever sinking to studio hackery. (His debacles, like *The Wiz* or *A Stranger Among Us*, seem to have been freely chosen, embraced with as much gusto as Preminger's *Rosebud* or *Skidoo*).

Significantly, Peter Bogdanovich, in his mammoth book of interviews with important Hollywood directors, *Who the Devil Made It*, concludes the parade of Dwan, Hawks, Hitchcock, Ulmer, Siegel, Aldrich, etc., with Sidney Lumet; and it is tempting to think of Lumet in these terms, as a throwback, the last of the old-fashioned prolific filmmakers. Tempting, but admittedly, they were all better craftsmen.

A more useful comparison might be to other directors of his generation who came to films (usually from live TV) in the early sixties: John Frankenheimer, Arthur Penn, Robert Mulligan, Alan Pakula, Irv Kershner. At the beginning each had his auteurist champions in *Cahiers*, *Positif* and *Movie*, while Lumet was being dismissed as a social-conscience Stanley Kramer type; yet I would submit that, over the years, they all ran out of gas or lost their edge, and that Lumet has given us more pleasure, on the whole, than his contemporaries. He has stayed the course.

Then why aren't we more grateful? Why are film buffs so reluctant to welcome Lumet—if not into the "Pantheon" (to use Andrew Sarris's categories), then at least to liberate him from the Sarrisian hell of "Strained Seriousness" and grant him a corner in "Lightly Likable," along with such veteran entertainers as Michael Curtiz and Delmore Daves? Because Lumet *is* maddening. His virtues (humanity, strong direction of actors, vigorous storytelling, novelistic background textures and lively minor characters, an amazing feel for New York City) are inextricably knotted up with his vices (visual sloppiness, improbable plotting, a penchant for moralizing, cliché, weak direction of actors). Just when you want to venerate him, he disappoints, and just when you want to discount him, he entertains.

Night Falls on Manhattan, his latest film, is typical Sidney Lumet: terrific for a while, until it stops being terrific. The opening promises much, with an elegant graphics title sequence, and a pumped-up quarter hour showing a cops' stakeout of a drug kingpin that goes awry. The black kingpin (sharply played by Shiek Mahmub-Bey) shoots his way out of the trap, three cops die in the crossfire, one is badly wounded, patrol cars converge on the hauntingly dismal ghetto street, sergeants chew each other out for stepping on jurisdictions.

As in *Dog Day Afternoon*, Lumet is in his element here: big-city chaos. The more bureaucratic complication, ethnic tension, anarchy, foul-up, the happier his direction becomes.

Another thing that gets Lumet's juices going is the portrayal of white middle-aged men: hard-boiled, saggy-eyed, browbeaten, torn between exhausted indifference and payback revenge or cupidity. Lumet's penchant for the theme of police corruption grows directly out of his feeling for the trials and uncertainties of the middle-aged, because a lot of his "dirty cops" are ethically compromised but by no means evil veterans looking for that final nest egg.

In short order, the story introduces us to a quintet of middle-aged secondary leads, all vividly etched: there is District Attorney Morgenstern (in a funny, manic turn by Ron Leibman), a tough liberal who speaks Yiddish-inflected New Yorkese and insults his bowtie-wearing WASP subordinate, Assistant DA Elihu Harrison (Colm Feore), for being bloodlessly patrician; the killer's defense attorney, Sam Vigoda (in a controlled, for him, performance by Richard Dreyfuss), a radical William Kunstler type who wants to blow the lid off police graft; an honest Irish cop who gets wounded on the stakeout (Ian Holm); and his Italian partner (James Gandolfini), whom we come to learn has been taking bribes from the drug kingpin. Gandolfini is magnificent in his projection of amiable venality. He is—or should be—the soul of the film, because, in Lumet's hands, corruption comes across as familiar, almost likably human, whereas virtue and idealism remain sterile, opaque.

Unfortunately, this being a major release, it needs a hero to complement all these lively secondary characters, and here is where Lumet stumbles badly. He gives us Sean Casey (Andy Garcia), rookie Assistant DA and son of the Ian Holm character. Leave aside that Garcia's accent makes him preposterous as an *Irish* cop; here he has a coiffed, poor man's matinee-idol prettiness, and cannot rise to the challenge. In days gone by, Lumet would have cast Al Pacino for the young man's role, and Pacino would have brought a wayward, disturbing electricity to it, not to mention a precociously middle-aged, scarred face. Garcia hams up badly a few speeches where he is called upon to express self-righteous shock at police taking bribes from drug dealers. Why Sean, the son of a cop—an ex-cop himself—should be so astonished about patrolmen on the take is beyond me. It's not all Garcia's fault; the script (by Lumet himself) gives him nothing to work with beyond a White Knight's moody naïveté. It also saddles him with a thin, halfhearted love interest: Peggy (Lena Olin), a lawyer in Sam Vigoda's office. Lena Olin has come a long way from the luscious vamp of *The Unbearable Lightness of Being* and *Enemies*; to be blunt, she has put on a lot of mileage, and looks too old for the part. In a forties movie, her foreign accent and bold seduction of the hero would have tipped us off that she was a counterspy, not to be trusted; here, she is insipidly stumbling around, reluctant to marry a man she perceives as too good for her.

Lumet knows how to keep the narrative charging forward. The trouble is that he does it by ignoring the contrivances that get us from Point A to Point B: the killer gives himself in (why doesn't he run for it?), the case is turned over to the inexperienced Sean, who wins it, of course, by insulting the defendant's sneakers (huh?); Morgenstern has a heart attack and Sean runs for DA and wins in a cakewalk; he prosecutes police corruption, only to find his father and father's partner not entirely innocent; he is faced with countless moral dilemmas, which occasion naïve outbursts.

In contrast to Sean's farfetched callowness is a brilliant cameo bit (by Paul Guilfoyle) as the Internal Affairs investigator, who knows exactly how the investigation is going to pan out—at what point the cops protesting their innocence will begin to rat on each other, etc.—and plays them against each other, adding cynically predictive commentary all the while. This character is like a refugee from *Prince of the City* or *Q & A*, bringing in a larger understanding of civil processes that the increasingly silly plot of *Night Falls on Manhattan* seems to have forgotten. But this too is typically Lumettian: the allusion to a complex, sophisticated code of urban relationships just outside the film—a history of deals and accommodations between ethnic, social and political forces, particularly as it relates to New York. Lumet shows us the city, to quote critic Kent Jones, "as an organism whose bodily fluids constantly pour into the oddest corners of existence." Crazy as it may sound, the closest analogy that springs to mind is Balzac: the way that novelist will, even in his weaker novels, assert a web of social cues that ties the work in question to his whole *oeuvre*. If Lumet had had the good sense to repeat, like Balzac, certain characters from story to story, we might better glimpse how his individual films represent fragments of a larger tapestry, a *Condition Humaine*.

Lumet himself compared filmmaking, in his Bogdanovich interview, to "making a mosaic. You take each little tile and polish and color it, and you just do the best you can on each individual tile and it's not until you've literally glued them all together that you know whether or not you've got something. Those of us who have had good work can admit the truth, which is: good work is an accident. That's not being falsely modest, there's a reason that the accidents are going to happen to some of us and will never happen to other people: we've got some sort of knowledge, or instinct, of how to prepare the ground for the accident to happen. Because some people work in a way that they shortcut any chance of the accident happening."

I think this honest statement says a lot about what makes Lumet's films so exciting, jumpy and inconsistent. In working with each piece as a mosaic tile, Lumet tends to lose sight of a visually systematic approach to the shot: one scene will have breathtakingly composed overhead locations; the next will resort to a TV-movie mishmash of close-ups and countershots; some images will be carefully lit (or underlit, as when Andrzej Bartkowiak was Lumet's director of photography: see especially *The Verdict*); others will be grainy and slapdash. In the same interview with Bogdanovich, Lumet listed (surprisingly) Carl Dreyer as the director he respected most. But it is Dreyer who eloquently lamented the absence of a consistent visual approach in Danish film, and who wrote: "What one feels regarding the photography of this film is first and foremost the absence of an artistic will that sets up a goal for itself and consciously works toward it."

We cannot say that Lumet rigorously works toward a conscious visual goal. He is the anti-Bresson. But he does have, I think, an artistic will: to complete a picture, whatever compromises that necessitates, and try to get onscreen some of his own edgy life force. I watch Lumet's backgrounds with some of the same pleasure that I do the wry institutional documentaries of Fred Wiseman, even if I have to roll my eyes at times at the foreground story.

Night Falls on Manhattan ends with a somewhat corny, patriotic speech in which DA Sean Casey addresses the new recruits about the duties and hardships of being a prosecutor. All along, the other characters have been trying to tell Sean that his approach to morality is too black and white, too much like a Boy Scout: "You want clean hands? Become a priest." In his concluding speech, he shows he has internalized this lesson of moral grays and abandoned the inhumanity of perfectionism. But I also think the speech is meant as Lumet's aesthetic apologia, as though he is trying to tell the audience: Don't expect perfection here, I don't shoot fifty takes, I bring my films in under budget, which means I make a lot of compromises. Which means some parts are better than others. Sometimes I get lucky—there are happy accidents. I do what I do, and I hope that's good enough.

For me, Sidney Lumet may not be Max Ophuls, but he's kept me entertained, and that's good enough. Even with all its contrivances, *Night Falls on Manhattan* still offers more complex adult characters and a larger worldview than 95 percent of the current releases.

THE EXPERIMENTAL FILMS OF
WARREN SONBERT

I first saw the work of Warren Sonbert at a one-man screening around 1967, at a funny little theater in the basement of the Wurlitzer Building on 42nd Street, where the Filmmakers Cinematheque then held forth. The program included his *Amphetamine, Where Did Our Love Go, Hall of Mirrors* and *The Tenth Legion.* Not a diehard fan of the New American Cinema but an occasional nibbler, who went to underground screenings out of an odd combination of civic duty and derelict voyeurism, always expecting the worst, or very little, I was almost jolted out of my chair by Sonbert's electric, bouncy, alive, humorous, roller-coaster rides. The world was in them, the city world, or let us say, to be candid and narcissistic about it, a world that felt like my own, a New Yorker in his early twenties: the ups and downs of that life, one moment crashing a fancy party and the next crossing a grimy 8th Avenue or yawning and waiting in line for a movie.

In addition to all the glitter and lights, there were ordinary lackluster moments as they so rarely appear in films about New York. I remember a shot of some college students gazing out the window of a lecture hall before their teacher had arrived, in *The Tenth Legion*, and thinking, "How daring, he's letting us know that these young debauchees also have to go to school; there's something very touching about that."

And the films themselves were sexy. I don't mean to say that the actors took their clothes off, they didn't, but what was sexy was the extremely fluid way the movies were put together. The sound track of soul songs had something to do with it, but even more so the long hand-held tracking shots that followed in "real time" someone walking down corridor after corridor, or the merry-go-round shot that metaphorically described an attitude toward the cosmos as much as did Godard's swirling coffee cup. The shots took us over like a wet dream. It was as if Hitchcock's 360-degree turn around the lovers, Stewart and Novak, in *Vertigo*, that saturation of love and impossible yearning and doubt and fulfillment, had started to infiltrate *all* of Sonbert's images. It was a lover's cinema. The filmmaker was in love with the world, or was amused and saddened by it, so obviously that he had only to point his camera anywhere, it seemed, and it would fill up with feeling.

Another thing I liked about Sonbert's films: there seemed to be no conflict in him between narrative and nonnarrative cinema. He was comfortably at home in the experimental cinema tradition, yet he was also a grateful offspring of Sirk and Borzage and Hawks. In his column Jonas Mekas had called Sonbert "post-Godardian," an interesting idea, but to me Sonbert was coterminous with Godard, in the romantic way he filmed images off movie screens (paying tribute to *Contempt* and *North by Northwest*), in his choice of at-loose-ends character types and in his "breathless" pace. Sonbert's plotless films felt narrative; though they told no story, they suppressed none either. Perhaps they were telling the story of life.

I found myself thinking a good deal about the people in Warren Sonbert's films. He was taking us behind the scenes and showing us the sort of young ambitious bohemians who were very much a part of sixties urban chic. It was the world of boutiques and discos and art openings, Andy Warhol and Henry Geldzahler. These were not flower children but grant-getting types who wound long white scarves around soft black leather jackets. King's Row and Portabello Road had left their mark on the fashions: mini-skirts and hot colors and synthetic rayons and sparkle dust and boots. When Susan Sontag defended young people in *Against Interpretation* by saying they wanted to look beautiful and what was so bad about that, these were the folks she meant. But Sonbert, engaged as his films are with fashion, did not, to his credit, photograph the subjects like *Vogue*. Instead he gave us the private moments of people we slobs in the audience were curious about. We saw both their scarlet blouses unbuttoned to the fourth button and their pimples and eye-bags of fatigue, or dirty-blond hair that needed a washing. Moreover, they were filmed in context, in their apartment or on their street or relaxing with their friends, so that the very same person, like Gerard Malanga or Rene Ricard, who had been encouraged to project his personality as that of a fabulous monster in an Andy Warhol movie, would pop up in a Warren Sonbert film a week later looking very normal and scaled down, sniffing at a painting in a gallery opening, one guest among many.

Sonbert seemed to be evolving a typology of Bohemia, filming his subjects in their haunts in somewhat the same way that August Sander approached his portrait of the German people by photographing subjects in their workplaces. Like Sander, there was more than a hint of psychological astuteness and clinical objectivity in these portraits.

And there were moments when loneliness was allowed to enter. Someone would be lying on a bed, thinking, off somewhere in his mind, or waiting for his lover to return from the other room. Sonbert had a good way with couples: his *The Bad and the Beautiful*, consisting of several edited-in-the-camera portraits of twosomes, tells us everything we need to know about couple-love, the tenderness, the silly horsing around, the compromises, the dead spots, the clinging to each other. It is a heartbreaking movie.

Though only an adolescent when he made these movies, Sonbert had the knack of creating an intensely elegiac mood about the present, as though he knew how quickly all these sixties costumes and postures would fade. His titles and song choices ("Where did our love go?" etc.) accentuated the anticipated loss as much as the haunting camera tracks which seemed to be searching for the separated lover.

To sum up: these films were fluid, they were rough, mostly edited in the camera, they were highly poetic and charged with feeling, they gave us city life. And they swung.

A few years later, I dropped in at the Whitney Museum to see what Sonbert was up to in his latest work, *Carriage Trade*. This was a disappointment. Gone were the long-duration takes, each shot now lasting only a second or two before giving way to the next. It was like a collection of postcards from around the world: vaguely amusing but finally canceling each other out. I missed the long juicy sequences that established character and locale. Nothing had a chance to build. Gone also was the bouncy Supremes & Company sound track, replaced by austere silence. Probably I did not see the film intelligently enough; I think I would like it now, in the context of knowing where it would lead (*Rude Awakening* and *Divided Loyalties*); but at the time I reacted only as a disappointed art consumer who does not want a beloved artist to change his style.

[Later, I was even more horrified to learn that the filmmaker had cannibalized *Tenth Legion*, cutting snippets of it into *Carriage Trade*. I continue to think that Sonbert has an inaccurate underestimation of his early films, wanting (like many artists) only to be identified with his recent mode and rarely showing or encouraging to be shown those youthful works, with the result that they exist for the most part only in people's memories. What a shame! If nothing else, Sonbert was one of the best historians recording that era.]

Rude Awakening (1976), his next movie, impressed me deeply. Though it was an extension of the style begun in *Carriage Trade* (short burst of images, no sound track), it took that method and refined it, tightened it, purified it. The film was a rigorously formed abacus of essences. Chamber music. It was obvious that this filmmaker knew what he was doing and had supreme control of his material. Also, Warren had made great technical strides as a motion picture photographer: his images looked burnished, classical. The lighting and color were more controlled. There were no more of those Abstract Expressionist-type accidents incorporated into the work, like the end-of-roll yellow blips or sudden light changes in his early films. He was after something else. As for his subject matter, he had gone beyond the bohemian scene (which was still included) to encompass more of the world: animals, children, workers, plants. The audience at Anthology Film Archives kept giggling and laughing appreciatively, but I was having an entirely different response. The film struck me as unflinchingly sad. (Another time, when my girlfriend saw it, she burst into tears—a response which understandably pleased Warren.) I wrote a brief note on the film for *The Thousand Eyes*, to help publicize its next showing:

> *Rude Awakening* is a dazzling funny, severe film which speculates about the value of human activity. Comparable in encyclopedic thrust to Vertov's ebullient *Man with the Movie Camera*, it differs from that tradition in being more compressed, more *cutting*. Sonbert is fascinated with spectacle (ice follies, bal-

let, street fairs), with everyday labor (butcher shops, frankfurter stands) and recreation, but underneath all this motion one senses a futility. Like the shot of people thwacking each other with fake swords in the Renaissance Fair, the images express playfulness, energy and impotence. They are held on the screen just long enough to bring us into a sense of comic contradiction: cutting used for undercutting. Each shot is another slice as harmless as a paper cut, but after a while one experiences the accumulated sadness behind all the joy and motion, and the title, *Rude Awakening*, becomes more fitting and darker in its double-edged irony. What sets Warren Sonbert apart from most other "nonnarrative" experimental filmmakers, aside from his impeccable craftsmanship, is his ability to bestow the psychology of narrative cinema, of a Preminger or Sirk, onto his images of people. The connection between shots, even without a story line, has an intuitive rightness that feels mysteriously syllogistic, though the fun is in knowing that much of this meaning may be audience projection while some may have been the filmmaker's intention. Sonbert lets you choose.

Warren's next work, his most recent to date, was *Divided Loyalties* (1978), which in some ways struck me as even stronger and tighter than *Rude Awakening*. It had great moments of humor, some breathtaking vignettes of human interaction, some lovely celebrations of the act of seeing. (It even has me in it for a few seconds.) The film is the ripening of a method and the successful proof of his new manner. Nevertheless, I think it must lead to a branching out into something else if Warren is to grow as an artist and not merely repeat himself. Elsewhere in this issue you will no doubt read many encomiums on these two recent films. For variety, I would like to spend the rest of this article raising some nagging questions and doubts about Sonbert's latest film work.

First, a picky one: there is too much overlap and repetition in the two movies. Elevators, car trips, stage shows, be-ins, etc.—one film begins to look like the outtakes of the other.

Second, I wonder about the tight corset of the brief shot. Why must everything skip by in only a few seconds, like a still photograph, so that the moment you have "read" the scene, it is already being replaced? The editing principle behind *Rude Awakening*, which Warren once explained to me (I hope I'm not giving away any trade secrets), of alternating a vertical shot with a diagonal or horizontal or whatever in sets of four, while also alternating shots of people with shots of nature—this whole schema strikes me as arbitrary and barren. If the images in these two movies mysteriously connect, one with the other, it is probably in spite of this lines-of-force Eisensteinian editing formula. Here the seventies influence of conceptual art, of grids and preconceived stencils applied to material, seems to have pushed Sonbert into a stiffer purity not always consonant with his gregarious talents. I prefer *caméra-stylo*, to write with a camera whatever you're thinking.

Third, and perhaps most problematic, is the philosophy or "meaning" of these films. We start with the titles. *Rude Awakening* reveals the sardonic, partly sadistic whack which these amiable images, taken together, are meant to give. "Wake up! You're fooling yourselves!" Sonbert the teacher is administering his lessons on our bottoms: we are not to hope for lasting satisfactions, pleasure holds only a few seconds and then dissolves, a polymorphous flash that leads nowhere. A world-weary disappointment, a bitter choked laugh, lies over the images of people relentlessly busying and entertaining themselves. On the one hand, futility of endeavor; on the other hand, a tension which is raised but not permitted to be released. *Divided Loyalties'* title points to this unresolved (possibly irresolvable) tension: the urbanite's confusion of riches, unable to choose between too many parties and cultural events on the same night; politically, the inability to choose sides; romantically, the conflict from having several lovers, or bisexuality; geographically, not being able to make up one's mind where to live. As images on a film, it works itself out as one reality canceling out another, without development.

The original title of *Divided Loyalties* was *Industrial Keys*. The young Orpheus is awakened rudely to a world in which industry holds all the keys, and even personal life has a manufactured, industrial quality, as Adorno would say. Warren Sonbert's films have always had a trace of sociological inquiry, and in *Divided Loyalties* one can almost make out the beginnings of a critique of modern society: from the furs and tuxedo set at the opening of San Francisco's opera season, to the mangy train tracks of the Chicago Loop, to factories and impersonal glassed-in elevators. Collective action is also treated sardonically, in the gay lib parade sequences, as one more illusion or pretense to be punctured (we see a cemetery after a gay be-in). However, the mosaic technique as Sonbert (unlike Vertov) uses it does not take responsibility for direct political or social statements that can reasonably be attributed to the filmmaker. Indeed, we can assume nothing but a pileup of ironies which imply, in the worst circumstances, a shrug of indifference.

A frightening emptiness dogs these films. Perhaps their real program is spiritual; and Sonbert is trying to induce a state of nonattachment, acceptance of the void, a pulling-down of vanity. The Buddhist text echoes him precisely: "Form is emptiness, and emptiness is form. Emptiness is not different from form, form is not different from emptiness." That may be the philosophy over the long haul, the twenty-year plan, but in the meantime what we are getting is not so much wisdom as the jaded sour dregs of sated youth. Warren needs to pause for a moment and catch his breath. Part of the problem with these films is that they have lost their geographical anchor. They are no longer rooted in the psyche of a place (like the earlier New York films) but wander everywhere. Sonbert has become a "citizen of the world." He can bring us back dancing bears from Berlin circuses and elephants from India, but the weariness of the travel begins to tell. The poet who tries to see everything ends up becoming a sort of globe-trotting opportunist/journalist/tourist collecting mere *spectacle*, in lieu of knowing the life of the people around him, or what is in their hearts. He is everywhere curious, everywhere estranged. Nothing is allowed to deepen. It's all entertaining but empty, he reports back to us.

There is at the moment a great deal of support in avant-garde culture for art which wanders around in a sort of Möbius strip; a floating lyricism coupled with a sort of punitive blockage of anything building to a climax. The sense of sterility in life (or of a mindless bubbling fecundity of no real issue, which comes to the same thing) leads some artists to affect a sniggling negation of human hopes and of anything adding up. Things just go round and round, everything's tacky, nothing's first-rate or authentic or real. . . . Ashbery says all that beautifully, combining a world-weary uncovering of cliché with a hunger for fresh perception. I'm not sure it's right to put all this on Warren's films, because he is such an entertaining materialist. But it's clear that even in his footloose early work there is that "life is just a hall of mirrors" claustrophobia, the endless walking down long halls that go nowhere, the merry-go-round symbol which can be seen in an ominous as well as a joyous light. There the circumscribed trap was expressed spatially; now it's more temporal (no one is allowed more than fifteen seconds onscreen). And now it's more connected to a severe aesthetic that inhibits release.

When a young modern artist wants to do something new, he generally goes through a puritanical period where he tries to frustrate his audience's expectations of pleasure. This is understandable: the artist has to break the socialized boundaries of conventional catharsis, be it in films or music or literature, and search for greater rigor. But having done so, the artist, continuing to grow, often comes back to the realization that pleasure is not so bad after all, that the audience is not cheap to want release, and that the stock-in-trade of art is, in the long run, sensuosity and generosity. I am not saying that the news needs to be good, but at a certain point it needs to be ample, full-throated, maybe even ragged the way Jean Renoir is ragged sometimes. A purity achieved too early can be a danger for a young artist.

I have no way of knowing what Warren Sonbert's future direction will be. He is still growing, he is extremely gifted and capable of anything, and I, as an admirer, wish him the heights. I daresay that Warren's films have not yet caught up with the full capacity for enjoyment and complexity of the man himself. When they do, we have something wonderful to look forward to.

The subtext running underneath much of this essay was my friendship with Warren Sonbert. True, I barely alluded to it in the piece, but that was because Film Culture, *the journal of experimental cinema, had asked me to write something for its special Sonbert issue, and I assumed they wanted a discussion of his movies, not the particulars of our friendship. Yet I was trying to speak directly to Warren with every line I wrote. The essay was a calculated intervention—a risky and perhaps impertinent attempt to prod a friend, whose work I respected but who seemed mired in repetitious strategies, to extend himself. As it happened, Warren took the criticism with his usual good grace, and went on making the same kind of film over and over. This either spoke well of his confidence that he was on the right path, or ill of the conceptual dead ends that seem part and parcel of membership in the avant-garde. Once you join that particular club, it seems to me, you enter a self-reinforcing, closed circle, encountering very little candid criticism from your peers. What little criticism does exist is usually on the order of keeping you from more bourgeois, mainstream directions—from straying, that is, into what used to be called "Kracauerite" (i.e. naturalist/realist narrative) filmmaking.*

Warren actually did write a script for a much more ambitious—overly ambitious—project: it revolved around multiple characters, intercut with scenes from Richard Strauss's opera Capriccio, and was set in the Nazi era. But he never came near to raising the necessary funds for it, so he went on making the short collage-diary films he could shoot with his 16mm camera, and living off adjunct teaching gigs and a trust fund. The American avant-garde film scene is a small world, with rewards that amount to peanuts (a few grants, a smattering of teaching posts, a dozen or so venues that will fly you in to show your film and give a talk); within that world, Warren was a Golden Boy. He was not above hustling for the crumbs, either; he befriended museum curators and film festival programmers, and applied gentle persuasion to arrange screenings of his latest work.

Warren was so charming, both physically and temperamentally, that he had only to arrive in a new city for strangers to start throwing him dinner parties. After he moved from New York to San Francisco, his return trips to New York were filled nonstop with seeing friends: he used to keep a piece of paper with a schedule of his ten or so daily dates or appointments, starting with breakfast and ending with a midnight drink. I hesitate to use the word "promiscuous," but at the peak of his roving days, before he settled down with Ray, his gentle older lover, he seemed to have erotic encounters at the glance of an eye. I found the extent of his sexual activity both impressive and threatening. (The "emptiness" I found in his work may have reflected my own puritanical uneasiness at an existence rife with orgasms.) The friendship between a gay man and a straight man has, in any case, complexities that require the utmost diplomacy to navigate. I think in our case most of the diplomacy came from Warren's end: he had many straight friends, especially women, and traveled easily in both worlds. One time when I visited him on the West Coast, staying at his Victorian house in the Castro area, he pointed out to me all the shops, bars and coffeehouses I might, as a heterosexual male, enter without feeling embarrassment or hostility. He could be amusingly mocking of the conformities and pretensions of gay culture. Still, the older he got, the more deeply identified he became with the politics of gayness. He also began writing very decent film criticism for a weekly gay paper, under the pseudonym Scottie Ferguson (the protagonist in Vertigo, in case you've forgotten). In the end he suffered the fate of many gay men—too many of my friends—losing his lover Ray to AIDS, and then dying a few years later of the same disease.

In Warren's last film, posthumously edited by his friend Jeff Scher, following the filmmaker's written instructions, there is a protracted sequence (itself a departure from the purist middle period) in a bullfight arena, the bull chasing the toreador again and again. I could not help but think of Death stalking Warren, and his trying to show us what it felt like to evade it as gracefully and as long as he did. My eyes filled with tears watching it; but I also wondered whether the sequence would be moving at all to someone who didn't know the circumstance under which it was shot. I could never quite figure out how much I was projecting onto his work, and how much was intended. So my ambivalence about his films, and their play of absence and presence, meaning and emptiness, continues long after he is around to smile and shrug off my questions.

I had wanted Warren to put more of his charismatic brio,

humor and understanding into the films he made. It had seemed to me he had trapped himself into a modality that wouldn't permit enough range. But maybe that's silly, or beside the point: you don't ask Sol Lewitt to give up his rectangles, or Robert Ryman his white pigment. It all depends, I suppose, whether you see avant-garde film as a subspecies of abstract art or as a specialized narrative.

THREE OZU FILMS FROM THE FIFTIES

The *oeuvre* of Yasujiro Ozu (1903–63) tends to provoke a religious hush, making it difficult for the critic to isolate the virtues and defects of individual films. Compounding the problem is Ozu's consistency: on the surface his pictures seem to share so many elements, resembling each other structurally and thematically, that it is not always possible even for an aficionado to disentangle in memory *Late Autumn* from *An Autumn Afternoon*, say. In fact there was more variation over the course of his long career than the static image we have of an Ozu movie generally suggests: consider the free-wheeling camera movements of his silent period, the neorealist *(Record of a Tenement Gentleman)* or melodrama *(Tokyo Twilight)* anomalies. Still, the charm of diving into Ozu's world is that one knows, more or less, what to expect: the subtly observant eye for family dynamics; the preference for character over plot; the serene acceptance of life's tragic limitations; the restrained cinematic style (camera generally placed low; mood-setting or palette-cleansing "pillow shots" which offer depeopled landscapes and interiors; uninterrupted autonomy of individual scenes). When so many movies try to take the viewer by storm, Ozu's gently invite you in. Artistically, he is the opposite of the bully. He is patient, alert. As Donald Richie noted in an appreciation of Ozu, "Actually, these films are not slow. They create their own time and clock-time ceases to exist; the audience is drawn into Ozu's world, into a realm of purely psychological time. What would at first appear a world of stillness, of total inaction, is revealed as mere appearance. Beneath this lies the potential violence found in the Japanese family system, and also the quiet heroism of the Japanese faced with his own family." Or the American with his. The major payoff in watching Ozu is that, formalist nuances aside, you are more often than not deeply moved by his characters' struggles, so penetrating is his wisdom about the tension between civilization and its discontents.

I have been going to Ozu movies for more than thirty years now. When the first selective retrospective was mounted at the Museum of Modern Art, in the mid-sixties, I attended as often as I could. It was something of a revelation, combining the satisfaction of discovering a new cache of Jane Austen novels with a cleansing visit to a Buddhist retreat. Inevitably, there developed a snobbish, cliquey sentiment around Ozu, equivalent to being in the vanguard of Monteverdi lovers. Later, the word spread, and there were fuller retrospectives mounted at revival houses and museums, where one could catch up with obscurities like *The Toda Brothers and Sisters*. I remember arranging a first date at *The Only Son*, a rather austere early sound picture by Ozu, shown at the late Gallery of Modern Art on Columbus Circle. It was a test: if the woman liked it, I was infatuated; if not, sayonara. She loved it, and, though we were incompatible in most other ways, we ended up messily entangled for seven years. I blame Ozu.

Nevertheless, I continued to worship at the shrine. During the eighties, when an Ozu retrospective again made the rounds, I found myself secretly growing impatient with some of the minor works. But the towering masterpieces, such as

Late Spring and *Tokyo Story*, seem to me part of our essential culture, able to be revisited as often as *King Lear* or *St. Matthew Passion*.

Here we have three Ozus from the fifties, recently reissued on videotape: *Early Summer, Floating Weeds* and *Good Morning*. The first is a masterwork, just a smidgen below the level of *Late Spring* or *Tokyo Story*; the latter two are intriguing albeit flawed. All three have been handsomely transferred to video, with crisp visuals and clearly legible subtitles. In some ways Ozu films do not suffer as much as the work of other world-class directors from being seen on the small screen, since he used mostly intimate, interior compositions with shallow depths of field, and stayed away from widescreen formats. On the other hand they do suffer precisely because television is a home medium, which treats most comfortably the familial and domestic. Ozu's family tableaus, lacking that larger-than-life projection which ennobled the quotidian and freed moviegoers to choose where to fix their meditative attention, become reduced, annexed as they are to the banal rhythms of the soap opera and the sitcom. Still, we know how to make these adjustments by now, adding a 20 percent quality surtax to the video image. And since Ozu's greatness is more a matter of script and acting than richness of visual field, we continue to have access to the best parts in these tapes.

Early Summer (1951) uses the favored Ozu storyline of a family trying to get their reluctant daughter married. (Often this reluctance has to do with her unselfish understanding that in marrying, she would be abandoning her parent to a lonely old age.) On one level an ensemble work—distributing its attention judiciously between a set of elderly parents, their grown children and spouses, the grandchildren, relatives and friends—its core of intensest feeling belongs to the marriageable daughter, played by the incomparable Setsuko Hara. Hara's great gift was to convey complex, thoughtful heroines

whose defiance and willfulness hide behind the sunny, acqui-
escent mask of a Japanese good girl. In the film, she is twenty-
eight, appealing but not getting any younger, an office worker
helping out the family's finances. Her boss, wondering what
her story is, gossips with a girlfriend of hers, who volunteers
the information that she used to collect Katharine Hepburn
photos. "Is she a lesbian?" he asks baldly. No, comes the answer. We deduce that it is Hepburn's independent, head-
strong quality that appeals to her. He admits that sometimes
she seems attractive to him, sometimes not. This crystallizes
the ambivalence around her and her vulnerability as a marital
candidate. Certainly we may find Setsuko Hara fetching
enough for any occasion, but the character she plays is meant
to be somewhat short of a beauty—and, in any case, too
proudly intelligent to avail herself of Pretty Woman privileges.

  Early Summer reunites Setsuko Hara with her co-star
from *Late Spring*, Chishu Ryu, the quintessential Ozu character actor. Ryu's specialty was the rigid, stern, scholarly, patriarchal figure, who, in the end, is kind enough to bend. In
Late Spring they had played father and daughter; this time
they are brother and sister. Since the father in *Early Summer*
is rather passive, older brother Ryu has become the functioning head of the family. He sets out to find a husband for
his sister. But she is too much the modern woman to sit still
for an arranged marriage. In the end, she thwarts his strategy
by impulsively selecting her brother's friend, a rather unsuc-
cessful widower with a child who is moving to the cold
northern countryside to take a job. There is no question of
romance either way: she candidly tells a woman friend that
she doesn't love him but will feel safe and protected with
him. As for the widower, we are given no indication that he
has even thought of his friend's sister previously as a potential mate: the final deal is cooked up between the heroine
and the widower's mother, and he merely accepts their agree-

ment with baffled resignation. But her own family is angry that she decided to act alone, without consulting them. This is not the Japanese way. Besides, her mother confesses, she had had high hopes at one time that her daughter would make a good catch, snare a wealthy man and live in a big house. "When she graduated from high school everyone was talking about her." The disappointment that parents feel in their grown children is characteristic of Ozu. As for the brother's anger that she has chosen his friend, this is more psychologically loaded. For all their sibling tensions, there is the suggestion that she worships her brother, and is marrying his friend as a surrogate for him.

So we are left with a bittersweet ending. The main goal has been accomplished, the potential "old maid" has been married off, but the family has been broken up in the process, and financially straitened with the loss of her salary. As the bride's elderly father tells his wife: "We shouldn't want too much."

One of Ozu's subtlest moves is to take us close enough to a heroine who so keeps her own counsel, by presenting us with varying degrees of candor and reserve. Within the family she is most formal and dishonest, or at least unforthcoming. When an aged uncle drops in and teases her in front of her brother about her unmarried status, she giggles, hides her face and runs away. In a later scene, alone with the same uncle, she responds to a similar prodding of his by saying, "Find me a man." We see her several times in the company of her women friends, both married and unmarried, who bicker hilariously and ritualistically about which side is better off. Alone with her confidante-friend, she is utterly unbuttoned, even mimicking satirically the hick accents of the country folk who will be her new neighbors. The film is filled to the brim with sharp character details, showing us once again what superbly economical dialogue-writers Ozu and his favorite screenwriting collaborator, Kogo Noda, were. And, contrary to the notion that Ozu never moved his camera in later years, there are some lovely tracking shots.

Good Morning (1959) was intended as a popular comedy. Ozu, one senses, pulled some of his punches and reigned in the darkness to achieve that purpose, and the result was one of his most successful films. It was also Ozu's second color film (the previous year's *Equinox Flower* his first), and the transition from his customarily restrained black-and-white to the kindergarten-cubby glossy, optimistic brashness of Agfa-color is a little startling, as if he had borrowed Doris Day's cinematographer. But perhaps this Hollywood fifties comedy look is fitting in a film which revolves around the strain on traditional Japanese society to adapt to American consumerism. In an old, lower-middle-class neighborhood where the housewives without a washing machine enviously eye the one who has it, two little boys covet a television set so that they can watch wrestling and baseball games. Ozu was a master at handling child actors, and the two brothers come across adorably in their brazen outspokenness. When their stern father (Chishu Ryu, naturally) tells them they are talking too much and should shut up, they go on a silent strike, punishing him by literally enacting his request. Eventually, their father relents and buys a television set, though he has already gone on record as saying TV will produce a nation of idiots. Meanwhile, the neighbors continue to fester with busybody gossip, grudges and rivalries. What the family was in *Early Summer*—a prison of inescapable pressures to conform—the neighborhood is in *Good Morning*. (The title comes from the little boys' insistence that adults also talk too much, spouting commonplace inanities.)

Good Morning is delightful the first time you see it; it works like a charm. But it doesn't deepen on subsequent viewing, partly because its "fart" jokes become tiresome and partly because its very construction so neatly alternates themes, that craft triumphs over complexity. Even the ever-respectful Donald Richie admits in his book that this is Ozu's most "schematic" film. It reworks materials from his earlier, silent masterpiece *I Was Born, But* (the two little boys went on a hunger strike in that one), but without the kicker of the boys becoming ashamed of their father for kowtowing to his boss. Here, there is nothing to challenge the father's authority but a mundane, easily satisfied acquisitiveness on his sons' part.

I once asked the knowledgeable Kyoko Hirano, film programmer of the Japan Society, why Japanese films of the prosperous, Sony period were not as deep as in the golden age of Mizoguchi, Naruse, Kurosawa and Ozu. Usually one thinks of culture as following money, yet the Japanese filmmakers of today, talented as they are, seem to lack that profound sense of *aware*, the transient sadness of things. Very simple, she said. Japan used to be a poor country, and that poetic sadness was an outgrowth of material sparseness. But now it has become mainly middle-class, and the typical, consumerist Japanese no longer feels that "cherry blossom" poignancy which Westerners had assumed was an ingrained feature of Japanese culture.

Good Morning seems to anticipate at times this Japanese future. Ozu's next motion picture, *Floating Weeds* (1959), looks backward. "Though this is a contemporary film," he said, "in mood it really belongs to the Meiji period." A remake of his 1934 silent *The Story of Floating Weeds*, about a troupe of traveling players, it benefited from the great Japanese cinematographer Kazuo Miyagawa, who had shot Mizoguchi's *Ugetsu* and Kurosawa's *Rashomon*, and who brought a lush density of color and compositional perfection to Ozu's dramatic scenes and cutaways. The establishing scenes in the first half are particularly fascinating, as the troupe fans out over the town—the male secondaries trying to make time with the village women while selling tickets to performances, etc. The troupe's leader is a dictatorial, washed-up ham (played with piglet-eyed opacity by Ganjiro Nakamura, an actor Ozu seemed to favor precisely because of his inexpressiveness) who has steered his company back to this town so that he can look up his old flame and their illegitimate son. The boy, now about to start college, does not know that the visiting actor who has always been presented as his "uncle" is really his father. The old flame, played by the great character actress Haruko Sugimura (the selfish daughter in *Tokyo Story* and the money-lending ex-geisha in Naruse's *Late Chrysanthemums*), is unfortunately given little to do as a sweetly patient, forgiving woman who would like the actor to settle down with her in old age. The real fireworks come when the troupe leader's mistress/leading lady (the voluptuously overripe Machiko Kyo) jealously sniffs out his old involvement. She confronts him, in a beautifully shot downpour: he calls her a bitch and an ex-prostitute whom he "saved," while she reminds him of the many times she bailed him out from financial jams by flirting with theater owners. They are two of a kind, both tough, gamy birds, and their crude language will come as a shock to those who associate Ozu with good manners. The old actor wants to distance himself from this seedy vulgarity, and settle down with his ex-flame and son. But the young man rejects his father when he learns the truth, and runs away with the troupe's pretty ingenue.

This whole subplot in the second half, involving the young man, is wooden and melodramatic. It reminds us not only how poorly suited Ozu was for melodrama, but also how bland and weakly realized most of his young male characters are. The handsome, youthful male lead, the staple of American movies, seemed an embarrassment to Ozu, who much preferred to concentrate on boys or elderly men—when not depicting his juicily thoughtful heroines. The soundstage tinniness of these father-son confrontations suggest that, alongside the rich Buddhist emptiness, or *mu,* that Ozu was able to achieve, there were times his later films struck a less profitable emptiness, which came from scraping away too much.

The richness of the first part seems all but kicked away in the second half, as if Ozu had lost interest in his hammy, overemotional characters. The exception is whenever Machiko Kyo appears on the screen; she maintains an operatic presentation of self entirely suitable to the screenplay's theatricality. In the last scene, their troupe dismantled by debts, she and her aged actor-lover go off together in a train to start anew. They belong together, these callous troupers, and she attends to him, pouring him wine with touching forgiveness, in a moment that redeems all the wobbliness of the film's weaker parts. Even in his less inspired films, Ozu was always able to reach into himself and produce such moments of gestural wholeness. In short, it is always a good thing to see an Ozu film, even if not every Ozu is equally good.

CAN
MOVIES
THINK?

THE PASSION OF PAULINE KAEL

Pauline Kael has just turned seventy. An important birthday: her house in the Berkshires is filled with flowers from well-wishers. "I don't want you to get the wrong idea there are always this many flowers around," she says with her nervous, melodic laugh. The rooms of her handsome, two-turreted stone and shingled house evidence a fine eye for American antiques: stained-glass lamps, wooden writing desks, quilt-covered beds—each item a bargain purchase, she notes with pride. Until recently, Kael—child of the Depression and bohemia—has had to struggle financially. Now, it seems, her life is serene, well ordered, almost pastoral. A copy of *The Hobbit* lies on her dining room table, a birthday present from her seven-year-old grandchild, Willy, who has had it read aloud to him and now wants to discuss the story with her.

Can this pleasant, obliging grandmother in sneakers, who is fixing my lunch and who reminds me uncannily of my aunts, really be the scourge of film distributors, the storm center of a dozen controversies, the acute and sometimes acidic critic whom Meryl Streep said she would kill if she could?

Kael seems the most unself-doubting (or well-guarded) person I've ever met, so logically consistent is she in her own eyes. The split occurs in others' perceptions of her. Her friends and fanatical fans see her as the most generous person alive, the best film critic America has ever had and the keenest writer of critical prose since Shaw and Orwell. Her detractors regard her as a conniving empire-builder and a reviewer of limited filmic sense whose judgments are often distorted by personal obsessions and vendettas. Rarely does one encounter an in-between position.

As it happens, I occupy a middle ground. Before I ever met Pauline Kael, I thought of her as one of several film critics I liked to read, each of whom balanced the others with strengths and blind spots. Vincent Canby might have a lighter touch with everyday movies, Andrew Sarris a deeper grasp of film tradition, J. Hoberman a more adventurous coverage of offbeat pictures and Manny Farber a stronger insight into film as a visual medium. But no one can *nail* a picture with Kael's passion.

Among her many virtues, she is a brilliant observer of acting styles, and can capture in apt metaphor the look and bounce of a performer. "Astaire's grasshopper lightness was his limitation as an actor—confining him to perennial gosh-oh-gee adolescence . . ." she will write, or summarize Faye Dunaway's appeal with: "Perfection going slightly to seed is maybe the most alluring face a screen goddess can have." She understands the morality of narrative structure, zeroing in unerringly on those script imbalances brought about through self-approval, hypocrisy or panderings to the *Zeitgeist*. She has an eye for good editing—less so for the rigors of camera composition. Hence, it comes as no surprise that she is strongest on comedies, weakest on Westerns. A dedicated fan of independent women characters and witty repartee, she was inevitably drawn to thirties screwball comedies. Most American comedies are gender-driven: Kael delights in disentangling the most gnarly problems of relations between the sexes. She can answer the question "What do women want?" But she does not like to watch men interacting with other men on the range. She is snortingly contemptuous of the virile claims of aging male stars like John Wayne and Kirk Douglas, "grinning with their big new choppers, sucking their guts up into their chests, and hauling themselves onto horses." She has a real distaste for the male valedictory mode, which causes her to dismiss much of John Ford's later work, including a beautiful elegiac work like *The Man Who Shot Liberty Valance*. Her coolness toward the Western goes hand in hand with a lack of feeling for the spatial qualities of film—for *mise en scène*.

Her insensitivity to formalist rigor and precision is her greatest limitation as a film critic. It causes her to overpraise certain visually muddy directors, like Hal Ashby, and then express disappointment later on when their mediocrity becomes undeniable. She will write intelligently about film technique when it suits her, but the rest of the time she dismisses formalistic concerns as a sterile, academic interest—a boy's game. Her real genius is sociological. She can show how and why a particular film is reaching audiences by analyzing the social currents of the moment. She is devastatingly sharp on trendy, overrated films to which the public responds for fuzzy-headed, narcissistic reasons (*Blow-Up*, 8½, *Butch Cassidy and the Sundance Kid*, *Network*, *Rain Man*). Ironically, she can turn around and enthrone certain other underbaked, overrated films, like *Bonnie and Clyde* or *Last Tango in Paris*, because to her they touch a nerve, catch the spirit of the moment.

No one has written better about the appeal of "trash," or the tangential pleasures we get from movies that aren't very good (a sexy actor, a song, an outrageous scene). She tends to forgive silliness in the name of "fun," while being extra-hard on serious-mindedness or artistic pretension. Her position that "Vulgarity is not as destructive to an artist as snobbery" sometimes leads her into a distorting antagonism toward the art film. "The educated person who became interested in cinema as an art form through Bergman or Fellini or Resnais is an alien to me (and my mind goes blank with hostility and indifference when he begins to talk)." I flinched when I read that. Fortunately, Kael's occasional anti-intellectualism is counterbalanced by her immense cultivation. When she discusses dramatic classics like *The Trojan Women, Henry V* or *Long Day's Journey into Night,* one realizes she could have been as gifted a literary critic as a movie reviewer. She seems also well versed in painting, music, dance. Would that her imitators had an equal measure of erudition to buttress their indulgence of pop culture.

Kael's first book, *I Lost It at the Movies,* opens on the heights, in the early sixties, as Kael juggles discoveries of the New Wave (Godard, Truffaut) with praise of the classics (Renoir, Ophuls, De Sica), appreciations of new humanist cinema (Kurosawa, Satyajit Ray) and shrewd dissections of popular American movies of the day *(Hud, West Side Story).* At the outset, ex-art-house-programmer Kael displayed more of an international, film-historical side. Her feisty, experienced, candid voice seemed fully formed from the start. Indeed, the *Hud* review, which opens the book, is a classic demonstration of how to do a personal essay in the form of cultural criticism.

"My father, who was adulterous, and a Republican who, like Hud, was opposed to governmental interference, was in no sense and in no one's eyes a social predator. He was generous and kind, and democratic in the western way that Easterners still don't understand: it was not out of guilty condescension that mealtimes were communal affairs with the Mexican and Indian ranchhands joining the family, it was the way Westerners lived." Kael is already a sharply etched character in her criticism: the worldly, anti-puritanical moralist, filial defender of adultery and the body's prerogatives; the native-Californian ranch girl intellectual, razzing the East Coast liberal Establishment.

Though Kael regards the criticism she did for *The New Yorker* as her most important work, in some ways I prefer her first two collections, *I Lost It at the Movies* and *Kiss Kiss Bang Bang*. Perhaps the fact that these early reviews were written largely for periodicals like *Partisan Review* and *The New Republic* enforced a more intellectually responsible tone. In 1966, in *The New Republic*, she is criticizing "American works that are out of control" and warning against the prejudices of a generation for whom "art is the domain of the irrational." By 1976 she has seemingly joined that generation, writing in *The New Yorker* that "what we all sometimes want from the movies" are "sensations we can't control, an excitement that is a great high."

The seventies were a heady time for Kael. She became the champion of a core of "personal American" filmmakers: Robert Altman, Martin Scorsese, Francis Ford Coppola, Sam Peckinpah and Brian De Palma. To her credit, she was open to the new, and saw immediately what was exciting about movies like *Mean Streets*, *M*A*S*H*, *The Godfather*, *The Wild Bunch* and *Carrie*. But she got carried away in comparing these films to the American Renaissance of Emerson, Thoreau, Whitman and Melville. ("A few decades hence, these years may appear to be the closest our movies have come to the tangled, bitter flowering of American letters in the early 1850s.") She didn't seem to notice that a well-done, if thin, genre spectacle like De Palma's *The Fury* lacked the intellectual layering, the moral wisdom of a *Rules of the Game* or *Magnificent Ambersons* (much less a novel like *The Scarlet Letter*). In the end, things balanced out: though never recanting an enthusiasm, years later she would sometimes acknowledge, say, the shortcomings of Scorsese's *Goodfellas*, or the vapidity of Bertolucci's *The Sheltering Sky*. But initially, as with any lover, she was not to be disturbed.

As a critic, Kael likes to fall in love. She has crushes on films, dates with movies, she endorses those that turn her on and is disdainful of those that don't. Eroticizing the film-going experience, she speaks of "the special aphrodisia of movies—the kinetic responsiveness, the all-out submission to pleasure." The advantage of this position is its gusto and honesty; Kael is not afraid to admit that one of the chief reasons we go to movies is their contribution to our sexual fantasies. She is quick to pick up on the "tarty walk" of Lena Olin, or Marilyn Monroe's "tempting bottom"—and just as quick to alert us that Richard Benjamin lacks "sexual assurance."

The downside of exalting the aphrodisiac aspects of film is that it gives short shrift to a more contemplative, spiritual type of movie. She has little to say about Dreyer, Bresson, Ozu, Marker. A more serious drawback is that she is better when she doesn't fall in love: her mixed reviews are more stimulating than her raves. Ambivalence brings out her analytical intelligence, enthusiasm stunts it. Kael's rave of *The Godfather, Part II* is finally a dull pileup of encomiums; by the time she places Coppola alongside Tolstoy, it's enough already.

The New Yorker supplied her with security and the chance to write regularly and at length. But it also encouraged her bad habits: not only prolixity and redundancy (which she acknowledges), but insiderism, excessive quoting of friends' bon mots, verbal inflation (a fondness for words like "beezie-wheezies" and "stiffs"), special pleading for favorites (Bertolucci, Louis Malle, Robert Towne, Irv Kershner, Peckinpah, Philip Kaufman), an increasing tendency to scold and an oversymbiotic merging with the readership (her "we/you" mode).

Kael's *Bonnie and Clyde* review, the first major piece she did for *The New Yorker*, was a daringly complex piece of analysis; but it also initiated a steamrolling approach. If you didn't like this movie, it was because you were afraid of the truth, out of touch with your feelings. It began: "How do you make a good movie in this country without being jumped on? *Bon-*

nie and Clyde is the most excitingly American American movie since *The Manchurian Candidate*. The audience is alive to it. Our experience as we watch it has some connection with the way we reacted to movies in childhood: with how we came to love them and feel that they were ours—not an art that we learned over the years to appreciate but simply and immediately ours."

Notice the almost demagogic use of first-personal plural as a way for Kael to identify herself with the "correct" instincts of the mass audience, whose spokesperson she becomes. "The audience is alive to it"—but is that the same audience who "jumped on" it? Surely not. The jumpers must be the snobs, for whom film "art" is a learned discipline and not a birthright. Kael, in writing for the *New Yorker's* educated albeit nonexpert audience, came to adopt a curiously jingoistic populism, flattering their ignorance of the art of film by telling them they already knew everything they needed to by national inheritance.

In her famous review of *Last Tango in Paris*, again she impugned the motives of those who might disagree: "There are certain to be detractors, for this movie represents too much of a change for people to accept it easily or gracefully. They'll grab at aesthetic flaws—a florid speech or an oddball scene— in order to dismiss it." I'm glad Kael liked *Last Tango*, but did she have to characterize those who didn't as cowardly? This bullying side of Kael has its generous aspects: she is so sure she is right that she wants you to enjoy the same pleasure she did—and so maternally protective of the artist she likes that she will do anything to fight off his "detractors."

Take this extraordinary passage, for instance, in her review of De Palma's *Casualties of War*: "Some movies—*Grand Illusion* and *Shoeshine* come to mind . . . can leave us simultaneously elated and wiped out. Overwhelmed, we may experience a helpless anger if we hear people mock them or poke holes in them in order to dismiss them. The new *Casualties of War* has this kind of purity. If you meet people who are bored by movies you love such as *The Earrings of Madame De . . .* or *The Unbearable Lightness of Being*, chances are you can brush it off and think it's their loss. But this film is the kind that makes you feel protective." This use of the "you" pronoun is so restrictive as to fit only one individual: Pauline Kael.

I regret to say I found *Casualties of War* decent but hardly memorable. Moreover, Kael seems to have forgotten that she spent a lifetime poking holes. And we love her for it: it's what a critic's supposed to do. But we also admire her for the naked courage of her emotional responses: her "helpless anger." What other film critic would admit to that?

From the seventies on, Kael's true subject became American society. She homed in on the new releases as a barometer of changing mores; and her analyses of the drifts and undercurrents in the American unconscious are very valuable. Meanwhile, she lost track of world cinema. She wrote no reviews of some of the more interesting developments in film of the past three decades: Fassbinder, Tarkovsky, Rivette, Chantal Akerman, Raúl Ruiz, Imamura, Oshima, Sembene, Chen Kaige, Zhang Yimou, Hou Hsiao-Hsien. In neglecting foreign films, perhaps she could more successfully argue that there was no middle ground between her handful of rogue geniuses (Peckinpah, Altman, etc.) and the studio hacks.

During the dreary *Top Gun* eighties, Kael has expressed her dismay at the dip in movie quality. The decade that began with her castigating educated filmgoers for their squeamishness (in "Fear of Movies") now finds her deploring the senseless car crashes and bloodbaths. One senses Kael's increasing weariness as she faces the cynical banalities of most studio product. It is a relief to watch her exercising her intelligence on a noble, mature masterpiece like Visconti's *The Leopard* (rereleased in an uncut version), rather than ferreting out the dubious merits of Towne's *Tequila Sunrise*.

But whether commenting on masterpiece or clunker, Kael is always a pleasure to read. What will Pauline say about the newest film? Will she skewer your favorites or your *bêtes noires*? When she is on a roll, irreverently dissecting a movie you also think is not so hot, it's a consolation you wish would go on forever.

The first time we talk, over dinner at Hubert's, I notice Pauline's hands and mouth trembling. She has given up alcohol (a previous liking), sugar and cream, on doctor's orders. Like film buffs everywhere, we compare movies we love as a quick diagnostic probe of each other's character. Having read so much Kael recently, in preparation for this profile, I already know what she thinks about most filmmakers, and can anticipate and partner her opinions. I find myself suppressing my own disagreements, afraid lest she take me for one of the enemy camp and clam up. Then it dawns on me that I am agreeing with her not because she is bullying or overbearing, but on the contrary, because she seems so sweetly desirous of a meeting of minds that will place us together in the inner circle of good taste. She makes it so clear that she would *like* to think the best of you—and the best usually means that you agree with her.

One of the conversation's themes is her pain and puzzlement at the friendships she has lost through her reviews. Woody Allen used to be a friend, until her *Stardust Memories* piece. Ditto, Coppola. If she gives someone a good review, says Kael, they seem to think it their right to be only well reviewed from then on, and take it as a betrayal if she subsequently says something negative.

I ask if she thinks being an older woman inclines filmmakers to project maternal, nurturing qualities onto her: hence their sense of betrayal when she fails to be entirely supportive.

"I hadn't considered the maternal aspect. But I think I've definitely been given a harder time in the press for being a woman. I'm called 'shrill' and 'aggressive' and 'opinionated'—which they would never call a male critic. I've been referred to in print as a 'cunt' by people I'd praised. The first time was by John Huston. We'd been friends and I'd defended him for years. But I wrote that *Night of the Iguana* was a lousy movie. So he called me a 'cunt' to an interviewer. Then he wrote me a personal letter of apology!" she says with a disbelieving laugh. "Of course the article would reach hundreds of thousands, but the letter would be read only by me.

"You can't get too close to these filmmakers," she adds. "They're very devious. Also, it's hard to write about them once you know them well, because you understand too much what's behind the films. On the other hand, one tends to make friends with people who are in the business, so it's difficult."

We gossip about the appetites of various directors: Rossellini's womanizing ("A few days before his death, he was staying up till two in the morning trying to impress some twenty-year-old nitwit," Kael sighs), Truffaut's attraction to "vacuous young girls," Welles's and Peckinpah's preference for "these little muchachas." Of all the directors Kael mentions, it is Sam Peckinpah she speaks of with the deepest feeling.

"He started out as an actor, you know, in a Pasadena playhouse. He'd invented that whole cowboy he-man past after the fact, and then he felt he had to become that way. But he was such a dear man. Peckinpah would write me letters full of juicy descriptions of producers and their wives and mistresses. We'd go to parties together at these big homes, and sometimes he'd arrive so drunk I didn't know how we'd get out of there safely."

I am reminded of Kael's lovely essay "Notes on the Nihilist Poetry of Sam Peckinpah," and her fondness for certain

Hollywood "bad boys": Peckinpah, James Toback, Robert Towne. I wonder if her attraction is purely vicarious, or if she had been involved with that sort of self-destructive, excessive type in her past. But whenever I ask Kael personal questions, she seems very resistant and steers the conversation as quickly as possible back to films. She will say nothing more about her reputed three marriages (the first two husbands' names have never even appeared in print) than: "We all make mistakes when we're young. Do we have to talk about that old stuff?"

It's clear from remarks in her books that she doubts the endurance of love or the value of marriage. In conversation, Kael seems to consider most men fools in their sexual behavior (as well she should). One senses she has been romantically disappointed often, and now is fiercely independent, free of all that messy longing, a victorious side effect of aging.

Five hours of stimulating talk end with my feeling giddy, slightly guilty for overtaxing her—and realizing that the real Pauline has evaded me. To get a grip on her life, I'll have to search the archives and talk to others.

Pauline Kael was born in 1919 in Two Rock, California, a town some thirty miles north of San Francisco. Her parents, Isaac and Judith Kael, were Polish Jews who emigrated to America, where Isaac saved enough as a salesman and storekeeper to buy a chicken farm in Petaluma. The youngest of five children (her two older brothers became businessmen, and her two sisters have had distinguished teaching careers), Pauline spent her first eight years on the farm. It was an experience that marked her with a prickly pride in the Western way of life, and an outsider's chip on her shoulder regarding the intellectually snobbish East Coast.

Kael's family was big on reading, music—and the movies. Pauline went along with her older brothers and sisters to the local movie house, and remembered years later, far better than they would, their early crushes on silent screen stars. She already had a phenomenal gift for recalling whatever she saw onscreen, which would allow her to write, sometimes decades after the fact, descriptions of film scenes still vivid in her mind.

In 1927, Kael's father lost his money in the stock market and had to sell the farm and go back to grocery-selling in San Francisco. "It was hard for him at fifty to start all over again," she says. "He tried, but he was a broken man." In Isaac Kael, resourceful inventor of a new farmer persona and dashing, adulterous cowman who died before reaching old age, one glimpses, perhaps, the model of the Sam Peckinpah type.

Kael went to Berkeley in 1936, in the midst of the Depression. "There were kids who didn't have a place to sleep, huddling under bridges on the campus. I had a scholarship, but there were times when I didn't have food," she told Studs Terkel in *Hard Times*. On the other hand, "a lot of the kids were well heeled. I still have a resentment against the fraternity boys and the sorority girls with their cashmere sweaters and the pearls."

Studying philosophy, she worked through college as a reader and teaching assistant. Eventually, she fell behind in her own course work and dropped out, six credits short of graduation, for lack of the $35 summer session fee.

"Do you regret not having gotten your college degree?" I ask.

"No, it doesn't mean a thing. I have all these honorary degrees. Anyone at seventy who's worried about a degree might as well forget it."

Kael wandered off to New York City for three years and lived with the poet Robert Horan. At the time she was interested in becoming a playwright. Then she returned to San Francisco, where she became involved with the poet and filmmaker James Broughton. Broughton's lasting importance in Pauline's life is that he fathered her only child, Gina James (named after his first name). I spoke by phone to Broughton, one of the major figures of American avant-garde film, who has made twenty-two movies, including the classic *The Bed.*

"In 1947 we were closest. The poet Robert Duncan introduced us. Pauline was working at Brentano's bookstore. I was making *Mother's Day*, my first solo film. She was very helpful in getting costumes and props, dressing the actresses with funny hats. But she also sneered at our avant-garde films—she's good at sneering. We were together that summer in a simple cottage in Sausalito. Pauline was always getting in terrific arguments about art with the painters who came around, and they'd leave antagonized. She can be very sweet, the velvet glove—but jungle red underneath. I've seen her say devastating insults in the sweetest tones."

"How did you break up?" I ask.

"I don't remember—it was obviously an incompatibility," says Broughton, whose acknowledged bisexuality may have been a factor. "She never wanted me to marry her, I know that. It's a sort of Virgin Mary archetype: she wanted a child but not to have to marry or live with a man. Once she got pregnant, she departed. It's curious how the pattern is repeated. Gina isn't married now and she has a child by herself."

Gina was born with an open heart, requiring costly medical attention, and Kael took a series of jobs allowing her to look after the child at home: seamstress, cook, textbook editor, ghostwriter and answering service operator. Around 1954 she also began writing her first film reviews, which were received with far more excitement than her efforts at playwriting.

KPFA, the Pacifica public radio station, asked her to do a regular show (without pay) on the movies. Ernest Callenbach, longtime editor of *Film Quarterly*, remembers the program's format: "First she'd invite a miscellaneous gaggle of people over for dinner at her house in Berkeley; they'd all drink a fair amount, and they'd see a movie and then show up at the studio a little sloshed and excited and talk about their reactions to the film. Her show was very popular; she had a sassy, caustic voice and it penetrated your mind. Her voice was also powerfully attractive to some men, who called her for dates. 'Well, honey,' she'd say, 'maybe you ought to tell me what you think I look like.' They would answer things like 'tall, blond, statuesque.' Pauline would say with that great laugh of hers, 'I don't look at all like that, but if you're ready for anything, come on by.' "

One of the men who contacted Kael after listening was Edward Landberg, who had started his own repertory movie theater and invited her to help him program it. She ended up managing the theater, booking films, taking tickets, answering the phone. The Cinema Guild and Studio became an enormous success, the first superior repertory cinema in America, some say, and also the first twin movie house. Key to its popularity were the program notes Kael turned out, which were far more candid and informative than the usual brochure blurbs. Many Berkeleyites gratefully remember these legendary film notes as providing, in painless form, the basics of a film education. They were also the forerunners of her brief reviews at the front of *The New Yorker*; they taught her how to write succinctly and provocatively.

In the process of working together, she and Landberg became lovers and ended up getting married. The marriage lasted only two years; he went off to Los Angeles while she stayed behind to run the theaters. When he came back with a new wife, they had a business argument—he claimed Kael was worried that his new wife would take out too much money; she, that Landberg wanted to underrepresent the gate to distributors—and she quit.

"What happened to Landberg?" I asked Pauline.

"He fell apart. Too much LSD. For a while he became a sort of guru. It's very sad. He was like a lot of those people in Berkeley, who were very talented and intelligent, but who disapproved of you if you succeeded."

"I must warn you that I'm not a fan of Pauline Kael," says Ed Landberg, who has agreed to meet me for an interview at a Thai restaurant in the Berkeley flats. He is a short man with a white goatee and bloodshot eyes; he is wearing a vinyl tan jacket over a blue pullover, and shabby, stained pants. A Viennese émigré with traces of an Old World accent, he has a certain warm cosmopolitan modesty, at odds with an edgy suspiciousness. He pulls out a large folder of poems and begins reading by way of introduction. The poems are fairly oblique, part Berryman satiric, part mystical— not very good. From time to time I catch a line about Miss Quill, his code name for Kael. Then he puts the poems away and we talk.

"I had founded the Guild in 1952. I heard Pauline Kael speak on KPFA, and I read a few of her pieces, in *Partisan Review* and *Sight & Sound*. She struck me as a bright, witty, gifted writer, a good wordsmith. So I sent her a note. At first I found her stimulating. But within a fairly short time the stimulus wore off."

"Why?"

"She was a very vain, aggressive woman. She had to be right in all things. She had to be kowtowed to. She was desperately in need of adulation and it didn't matter who it came from. As long as people flattered her, they were welcome. She certainly was sufficiently intelligent to be able to tell flattery from the real thing, but it didn't seem to matter. She had a solid coterie of fifteen to twenty people around her in this 'salon.' She attracted a lot of gays because she was essentially their Queen Mother. There would be this constant aesthetic chitchat—about nothing. When you think about someone who wants to talk about nothing but movies—no matter how good the movies are—think about the emptiness."

"Why did you get married?"

"It was a matter of convenience. I don't think either of us really wanted to get married. It was pretty much a business arrangement. There were certain economic advantages: she was good for the theaters, and they helped keep her alive. I will say she was a very good housekeeper and cook."

After his remarriage, Kael quit the theater with a flourish, printing her letter of resignation on the program calendar. "When she showed me all the copy for the new program except one page, I began to smell a rat," says Landberg. "I went down to the printers. Sure enough, she had put in her 'I'll be seeing you' note. It wasn't a resignation letter, it was a betrayal. All this stuff about 'irreconcilable differences with the owner.' I did a stupid thing: I tried to hatch out the message. But you could still read it through the hatchings."

After her departure, the theaters continued to thrive, says Landberg with touchy pride. "In fact I did an even better job with publicity than she had. I became a wealthy man. I expanded to four screens."

"Then why did you give up the business?"

"To anyone who has what I have, a—messianic drive," he says hesitantly, as though aware he is about to lose me, "it could never be realized through showing movies. I began to receive messages, in the way of Joan of Arc. I was receiving Revelation; or if I wasn't, I thought I was. The way it works is that the pineal gland is the organ for hearing God—"

"Wait a minute, what do you mean, a 'messianic drive'? Do you mean that you consider yourself . . . the Messiah?"

"Well, it's obvious I can't be Jesus. But if I'm anybody, it's Elijah. And if I'm right that I'm the Final Prophet, then they'll have to hand over the Covenant to me. And then the world will be saved."

He flashed his dimpled smile, which still contained a shade of the boulevardier's skepticism within the fanatic's glare; and I saw how he must have been an attractive man years ago. It was, as Pauline had said, sad. How else could he top his ex-wife's fame and cinematic crusading, except by saving the whole world?

Kael eventually demanded a salary to continue her show. "It was a major crisis for KPFA because no one was paid there," explains Ernest Callenbach. "She made a farewell broadcast which flat-out attacked KPFA for not supporting her. It was a godsend, actually, since it forced her into print."

The most controversial essay she wrote for Callenbach's *Film Quarterly* was "Circles and Squares," a critique of director-centered, auteurist film writing ("the *auteur* theory is an attempt by adult males to justify staying inside the small range of their boyhood and adolescence . . .") and of its main American proponent, *Village Voice* critic Andrew Sarris. This led to a good deal of bad blood between Sarris and Kael over the years. "When I wrote the piece," she explains, "I thought of it as good intellectual fun—you know, a debate. I had Chick Callenbach send a copy in advance to Sarris so that he could write a reply. I was very surprised to discover how hurt he was by it. I wrote him a note saying we should meet. But it didn't work. He continued to be offended." Says Sarris: "I was somewhat taken aback by her apparent conviction that she had done me a favor by blasting me in print. She insisted that I should be grateful for her having shown me the error of my ways."

"The funny thing," observes Callenbach, "is that neither Pauline nor Andy had a theoretical bone in their bodies. I think she just felt deeply offended by his attempt at system-making, and its threat to the immediacy of reaction which she saw as the basis of film love. She later gave a famous address at Dartmouth against film education courses. 'If you don't think education can ruin film,' she said, 'you don't know the power of education.' "

Kael tried hard to land a film reviewing job with a San Francisco newspaper, so that she could stay on the West Coast. But, according to her friend, jazz critic Grover Sales, "Pauline made them very nervous—maybe because she'd attacked the local critics so often. San Francisco's a small town and they wrote her off as some kind of nut. Pauline said, 'San Francisco is like Ireland. If you want to do something, you've got to get out.' "

A hectic freelance period followed, during which she wrote for *McCall's*, *Life*, *The New Republic*, *Vogue*, *Mademoiselle*, *The Atlantic*, *Holiday*. She was becoming a nationally known writer; but she was also having run-ins with editors who rewrote or rejected her copy. A particularly scathing review of *The Sound of Music* for *McCall's* (she called it "the big lie" and *"The Sound of Money"*) helped get her fired from that family magazine. When William Shawn, editor of *The New Yorker*, approached her in 1968 with an offer to become their regular film critic half a year (the other half going to Penelope Gilliat), and promised not to interfere with or shorten her copy, Kael had found her niche at last.

She had to relocate East for the job, since movies open up there faster. "It was a wrenching move to go from California to New York—a hard city to adjust to at my age. And let's face it, everything in the West is better."

There were other adjustments: Pauline Kael, the Westerner taking potshots at the Eastern Establishment and the "fuddy-duddy" journals, the working woman who resented the privileges of the "well heeled," suddenly found herself ensconced in the most comfortably middle-class, prestigious journal of all. "At first, I didn't fit into *The New Yorker*," she admits. "I seemed too rambunctious for its pages. You couldn't even say a word like 'constipation' because it would make people think of shitting! But gradually things have turned around so that now people associate me with the magazine."

Indeed, the marriage between Kael and *The New Yorker* is one of the most long-lasting and mutually beneficial in modern magazine history. Her own influence shows in the way the weekly has lately become more trend-conscious and visceral. "That refined genteel tradition is a dying tradition, and I think it deserves to die because it says we're really above the art," notes Kael. "When I was a kid, *The New Yorker* had a gentleman critic in just about every art form. And even though some were very good and knowledgeable it used to drive me crazy because they were so superior to what they talked about."

Kael's own method was to get *down* with a movie, turned on by its sexy, animal energy—even, at times, by its violence. She has frankly acted like a booster or salesman. "If I have reservations about a film that I think is marvelous and that people should see," she once revealed, "I don't discuss those reservations in the review, because people will immediately seize on those as a reason to stay away." Inevitably, her enthusiasms sometimes resulted in hyperbole, as when she compared the importance of Bertolucci's *Last Tango in Paris*'s premiere to that of Stravinsky's *Sacre du Printemps*. And just as inevitably, there came a backlash: Kael was attacked by Renata Adler, Sarris, Richard Gilman and John Gregory Dunne.

"People don't understand something about Pauline's particular take on reviewing movies," says her friend Joe Morgenstern, the journalist and *Wall Street Journal* film critic. "When she writes something excessive, it's often out of a desperate need to invent a better movie than the one she's seen. She's a romantic who gets smitten by certain movies—she loves their promise and refuses to be worn down by their defects. She falls prey to her capacity for excitement, which is a pretty honorable flaw."

Renata Adler's 1980 attack in *The New York Review of Books* was singular, not only because of the schoolyard excitement of a fight it brought to the literary world, but because of the rarity of one contemporary prose stylist analyzing another's devices so closely (if vituperatively). Adler accused Kael of "compulsive and joyless naughtiness," "strident knowingness," "*ad hominem* brutality and intimidation" and "relentless, inexorable" images of "sexual conduct, deviance, impotence, masturbation," as well as "indigestion, elimination, excrement." One read it at the time with uneasy fascination, thinking that Adler was definitely onto something with her attempt to decode Kael's recurrent erotic metaphors and obsessive figures. The problem was that Adler knew so much less about movies than Kael; that every good writer could be said to have psychosexual obsessions; and that Kael's collection, *When the Lights Go Down*—far from being "worthless," as Adler had sweepingly concluded—turned out to have a high percentage of thoughtful reviews.

Pauline Kael made it legitimate to go into film criticism as a profession, and her influence on a whole generation of film critics has been immense. Some younger critics have been accused of aping not only her opinions but even her pronouns and syntax. These imitators are called, in the trade, "Paulettes"—a category which resembles the Mafia in that many insist no such entity exists, while others see its conspiratorial roots everywhere. Among the critics mentioned as having at one time or another been a "Paulette" are Gary Arnold, David Denby, David Edelstein, Steve Farber, Hal Hinson, Elvis Mitchell, Terrence Rafferty, Peter Rainer, Lloyd Rose, Stephen Schiff, Paul Schrader, Michael Sragow and James Wolcott. Clearly the list covers writers of varying degrees of originality, but they share Kael's having helped most of them get jobs. The present Paulettes often seem to vote as a bloc for National Society of Film Critics awards. Kael bristles, however, at the notion she has a "party line" which others slavishly follow.

"I don't discuss movies with other critics before they write their reviews. It would be totally unprofessional, and frankly, I'm not that interested in spending my life on the phone with kids half my age."

One critic—among the many who asked to be anonymous—backed her up: "It's much more subtle than Pauline calling and telling them what to think. It's people trying to anticipate her taste. That's a hard game to play, but a seductive one, especially if you don't have an aesthetic of your own. Pauline's style is so addictive to people of the movie-based generation. It lets you be smart without being stuffy, to pick up on the vernacular and the conversational, to feel sophisticated without needing to acquire much historical background. Also, things have to be 'jazzy' for her, which young people like too."

"She's more than encouraging of young writers, she's insistent," notes Meredith Brody, a restaurant critic and screenwriter. "If she thinks you're expressing something well out loud, she tries to get you to write about it."

An ex-Paulette told me: "She gives you the impression that she cares more about your writing than you do yourself. It's a tremendous high to be appreciated by someone so powerful. Unfortunately there's the desire to keep that high going—addiction to her praise. It's not *her* fault, it's the fault of younger critics for allowing ourselves to be dominated by her."

But another anonymous informant told me: "Pauline is both the Good Mother and Monster Mom. She appears enormously nurturing, and then later there's this withholding. She'll call you up and say, 'It's not very good, honey,' especially when you've tried to stretch yourself into something new."

Joe Morgenstern vehemently denies this: "I've always found that when I've been at my most original, she's responded with enormous generosity. And when I've been most predictable, she's been tactfully silent."

Kael insists that it bothers her when people imitate her style, and that it's only people who don't know her who speak about her having a coterie. As with so many issues regarding this complex woman, it is possible to put a positive or negative interpretation on the same facts. Why call it a "coterie" and not a set of friends? What's wrong with being a mentor to young people, or helping them get jobs? Perhaps the truth lies somewhere in between. As Morgenstern puts it: "Pauline's generosity is intertwined with the enjoyment of refereeing and brokering and having an influence."

One ex-Kaelite willing to talk on the record was screenwriter-director Paul Schrader. "Pauline Kael was my mentor. She got me into this business. I was going to a religious school, Calvin College, and my college and my church forbade films—therefore I got interested in them. I took some film courses at Columbia. One night at the West End Bar I was vociferously defending Pauline's book *I Lost It at the Movies*, and Paul Warshaw, Robert Warshaw's son, said: 'Would you like to meet her? She lives nearby.' So he brought me over to Pauline's apartment on West End Avenue. We got to talking. I hadn't seen many films but I had strong opinions. It went on so late that I ended up sleeping on her sofa. The next morning she said to me, 'You don't want to be a minister, you want to be a film critic.' And: 'If you ever want to go to film school I can arrange it.' Not only did she help me get admitted to UCLA Film School though I didn't have the proper requirements, but thanks to her recommendation I also began reviewing for *LA Free Press*.

"I became one of a group of her satellites. At that time they were Gary Arnold, David Denby, Roger Ebert, Steve Farber. . . . The satellites would send her anything interesting by young critics. She read everything we wrote and would comment to us about it. She would call when there was some film coming up that she felt had to be supported, to rally around. You have to understand that this was the evangelical period of film criticism. We were all *committed* to film criticism; we really felt there was a need for what we were saying. And she's a proselytizer. She fills you up with energy and enthusiasm.

"Anyway, this satellite system increased her power and influence, naturally, since her opinion was multiplied in all these publications around the country. My falling-out with her occurred when there was an opening for a critic's job in Seattle. Seattle was one of the best film towns in the country, and she needed a voice out there. She wanted to put me up for the job. Ostensibly it was everything I was looking for. But the idea of being yanked out of the film community in L.A. spooked me, so I turned it down, and began writing screenplays, and fell out of that circle of critics. In a way, I had betrayed her investment in me."

Did he think this estrangement had a role in her criticism of his movies? I asked. (Kael had written about *Hardcore:* "For Schrader to call himself a whore would be vanity: he doesn't know how to turn a trick.")

"I don't take her criticisms of my films that seriously. Besides, I didn't end up making the kind of films I would have approved of as a critic myself." Interestingly, when Schrader's underrated *Patty Hearst* came out last year, Kael was one of the only reviewers to defend it.

"I always know when I've had too much to drink," Schrader muses. "Because I want to sit down and talk to Pauline. I miss those conversations we had around her kitchen table on West End Avenue."

Pauline is working on a review of *Batman* when I visit her in Massachusetts. She has just finished her second draft and is still not sure she has it right. It's especially important because she is pro-*Batman* and feels the movie has been mistreated critically. "Canby just didn't get it," she says, shaking her head. Kael often seems preoccupied with her more powerful *Times* colleague.

Gina comes by to type the penciled second draft. Her daughter does all the typing and driving for her. I've been told their relationship has been rather symbiotic: "When you meet Gina, you'll understand everything about Pauline." But, perhaps because I am unobservant, all I see is a pretty brunette, somewhat self-effacing and down to earth, struggling to paint and raise a child alone, who seems to have her mother's little tics in perspective.

Gina descends from the upstairs study a half hour later and says she has to go, handing the pages to her mother.

"So, what did you think?" asks Kael.

"That ending—it's really out there!" says Gina with a grin.

"You think it's too hypey? . . ."

"I don't *know!*" her daughter answers mischievously, unwilling to clarify, and departs.

"Does Gina edit your pieces as well?" I ask.

"She used to. She was great at it. But she said she felt she was too much inside my head, it made her uncomfortable."

Pauline takes me around her house and shows me photographs of Gina when she was a child, holding a beloved basenji dog, since deceased; then Gina around twenty, looking like the young Gene Tierney; then a whole suite of Willy, her grandchild. I am touched by how helpful Kael is, opening her whole life to my scrutiny, not really sure what I am looking for—as neither am I.

Later she shows me the draft of her *Batman* review. I make a few suggestions—the title seems weak, I tell her; the ending *is* a bit hyped, I don't tell her—and she disappears for some more rewriting. The phone rings; an L.A. friend reports the "depressing news" that Sheila Benson of the *L.A. Times* panned *Batman* but loved *Do the Right Thing*, which Kael disapproves of. "And to think, I recommended her for that job!" she says with a weary smile.

Though Kael may be right in claiming she does not discuss beforehand new movies with her fellow reviewers nor campaign afterward for film critics' awards, there is still the sense of a straw vote being taken, with various precincts around the country reporting in. The results are often disenchanting: she sees herself frequently as waging a lonely crusade.

That night, Pauline fixes me a nice, simple meal of tortellini and salad, with some leftover birthday cake. After dinner she retires for a few more hours of *Batman* revisions. In the morning she tries out new article titles on me. Gina stops by to type draft number three of *Batman*, while Pauline gets ready to start on a *Ghostbusters II* review. Her devotion to her craft is thrilling—it would be impressive in any writer, more so in someone just turned seventy.

"Tell me about growing older," I prod.

"What is there to say? It's not a happy stage. When your mind is working well, when you're clicking along as you're writing, you think, 'Oh I could do this forever!' But when you get up from your desk you're goddamned tired and your body doesn't want to move. It's only in terms of the alternative that it looks good. Some energy always feeds the writing, but the hell is waiting in line forty-five minutes for a screening you've been invited to, or the sheer physical fatigue of trying to get to a movie in time. I mean traffic is terrible in New York, you often can't get a taxi, I often find myself walking in the rain, and I'm a soaking mess when I get there. And in winter it's sheer misery at my age, flogging through wet streets."

"Can you foresee a time when you'd stop doing it?"

"I think about it all the time. But the fun of writing is still there. Things are coming up that I want to write about. And I need to earn a living."

"Writing is a funny profession, in that you can't retire," I say.

"You could be forced by physiology to retire. One thing is that it's harder to write when you get older. The words don't come as easily. Also, if you've written as much as I have, the phrases you've used before tend to come to mind. And you think, 'Omigod, this is senility!' But the real problem is the flow of language. Before, the words just piled up and came out of the pencil—and they don't pile up anymore. The circuits are not as accessible."

In 1979, Kael passed out in a screening room, and was rushed to the hospital. She was told that, with her heart condition, she had only a month to live. "I was supposed to go out to L.A. to give a lecture. The doctors told me that if I flew out I'd be dead before the plane landed. Finally I said, 'What the hell, I may as well go, I need the money!' " She laughs, recalling it. Since that time, she takes daily medication. One is aware of her as frail—probably very different from the hell-raising Pauline of days gone by, who could smoke a cigarette, apply lipstick and drink bourbon simultaneously, while letting fly a barbed remark.

In some ways, her old friends say, the change is for the better. "Pauline has mellowed," says Grover Sales. "She's less abrasive than she used to be. There's a sweet quality to her now. Success has been good for her."

In 1978, tired of reviewing, and, at fifty-nine, feeling perhaps that this was her last chance for a change of course, Kael took a leave of absence from *The New Yorker* and went to Hollywood. She was lured there by Warren Beatty to produce her friend James Toback's movie *Love and Money*. Beatty, executive producer on the film, told her: "We need a third intelligence." But there were casting problems, Beatty procrastinated as is his wont and conflicts arose between Kael and Toback, who is known as much for his excesses (gambling, picking up women) as his movies. "In retrospect she was right about a lot of things," says Toback, "but it was very difficult for me at that point to collaborate." Torn between her convictions about what the film needed and her loyalty to Toback, she withdrew from the project. But she stayed on as an "executive consultant."

Kael became answerable to Don Simpson, then head of production at Paramount, and the two did not see eye to eye. She was frustrated by rejections of her proposals and by encounters with Production Hell: she'd work on a script with a writer until it reached satisfying shape, only to have the studio demand heavy rewrites. Her phone calls were not always returned. She became a court intellectual, not taken altogether seriously. No doubt many in the industry who had long waited to see Pauline Kael get hers were not unhappy.

Kael declines to name which projects she worked on, but adds with typical poise: "When they took my advice the films turned out better, and when they didn't the films came out worse." She insists she had a pretty good time.

Her friend Joe Morgenstern says otherwise: "It was certainly a terrible, shocking experience for Pauline. She got a heavy reality bath when she came out here. It was out of an ardent love of movies that she threw herself into the arms of the movie goddess. And nothing came of it. It's never pleasant to be part of a movie that never gets made, or is made in a distorted way."

After six months she ended her film producing career and returned to *The New Yorker*, the job now sweetened by no longer having to share it with Penelope Gilliat. Kael had her revenge on the studios with a long jeremiad called "Why Are

Movies So Bad? Or, The Numbers." Some called it sour
grapes; others censured her Hollywood episode as a potential
conflict of interest. As I see it, Kael has far too much integrity
for that. The only reproach to be made about her Hollywood
ties is a tonal one: that inside tipster's tone that seems to
want to address the industry not just as a critic but a player.
Her *Greystoke* review, for example: "[Robert] Towne's script,
which I've read, was marvelously detailed. . . . [It] exists now
only in vestigial form; it's in some of the bits and pieces of
[director Hugh] Hudson's scraggly mess, and Towne uses a
pseudonym in the credits—P. H. Vazak, the kennel name of
the dog he loved, who's now dead."

If she is not as powerful in the marketplace as she once
was, that has perhaps more to do with the poorer quality of
movies today than with any personal decline. Indeed, her latest collection, *Hooked*, shows Kael to be just as feisty, probing
and passionate about movies as ever.

She's sometimes seen as *too* movie-mad. "As far as I know,
Pauline Kael has no general conversation," Richard Schickel
has said. "She only talks about movies. She's a bit of a mono-
maniac." Calvin Trillin quipped: "Ask Pauline Kael which is
more important—movies or peace in the Middle East."

"It's not correct that movies are her only life," says Joe
Morgenstern, who is closer to Kael. "But her movie life is as
intense as anyone's I know. We'll pick up the phone and talk
a little about the world, then get down to the meat of it:
'Okay, so what have you seen lately?' There have been times
when we've had intensely personal conversations—more
lately than when I first knew her. I'll tell her all my problems.
If I want Pauline to be the sort of friend she's capable of, I
have to push another button and say, 'Let's leave movies for a
while.' And she'll listen with sympathetic attention and be
very helpful. But there *is* that obsessive attachment to the
movies. She's really a very private person; even with all the
people streaming through her life and calling her on the

phone, she keeps to herself. Very often, I think, the movies are a defense for her against the messiness of the rest of the world."

There remains a puzzling gap between the appealing, warmly reasonable Pauline Kael I met on several occasions and the embattled, armored, self-righteous quality evinced at times in her public persona. When I am with Pauline, I see the world all her way. She has a kind of charisma: her voice is an amazingly caressing instrument, and she looks at you with those startled blue eyes, the way a child can seem to be all face vulnerably attached to a small body, and you want to protect her and win her approval. Only in leaving Kael-land do doubts enter.

The Pauline who never admits she is wrong, who will not allow those who disagree with her a dignified out but insists on portraying them as prim or hypocritical, who answers a question from the audience with "What kind of fink are you?" or some other putdown, yet who steadfastly remains surprised by the pain her harsher reviews cause—that Pauline seems either a little unconscious or not very given to examining her own dark side. "Her particular myth," says one informant, "is that everyone else has motives and an unconscious desire for power—except her. She alone is disinterested."

Perhaps doubt or self-skepticism would be a luxury in a woman of her generation who has had to battle for a place in a previously all-male club. Other achieving women her age or older—Martha Graham, for example—have had that same quality of refusing doubt. Reviewing is a profession, in any case, that tolerates little uncertainty, and Kael has excelled by trusting her gut intuitions. Still, that same approach, untempered, prevents her from adjusting her views in the light of later experience. Kael is famous among film critics for not seeing movies more than once. When I asked her why, she said: "Who wants to find out you were wrong the first time? Besides, most movies would bore me a second time." Another critic might think it worthwhile to find out which films could stand the test of multiple viewings—which got by the first time only on surface sensation and which deepened as art—but that would lead Kael into a sort of historical study at odds with her love of movies at first sight. Quite apart from her distrust of film scholarship—the one time she attempted it, *Raising Kane,* her ideas were rich but her research severely questioned—Kael freely admits that she is interested only in reviewing a movie in its own time, when it debuts.

Many have wondered whether Kael's formidable intellectual gifts are not sometimes misapplied to the latest studio bonbon. Does she regret not writing other books besides film review collections?

"No. People who review my books often say I should sit down and write a book on film aesthetics. I think I've been running a course on aesthetics for twenty-two years at *The New Yorker!* I would hate to write a book on film aesthetics that I think would be outdated by the time it was finished. Besides, I don't like reading film aesthetics books, I think they're a bore."

How about her memoirs, then?

"My editor, William Abrahams, has wanted me to do that for years. But I like writing about a subject and getting rid of it in a week and writing about something else. It's fun for me. Most of my friends have been in analysis for so long, I've heard them maundering about their lives for decades and I think, 'Oh God, I don't want to do that.' I mean it's all over now."

As I prepare to leave her house, Pauline Kael says to me, a little apologetically: "Are you sure you got all you need? I feel as if there should have been some 'revelation' to give you about myself."

"Don't worry, I got more than enough."

I mean that the one necessary revelation has occurred. I see Pauline standing there, fragile, complicated, full of old angers and new composures, and I feel her loneliness, her pride of achievement, her disappointments, her wisdom, her kindness, and for a moment I have the impression I understand her.

I wrote the bulk of this profile for a glossy magazine, now defunct, called New York Woman. *I was not entirely sure how Kael would receive it, since at the time it seemed to me I was trying to be as balanced as possible. It would be an understatement to say she was not pleased—as I began hearing from different sources shortly after it appeared. At first I told myself that her disapproval stemmed from wanting to be responded to with either love or hate, as though it were not my place to try to maintain objectivity toward her. But later, I came to feel that her real objection was that the piece was not innately sympathetic to her. And in this, I think, she was right. In her presence I experienced moments of real sympathy and fondness. Then I would go off and try to put it on paper and the critical voice would intrude. Part of the issue was that I began the piece not as a devoted Kaelite but as a respectful observer from another camp. My own cinematic perspective had been much more deeply shaped by Manny Farber and Andrew Sarris than by Kael, which made me feel a bit duplicitous in profiling her. In reading great gobs of her as research, however, I came to be astonished—not only at how often I agreed with her opinions, but at how high a level of prose she managed to maintain over decades of deadlines. Indeed (and how she would disapprove of that locution!), it seems to me that people will be reading her into the next century for the quality of her writing, long after its topical buzz is gone. I regard her body of criticism as foremost an achievement in American letters, to place alongside Edmund*

Wilson and H. L. Mencken. Still, we see movies very differently. Our disagreement may ultimately come down to the fact that I approach film primarily as an art form, and only secondarily as entertainment, whereas with her the order is reversed. She has made clear that she considers the "art first" orientation grotesque. Me, I can't help myself: I am so constituted that I would often rather see—for pleasure—a difficult new or obscure old movie than the season's biggest hit.

Kael has since retired from writing film criticism. It goes without saying that I miss her cantankerous, enthusiastic voice.

THE GALLANT ANDREW SARRIS

A mong the books that have most influenced me, transforming forever my understanding of a whole field—alongside, say, Jane Jacobs's *The Death and Life of Great American
Cities* in urbanism or Walter Benjamin's *Illuminations* in criticism—must be counted Andrew Sarris's *The American Cinema*. Actually, it was the first magazine incarnation of this
text, rather than its book form, that changed my life, falling
into my hands in 1963 when I was nineteen; and my copy of
Film Culture # 28, with its cover still of six chained maidens,
their nudity chastely covered with flaxen tresses like a sorority of Lady Godivas, remains in my collection of treasured
publications. One reason it is so dog-eared is that I was then
running a film club at college, and eagerly underlined all possible booking suggestions (Abe Polonsky's *Force of Evil*, Edgar
G. Ulmer's *Daughter of Dr. Jekyll*). Under Robert Parrish's entry was the madly tempting *"The Purple Plain* stands out in
the above list like a pearl among swine. What burst of Buddhist contemplation was responsible for such a haunting exception to such an exceptionable career?"

Part of what captivated me was Sarris's allusive, allitera-
tive, epigrammatic wordplay ("exception-exceptionable").

That combination of authoritative judgment and space restriction exerted such compressive force on his prose. Has anyone ever noticed what an irresistible subgenre of film criticism is this Wise potato chips approach? (See also Pauline Kael's short-shorts in 5001 *Nights at the Movies* and David Thomson's oft-revised A *Biographical Dictionary of Film*.) Who knows how many hours I have spent hopping from entry to entry, whole afternoons wasted or at least consumed in the decoding of these three's koans? But Sarris got to me first and shaped my tastes the most: initially it was because he provided a map, a system (essential to the young novitiate), but later, I realized, it was because I subscribed more closely to the value system, the humanist romanticism, beneath his judgments.

Long after I had ceased caring whether Sarris was wrong for not placing William Wyler or John Huston in the Pantheon, I continued to resonate to the waltzing fatalism of those directors he cherished most: Ophuls, Mizoguchi, Renoir, Murnau. . . . You might say that I had that same regretful, oxymoronic music in my soul that he was always alluding to when he wrote, say: "But ultimately there is no dramatic conflict between Boudu and his benefactors. They are all part of Renoir, part of his joyful sadness, part of the feeling he expresses so lyrically about the irreconcilability of life's choices." That ole irreconcilability, *yes!* The same critic who once confessed in *The Village Voice*, to my shock of recognition, that he would have a hard time getting laid in Stockholm, went on to allude in myriad sentences to the gap between libido and duty. He seemed to cherish movies because they spoke to one's half-buried desires, but then cherished most those with an "adult" (one of Sarris's favorite words) perspective, which acknowledged the necessity for sacrifice, whether gallant or otherwise. This applies not only to old films he praised in the past, such as Ophuls's *The Earrings* of *Madame De* or McCarey's *Love Affair*, but even recent movies he has admired, like *Flirting with Disaster* or *My Best Friend's Wedding* (speaking of reluctant sacrifice).

Though Sarris never used an explicitly psychoanalytic vocabulary, the Freudian in him—the late Freud of heroic restraint—emerges everywhere between the lines, in the simultaneous recognition of the price repression extracts and the necessity to maintain the discipline of civilization and decency in the face of discontent. Some of this I have gleaned from a patient reading of Sarris over decades; some was confirmed to me when, years later, I came to know him socially—and went to the Sarrises' parties, which were always divided evenly between film people and psychotherapists. Andrew and his wife Molly Haskell make no secret of the fact that they have been analysands forever.

Sarris's reviews tend to move from the specificity of proper noun, character and plot to some large, sweeping statement about the human condition, as grasped from a viewpoint of tolerance for people's need to reach for happiness, and the inevitable suffering when they don't get it. I would call this the "wisdom" perspective. He is always trying to move the reader to a more adult—by which I mean disenchanted but self-aware and, therefore, hopeful again—grasp of the patterns under human behavior. ("Behavioral," another Sarris word!) At his best, he is able to show how a film's technique, its story and the larger sociopolitical themes it touches upon all converge to create a certain aesthetic experience.

If *The America Cinema* had the most impact on me, my favorite book by Sarris has become *Confessions of a Cultist*, partly because in these reviews he seems most relaxed, most in tune with the films that were being released, and most able to keep all these factors of visual formalism and sociology in balance. Take, at random, this excerpt from his piece on Resnais's *La Guerre Est Finie*:

If *La Guerre Est Finie* is in some ways the most satisfying movie Resnais has made, credit is due largely to the lucidity and integrity of Yves Montand's characterization of Diego, a revolutionary engulfed by fears, fantasies, and futilities. However fragmented the director's feelings may be, Montand remains a rock of commitment, and with Montand's solidity as an actor serving as an anchor of style, a sea of images can be unified into a mental characterization. Whereas the awesome majesty of the late Nikolai Cherkassov obliterated montage in the late Sergei Eisenstein's *Ivan the Terrible*, the humanity of Montand domesticates montage in *La Guerre Est Finie*. We are no longer concerned with the pretentious counterpoint of love and the Bomb, past and present, illusion and reality, society and the individual, and so on. We are obsessed instead with the doubts and the fantasies of Diego. Through his mind passes what we know and feel about the heritage of the Old Left, that last, desperate camaraderie commemorated in kitchens and cemeteries as old comrades grapple with the old rhetoric they are doomed never to forget and the new reality they are doomed never to understand.

For Resnais it is enough to celebrate remembrance and mourn forgetfulness as fragments of personality and politics disintegrate in the void of time. Civilization is the process of trying to remember, and Resnais once did a documentary on the Bibliotheque Nationale as the supreme ornament of civilization. Cinema, however, is more than remembering and forgetting. It is also acting, doing, resolving, indeed being. Cinema, like life, is a process of creating memories for the future. Resnais has always drawn on the past without paying for the future. His cinema has been hauntingly beautiful if dramatically improvident in its ghostliness. His characters have been paralyzed by the sheer pastness of their sensibilities. Montand's Diego is no exception, but a marvelous thing has happened. Montand's dignity and bearing have broken through the formal shell of Resnais' art to dramatize the doubts and hesitations of the director. Diego has become a hero of prudence and inaction. He has shown what it is to be a man without the obvious flourishes of virility so fashionable today. (Even the stately explicitness of the lovemaking is a measure of the hero's stature.) To be a man it is above all necessary to be patient as one's life dribbles away on the back streets, blind alleys, and dead ends of political impotence. The at times agonizing slowness of *La Guerre Est Finie* achieves the pathos of patience by expressing a devotion to detail common to both Diego and Resnais. It has always seemed that Resnais was more suited to documentary than fiction because of a preoccupation with facts rather than truths. The parts in Resnais always seem superior to the whole, and if *La Guerre Est Finie* is an exception, it is because the integral behaviorism of a performer has buttressed the analytical style of a director. It is as if Resnais were dropping things all over the screen, and Montand were walking around picking them up. That *La Guerre Est Finie* finally makes us weep is a tribute to Montand's tenacity.

This is careful, cultivated, highly perceptive prose, much more serene and poised than one expects to find in a weekly column; and it reminds us what a fine writer Sarris can be, when he takes the trouble. I would single out for attention: 1) Sarris's deep grasp of film history (Eisenstein, Resnais's entire *oeuvre*), which helps place this particular picture in context;

2) his shying away from unpacking the Ideas in a film. As he says about *Pierrot le Fou*, in what could be a credo: "but the point is still to see what is felt rather than to figure out what is meant. . . ."; 3) the flexibility of his auteurism stance, as evidenced by his willingness to credit Montand with much of the film's tone; 4) his stoicism and generalized wisdom-teaching: civilization is remembering; to be a man requires patience "as one's life dribbles away"; 5) the formal analysis of montage and *mise en scène*, here given especially witty expression in the image of Montand picking up what Resnais has scattered.

I am more partial to Sarris's reviews from this period than to his polemics. The problem with the polemics (see *The Primal Screen*) is not so much that they seem dated, as that they raise the spectacle of an insufficiently acknowledged hostility in a critic whose strong suit is fair-minded balance. No regular critic of the arts can be entirely free of aggressive hostility; some of the best (such as Pauline Kael or John Simon) know how to dramatize their malice in an entertaining way. But Sarris has always been slow to anger, a reluctant counter-puncher, so that when he takes after an opponent he does so in a conflicted way, backtracking, qualifying and so on, and when he lands a direct punch its mean-spiritedness seems out of character.

The gleefully provoking Kael is perhaps the only female opponent who could have elicited from Sarris an ungentle-manly surliness. Since the closing of the "auteurist wars," what has become more and more noticeable in Sarris is the consolidation of his gallantry. He seems to go out of his way to endorse any movie with a strong woman character who is treated respectfully or emerges triumphantly (which sometimes results in overpraising flawed films like *Chasing Amy* or *Beyond Rangoon*). He has compiled lists of the year's best performances by actresses, however small the role or unsung the picture, dispensing what seems like a big, gushing valentine to what used to be called "the fair sex." He will rush to the defense of a maligned actress, as when he denounces "all the gleeful gossip about the commercial demise of Ms. Roberts. She has never been lovelier or spunkier or more intelligently womanly." Formerly I was tempted to see his wife's feminist hand in all this: but the more I came to know Molly Haskell, the more I realized that she tends to be both more tough-minded and less sentimental about women. No, Sarris's chivalry toward women is his own likably quaint feature, marking him as a man from a bygone generation.

I am amazed that Sarris can continue to write intelligently and open-mindedly about movies year after year in his *New York Observer* column. What I miss, to be honest, is his visual analysis; whole columns may go by without his saying a word about camera placement, *mise en scène*, surface textures. In its place is a great deal of social commentary—attempts to spar with the *Zeitgeist*—which frankly interests me less. Sarris has metamorphosed his persona into a somewhat grumpy, still liberal old geezer commenting on matters of race or economics or gender. I noticed the same thing happening to Kael in her last years at *The New Yorker:* an increasingly irritable attempt to monitor the *Zeitgeist*, while withdrawing a certain emotional energy from caring about movies themselves. The current Sarris will often use a film as a jumping-off point for a disquisition on some social phenomenon, or a chance to walk down Memory Lane (sometimes by quoting himself from an earlier review). He will also often announce a prejudice—such as indifference to a genre or to a certain performer—and disqualify himself in advance as the ideal reviewer for the movie in question, even as he grapples with a few issues it raises. Sometimes it is clearly a matter of passion spent and loyalty to one's youth, as when he announces his refusal to take the up-and-coming French filmmaker Olivier Assayas as seriously as the old New Wave directors. (As Lloyd Bentsen would put it: I knew François Truffaut, Mr. Assayas, and you're no François Truffaut.)

So essentially what Sarris's weekly column offers is the opportunity to watch him shifting through the celluloid sands of time, pronouncing on the day's headlines, and sharing his enthusiasms for some aspect of a new movie. It is a *column*, more than an actual review, and, as such, a basket for digressions. What is curious is that this onetime systematizer has lost the appetite to put the cinematic present in order. He likes movies, always has, and will respond with pleasure, if given half a chance, to the latest releases. Gone is the hierarchical itch, however. I miss the old lawgiver: it's a bit like watching one's once terrifying father sink into a mild, fond embrace of the moment.

But enough of the Oedipal subplot. Clearly Andrew Sarris's criticism has meant the world to me. If it no longer affects me as deeply, that is partly because I have become my own man through cannibalizing him. Isn't that what a *Festschrift* is meant to demonstrate?

I wrote this piece for a volume of essays in tribute to Andrew Sarris—an old-fashioned Festschrift on the occasion of his seventieth birthday. Though we don't see each other socially that often, Andrew is enough of a friend that I invited him to my wedding. The truth is, I participated in this collection with some reluctance, because it is hard to write about one's friends honestly, and I dislike writing dishonestly. I hope I have struck a middle ground between obsequious and underhanded.

THE LAST TABOO:

The Dumbing Down of American Movies

One day last summer my friend Lorenzo, an old pro screen-writer, called for some quick advice. He had been hired to do last-minute rewrites for a *Die Hard* sequel that was about to start shooting but still had script problems. One difficulty: how to get across with a line or two of dialogue that the Mad Bomber was brilliant. "Speaks five languages?" mused Lorenzo, thinking aloud. "That's old hat. Went to Oxford? Doesn't mean anything anymore. Help!"

"There's always the chemical wizard approach. Like in *Blown Away*: 'That guy can make bombs out of Bisquik.' "

"Please. A total fiasco, it lost a pile. What are the marks—the stigmata of intelligence? Come on, you're supposed to be an intellectual."

"He reads Adorno in the original German . . . ? I don't know what to tell you." I offered a few other lame ideas. One reason my friend's request for a mark of brilliance was so difficult was that, as we both knew, true intelligence is an ever-renewing process, not an acquisition. By now, I sensed that Lorenzo had given up on me, and we turned to the more enjoyable part of the conversation. But afterward, I thought, "Has it really come to this? That the last refuge of intellect in films—the only one allowed to demonstrate a brain—is the Mad Bomber character?"

Of course, intelligence has always been associated with villainy (Mephistopheles, Iago), and simple minds with virtue. The audience for action movies pays to see its stand-in, the medium-IQ hero, get the better of the twisted genius through physical effort and fortitude. And Americans have long felt, as Richard Hofstadter argued in *Anti-Intellectualism in American Life* (1963), a mistrustful ambivalence toward the brainy. Yet some sort of sea change does seem to have occurred recently: ambivalence's positive pole has dropped away.

Why is "dumb" such a powerful metaphor for the American mood? Conversely, why has it become so rare nowadays to see onscreen a lively, functioning intelligence—an articulate, educated, self-aware character with an inner life?

Granted, we have been passing through a particularly silly season. 1994–95 has been dominated by 1) recycled versions of old television shows, such as *The Flintstones, The Little Rascals, The Brady Bunch, Lassie, Maverick. . . .* These are, above all else, presold packages testifying to the staggering unimagination and timidity of studio executives, who will only green-light a project with some built-in recognition factor, and who narcissistically overrate the nostalgia value of the TV fare they grew up with; 2) action movies wherein a mad bomber or terrorist holds a significant portion of the civilian population at risk (*Speed, True Lies, Blown Away, Die Hard*). The best of these pictures, such as *Speed* and *True Lies,* lavish considerable narrative intelligence and cinematic craft on entertainments that essentially bypass the cerebral cortex; 3) films about cretinism, which give us a choice between hapless morons (*Airheads, Dumb and Dumber, The Jerky Boys, Billy Madison*) and helpful ones (*Forrest Gump*). The comic idiot film genre clearly points to audiences' needs to feel superior to others who seem stupider than themselves. Its demographic base is young teens, mostly male, who like to smirk at everything; perhaps self-contempt, as much as superiority, constitutes its emotional draw. I do not abhor this genre: it continues a legitimate vein of American film comedy, based on gracelessness, infantilism and irreverence for authority. Its roots go back to Harry Langdon and the Three Stooges, its *maître* is Jerry Lewis, its cousins the denizens of *Animal House*, Cheech and Chong and PeeWee Herman. Sometimes it offers a vehicle for a wonderful talent, such as the rubber-limbed Jim Carrey, whose *Dumb and Dumber* is a mildly amusing comedy (if weaker than his innovative *The Mask*); sometimes it bogs down in interminable longeurs, as *Airheads* does. Often, the characters in these films are not precisely stupid so much as arrested in childish behavior.

The idiot genre has been too decried by public pundits and columnists as an avatar of the decline and fall of American civilization. Myself, I am less troubled by its significance than by the anti-intellectualism I see in the high end of American movies: the independent, provocative, festival films such as *Pulp Fiction, Ed Wood, Natural Born Killers, Bullets over Broadway. Forrest Gump*, one of the top-grossing films ever, is clearly a phenomenon: a feel-good tragedy for the Prozac generation. Well made for what it is, it is a Smiles decal plastered onto a depressive's grimace: Vietnam vets with blown-off legs, women dying of AIDS, a whole society coming unglued; but with the right attitude, you can come smiling through. "Whistle while you mourn," as film critic Carrie Rickey summarizes it.

In the forties, Jimmy Stewart represented the figure of the typical American, harassed and desperately trying to act with dignity without being taken for a sucker. Now our typical American, our neo-Capraesque, is Tom Hanks's Forrest Gump, a mentally "challenged" optimist who lands on top mostly by accident. He represents one pole, the holy fool, while the opposite pole is taken up largely by serial killers, hit men, drug addicts and psychopaths.

What has been lost is the middle, in the form of that conception perhaps too easily dismissed as patronizing: the common man. In a 1945 classic, *The Clock*, two ordinary people, a soldier (Robert Walker) and an office worker (Judy Garland), meet in Grand Central Station and fall in love, and have to overcome various obstacles to get married before his two-day leave ends. Aside from the restrained beauty of the two performances and Vincente Minnelli's tactful direction, what lingers in the mind is the touching belief implicit in offering a story without melodrama about the problems of ordinary people.

In the Coen Brothers' recent, smirking *Barton Fink*, the eponymous playwright-hero is shown to be a sap merely by expressing concern for social injustice and the plight of the common man. The movie takes the position, as film critic Jonathan Rosenbaum astutely observes, that "The very notion of the common man is fraudulent," first by setting up an embodiment of the common-man cliché (in Charlie, played by John Goodman), then by undermining it with "a contemporary cliché that's every bit as hackneyed. When Charlie turns out to be the serial killer, we are offered the revelation that people who chop off other people's heads are nice, ordinary people just like you and me—'common folks,' in fact."

A good part of the hip filmmaking of recent years, inspired by the stylistics of David Lynch *(Blue Velvet, Wild at Heart)*, has set about to satirize the rancid, decadent, psychopathic underbelly of Middle America. This is wishful thinking. If only Middle America were so decadent. The older direction, to plumb the lives of ordinary Americans for stories about their daily struggles, seems no longer an attractive alternative to filmmakers.

I wonder to what extent the reasons are demographic—and racist. The increase in new immigrants and minority groups is met by an almost spiteful refusal to engage the premise of a common man. Historically, the common man in America has been white; and if the face of America seems to be turning darker-skinned, one impulse is to deny the very existence of a shared humanity by expunging the national archetype, the typical American. Part of this spite takes the form of an explosion in vulgarity (bathroom jokes, infantile silliness of the *Dumb and Dumber* variety) and silly characters, as though, unable to put forward a single adult model of commonality that would reflect the multicultural audience, there is an attempt to locate universality in a preadult, child mind.

Never, I think, have intellectuals been so alienated from American movies as now; never has there been a period when they less expected to see in motion pictures a vestige of their own commitment to the life of the mind.

Intellectuals have always been drawn to film. Not, be it said, for narcissistic reasons, to see mirror reflections of themselves onscreen, but for the movement and erotic glimmer of the material world. (Wittgenstein was said to rush off to Betty Grable movies when the mental pressure became too great.) Movies have offered a quick, painless way for those devoted to refinements and "elitist" esoteric problems to participate in, or catch up on, the interests of their fellow-men.

Nevertheless, before now there were always traces, subversive smugglings of higher culture and intellectual perspectives into American movies. Sometimes these would take the form of adaptations of the classics (now derided as overly literary, MGM-parvenu). Or an intellectual surrogate, a model of mature intelligence, would be planted in the story: an older minor character who seemed worldly, cultivated, wise, like the aunt in *Love Affair* or the uncle in *The Snows of Kilimanjaro*. Often, aspirations to higher culture would be asserted through a ballet sequence, or a scene of the family gathered around the radio, listening to an opera program. "Carnegie Hall" was a universally recognized trope; and numberless times a John Garfield type from the slums donned a tux to conduct some Rachmaninoffian schmaltz in the orchestra pit. Certainly, we can smile today at the clumsy culture-mongering of those interludes; but the very naïveté of these sequences reproaches us. For they point to a time in American movies when both high culture and popular culture references existed; whereas now, only pop culture has the right to be alluded to.

I think one of the main reasons why so many cultural references (particularly to classical music) found their way into American movies of the thirties and forties was the large enclave of German refugees in the Hollywood film community. They missed Europe; they deplored the blandness of American consumer culture; and they found every opportunity to sprinkle their screenplays with references to the Louvre or the Vienna Philharmonic. They also wrote in countless minor comic roles for displaced European character actors, as violin repairers, Pushkin-quoting janitors, etc.

These homesick refugees were joined by a second group of "émigrés," the ex-East Coast writers who had deserted Broadway for the gold of Hollywood. Herman Mankiewicz, Ben Hecht, Dorothy Parker, Robert Benchley and all from that tribe who saw themselves as cynical sellouts nevertheless managed to allude to the cultural life they left behind (sometimes rather floridly, as in Hecht's *Tales of Manhattan* and *Specter of the Rose*). Joseph Mankiewicz, Herman's younger brother, never passed up the opportunity to insert a little speech about the importance of reading and English teachers!

Those leavening émigré populations are gone. What we have today are young would-be screenwriters and directors pouring out of film schools, who either have no cultural memory or repress it, who want to make a tidy little film noir about two greasers (he sports an Elvis jacket, she a Marilyn wig), stuck in a nowhere town, who meet cute, fall in love and then find a gun. . . . The appeal of Nowheresville is especially ironic, given that many of these young filmmakers live in New York's Lower East Side or similar urban hangouts. They descend on the sticks for their six-week low-budget shoot, thinking they are being sympathetic to white-trash America when they are actually slumming. What the small town setting offers, in *their* imaginations, is the allure of Rural Idiocy, of a premental world, occupied by characters who have nothing in their brains but the indoctrinations of mass culture. (The serial killer just wants to be a star.) Believe me, I am not saying that intellectual life only takes place in big cities; but I *am* saying that the small town is appropriated precisely for its ostensible "emptiness," which sets into harsher relief the tale, enacted for the thousandth time, of sex, violence and ersatz celebrity borrowed from the icons of popular culture.

One is entitled to ask: Why this narrow obsession with a few pop culture idols, Elvis, Marilyn, James Dean? How can it be that a complex national culture should have allowed itself to be stripped down to such few, barren archetypes? Take Jim Jarmusch: a very gifted, intelligent filmmaker, who studied poetry at Columbia, he yet makes movie after movie about lowlifes who get smashed every night, make pilgrimages to Memphis where they are visited by Elvis's ghost, shoot off guns and in general comport themselves in a somnambulistic, inarticulate, unconscious manner. Quentin Tarantino, the great hope of new American cinema, writes a screenplay *(True Romance)* in which the main character is also obsessed with Elvis, talks to his ghost, gets involved in a life of crime, is chased by the Mob, etc.

His *Pulp Fiction*—admittedly an enormously inventive, entertaining and polished work—is also a celebration of mindlessness and an assertion that nothing exists but pop culture. Hit men muse over old TV shows and cheeseburgers, between killings. The characters act entirely reflexively, without ever thinking: guns go off by mistake, the prizefighter dumbly returns to his apartment to retrieve a family watch, knowing that a mob hit has been put on him. The one bit of "inwardness," Samuel L. Jackson's last-minute conversion to moral responsibility, seems a too calculated plant to show someone has a soul. . . . *Pulp Fiction,* for all its tricky constructional surprises, is so filled with comforting allusions to old movies, TV shows, movie icons (like the scene in the fifties-decor restaurant), that the audience can feel they are in on the joke, they are seeing something they already know. ("Look, they're quoting *Saturday Night Fever!"*) Indeed, the movie exists in a kind of echo chamber of recycled pop culture.

It seems we are stuck in an ever-shrinking set of referents: a barroom with a jukebox, a TV set, some movie posters and some virile specimens of white trash.

In a *New York* magazine article about the takeover of "white trash culture," Tad Friend noted: "But now screenwriters are obsessed with the idea of the road-tripping, spontaneous, and often murderous poor. (It is ever tempting for Hollywood to impute authenticity to the ignorant—and to give them bodacious bods.) . . . 'It's totally about sex,' says director John Waters. 'Extreme white people'—Waters' preferred term for the white under-class—'look incredibly beautiful until they're 20, and then they look about 50. It's a sexual fantasy for people in the movies, who don't meet those sort of people very much—it's the idea of the bad boy, the juvenile delinquent.' Movies give us an airbrushed dream of white trash: alluring and deadly."

I understand the attraction of this material, within limits, but what I don't understand is why there can't also be films which express more of the experience of the filmmakers' own lives—including their intellectual lives. The young French cineaste and his/her American counterpart live fairly similar lives: they hang out in cafes, read, go to movies and classes, talk endlessly. Yet a first feature by a French director about young people is very apt to show characters sitting in cafes, quoting Nietzsche and talking a lot, while a first American feature (like ex-NYU student Kathryn Bigelow's *The Loveless*) will more likely be about a lockjawed motorcycle gang who terrorize a small town.

I refuse to believe that the answer is simply economic ("You can't show brainy characters onscreen because no one will pay to see it"), since the vast majority of independent American first features are distributed very narrowly, if at all, and lose money anyway. They might even stand a better chance of turning a profit if they reflected more closely their college-educated audience's experiences. No, it isn't just economics, it's a matter of choice and taste: people without brains are cool.

Does this have to do with the post-modernist antagonism to psychology—its disdain for motivation and characters' past backgrounds, its preference for actions that seem random and mysterious, as a way of asserting more freedom for the human species? Whatever its rationale, the suppression of psychological understanding results in cartoonishly impulsive characters living in the eternal Now, who perform one *acte gratuite* after another. Hence the preference for serial killers, drugstore cowboys, hit men and their thrill-seeking, amoral molls.

One way to consider the dumbing down of American movies is to examine some recent portraits of intellectuals or creative thinkers on the big screen.

We can start with the figure popularly equated with intellect itself: Albert Einstein. On face value, it would seem daringly elitist to call a commercial movie *I.Q.* and use the famous physicist (ably mimicked by Walter Matthau) as one of its main characters. But, for penance, this Einstein is made to repeat a half-dozen platitudes that assert the heart's supremacy over the head. In other words, the great thinker must ritually offer his head to the audience's anti-intellectual prejudices. His scientist colleagues are portrayed as a bunch of desexed, impractical old ninnies who cannot even change a light bulb; his niece's fiancé is an adenoidal, snotty academic. The only virile, attractive, capable character is a garage mechanic with a big pompadour who has lots of heart.

In the previously mentioned *Barton Fink*, a leftish playwright goes out to Hollywood to write screenplays. There are suggestions that Barton Fink has been based on Clifford Odets; however, Odets was anything but dumb, whereas Fink seems incorrigibly dense—a fool who grasps no more at the end than the beginning. The filmmakers sneer at his intellectual pretensions (and by extension, the claims of the mind), while putting their main energy into a visual *exercise du style*, in the surreal *Twin Peaks* manner.

In Woody Allen's *Bullets over Broadway*, the hero is again a playwright who proves to be an inept faker, and who is unable to apply a scrap of intelligence to the chaos of his private life. Unable to solve his play's script problems, either, he turns to a low-life thug, who naturally has all the narrative solutions at his fingertips. *Bullets over Broadway* is, admittedly, uncharacteristic Woody Allen, both in its glib, impersonal filmmaking and its anti-intellectualism. Usually, this *auteur* has at least provided one thinking man's role: for himself. Curiously, he cannot seem to write a cerebral, reflective character for another actor or actress. Hence, those Woody Allen films without Woody in the cast have lacked a self-reflective core, a judgmental consciousness. For most Americans these past twenty years, the one recognizable "intellectual" onscreen has been the Woody character. In *Bullets over Broadway*, he shows again his unwillingness to share the mental laurels, while pandering to the audience's prejudice that writers and others who work with their minds are idiots underneath.

The creative intellectual's inability to learn anything of consequence from his or her experience is a constant in recent biopics, sometimes played for laughs, sometimes for bathos. Thus, in *Mrs. Parker and the Vicious Circle*, we are given a Dorothy Parker who may be clever enough to toss off *bon mots* but who is so pathetically self-destructive (drinking, chasing the wrong men) that all lesser brains in the audience are invited to feel superior to her. Poor T. S. Eliot, in *Tom and Viv*, seems so baffled by his marriage that you want to laugh at him. And Ed Wood, in the movie by that name, is championed for never learning, as though the inability to acquire craft and sophistication over time were an artistic gift. Wood, played with dimpled zest (and zero character development) by Johnny Depp, is as satisfied with his first takes on the initial day of shooting as every day thereafter, despite the fact that the results continue to be dreadful. He is another Holy Fool, a Forrest Gump with a megaphone, whose innocence is his strength and armor. As a movie, *Ed Wood* is ravishing to look at, another cinematic *exercise du style*; but again, one is asked to check one's brain at the door, identify with a character arrested in dimwitted self-admiration, and groove on the mysterious, ineffable, surreal charm of the premental.

The one thing that is seemingly impermissible to show in American movies today is an intellectual possessed of self-insight. The struggle to lead an unillusioned life is nowhere visible on our screens. Again, I don't think the explanation is strictly financial: some utter follies have found their way into production, $30 million lemons, like *Toys* or *The Road to Wellville*, that make you rub your eyes and wonder what the studio was thinking of. No, the reason is that it violates the last taboo: we cannot have thinking people who aren't taken in by themselves.

• • •

So far I have been focusing on issues of character and theme to explain the dumbing down of American movies. But it seems to me that formal matters—recent changes in the very grammar of film, as it applies to the nature of a filmed image, a scene, a screenplay, the editing process—may cut deeper and provide more serious causes for this leakage in intelligence.

Much of what dumbifies movies today starts with the screenplay. Perhaps more than at any other time, screenwriting has become coded into a step-by-step convention. Workshops like those offered by Robert McKee, taken by thousands of wannabe scriptwriters, break down the screenplay into bite-sized formulae. Manuals like Syd Field's *Screenplay* dispense wisdom like "The days of ambiguous endings are over," and decree with mathematical precision ("about 25 minutes into the film") where the first major "plot point" should occur. Tom Laughlin, of *Billy Jack* fame, offers a newsletter subscription guaranteeing you mastery over the nine plot points which will make a successful movie. Actually, much of what Syd Field and others like him say makes good sense. The problems occur when their prescriptions are applied too literally: the movie develops a homogenized, mechanical, predictable pace. Too many studio executives in Hollywood take Field's or McKee's ideas religiously; we were better off when the world was wired to Harry Cohn's ass.

The prevailing mantra in film schools is that movies are above all a visual medium: therefore, dialogue must be kept to a minimum, or you risk sounding "literary"; a voice-over is a "literary device" and a form of "cheating"; "literary" is bad. Translation: words and ideas are bad. The result is a fearfulness that creeps into the screenwriter's intestines whenever his characters start to speak up for more than two sentences.

One important result is that scenes are getting shorter. Sometimes very short indeed: in action movies, one character may say "Shit!," another say "Duck!" and that is all she wrote.

The shorter the scene, the less chance there is for that tension between characters to reach the danger point where true communication can break out between them. As scenes grow shorter, too much pressure is put on the wisecrack, inserted between expletives and hot pursuit, to carry the load of character shading.

The art of writing movie dialogue has become less a matter of constructing scenes than of coining one-liners that can be quoted as marketing slogans in trailers and advertising campaigns. Dirty Harry's pioneering "Make my day" has become Schwarzenegger's "Hasta la vista, baby" and on down to "That guy can make a bomb out of Bisquik."

In domestic dramas, more and more inarticulate characters find themselves onscreen, like the eponymous hero of *What's Eating Gilbert Grape*, whose every scene with another character turns on the drama of his not being able to say what he feels. In action movies, the hero does not have to say much at all; he can grunt and swear.

The other night I was watching a 1939 Clarence Brown picture set in India, *The Rains Came*, on American Movie Classics. I tend to watch AMC a lot, because of all the thirties and forties movies they show. Let's not overly romanticize that era: the thirties and forties turned out thousands of clinkers, and *The Rains Came* is in many ways one of them. But what struck me was that, despite the wooden acting and the ponderous, artificial colonial backdrop, the characters were allowed to talk to each other! Scenes went on and on between them—taken verbatim, I assume, from the Louis Bromfield novel which the screenplay adapted—and in those confrontations one's sympathies would shift from one character to another, as each struggled to make clear his point, his perspective, his worldview.

This experience has been duplicated many times, as I watch an old movie and luxuriate in the ripening exchange, at the same time sensing the exact moment, like an internalized wince, when the same scene would have been chopped off in a contemporary movie. I can almost hear the producer saying, "Cut! Too much talk!" When studio executives see a large block of type (connoting a long speech) in a screenplay, they often dictate that it has to be trimmed without even bothering to read it.

The influence of TV sitcoms and stand-up comedians should also be noted in the reduction of screenplays to strings of one-liners. So we have arrived at the movie convention that conversation is a Ping-Pong match, zinging one-line ripostes across the net.

Formerly, our movies were allowed to breathe. They had hiatuses: atmospheric cutaways or comic relief passages where the audience gathered its energies. (Howard Hawks, for instance, has been justly praised for the rhythm he developed of stress and relaxation in movies like *Rio Bravo.*) Today, we see increasingly a hyperkinetic type of movie *(Raiders of the Lost Ark, Terminator 2, JFK, Mississippi Burning, Speed)*, which, well-crafted fun though it may be, is nothing but high points; all the "slack" has been squeezed out of it, there are no moments to pause, to reflect, we keep rushing up and down the roller coaster of sensations, and the movie suffocates for lack of breath, it is as though a plastic sealant had been applied to its surface. When we leave the theater we feel bounced around, black-and-blue and strangely amnesiac, wondering: what was *that* all about?

JFK is a paranoid movie not only because it engages confusingly so many murky conspiracy theories, but because its bludgeoning montage technique, its avalanche of fragmented shots, does not allow you to take a step back and consider what part of its contents might be true and reasonable.

Underneath it all, the very nature of the shot is changing.

The pioneering films of Renoir, Welles and Ophuls (among others) in the thirties and forties had awakened a taste for a gliding, graceful camera that would track characters from room to room, exterior to interior. The 1950s may be seen as the golden age of this long shot, deep-focused, extended-take, spatially complex image: what French critic André Bazin and his New Wave followers championed as the aesthetic of *mise en scène*. Partly because CinemaScope's horizontality forced a slower cut, and encouraged the camera to explore the sides and backgrounds of the frame before cutting to another setup, partly because veteran directors like Ford, Hawks, Walsh, Hitchcock, Sirk, Lang, Ray, Mann, Preminger and Minnelli were all at the height of their powers during the fifties, and were sympathetic to a composed, deep-focus composition, the result was a feast of maturely classical, "realist" moviemaking, which linked characters to their environments, in a formal (some would even add spiritual) wholeness.

The sixties began the breakdown of this classical film grammar. Ironically, the very supporters of *mise en scène*, the New Wave directors like Godard and Truffaut, helped bring about its demise by their innovations: jump cuts and self-reflexive storytelling. Additionally, new (or newly rediscovered) technologies like the zoom, slow motion, freeze-frame, and split screen, began to be used like toys, puncturing the stately space of the classical composition. The era of fragmentation and rapid cutting had arrived. Television was certainly partly to blame, both for reducing the audience's attention span and for exerting a pressure on moviemaking toward quick close-ups and more shallow depth of field. Later, MTV would exert a specific influence in the direction of slick-magazine surreal, fricasseed visuals. Still, we might remember that, even without TV, "arty" film directors were moving away from the spatial integrity of classical filmmaking in the sixties: Arthur Penn's *Bonnie and Clyde* (1967) employed nu-

merous distancing and flattening devices, while Sam Peckinpah's *The Wild Bunch* (1969) used three times as many cuts
as a normal movie, not to mention slow motion and special
effects for blood.

In what way can I argue that the triumph of quick cutting, or montage, over a *mise en scène* aesthetic is somehow
connected to the decline of intelligence in American movies?
Well, it's like this: if we are no longer invited to enter an image on the screen and dwell there inwardly for more than
three seconds; if our eye is not given the time to travel from
one character's face to another's and then to the objects and
scenery behind or to the side of them; if we are being presented with too many close-ups that show us a very small
amount of visual information, which make one point and only
one point per shot; if we are not encouraged to develop *fi-
delity* to a shot, then we do not make as deep a commitment
to understand and interpret the material presented to us. A
scene is no longer, properly speaking, a scene; a shot is less
than an image. All is underselected; the necessity for rigorous
composition is negated; we are in a perpetual, perspectiveless
flux, a flux which defers judgment to a later, saner time,
which never comes.

A case in point is *Natural Born Killers*, directed by Oliver
Stone from a script by Quentin Tarantino. Not the worst film
ever by any means; in fact, filled with talent and brio. But in
the end this joyride (as in Stone's earlier movie, *The Doors*)
leaves us bewildered, as the first half hour's excitement gives
way to utter indifference. Masses of shots, some lasting less
than a second, are disgorged onscreen, and the serial killer's
hippie rationalizations ("I'm your shadow") are offered like
serious insights, and the net effect is that nothing is real, all
is presumably maya.

Thierry Jousse, editor of *Cahiers du Cinéma*, wrote a
piece in 1994 called "The Killers of the Image" in which he

tried to understand the long-range consequences of such filmmaking:

> Take, for example, Oliver Stone's film, *Natural Born Killers*. It's a child monster, a maelstrom of images, a whirlwind of colors and sounds, a sort of hash of gestures and movements, a magma of sensations and music. Can we speak here of the shot's composition? We need to find a new word to denote these incessant passages of images, simultaneously subliminal and convulsive—of electrons as much as projectiles. But decidedly, they're no longer composed shots. They're a space where everything is on the surface, like in a baroque sphere; where images never stop arriving, speeding into the eye and sliding over each other, in place of the old cinematic way, where the eye takes the road in order to scrutinize the shot. . . . It's a video environment, a big live show as well as a self-cannibalization of cinema by the media, or a sacrificial ceremony with the immolation of the frame and the invocation of new images.

Jousse goes on to say that the use of such images in Stone's and Tarantino's films approaches the sensation of a drug, a "film-trip." He likens the irresponsibility, the lack of consequences, in Tarantino's films to a cocaine high. "You could call it a stylistic exercise, but it's also the same sensation procured by cocaine, a drunkenness of the intelligence verging on the absurd, a feeling of superiority detached from reality. . . ." Ironically, Tarantino does not shun dialogue; in fact, his movies impress with their snappy talk. But the talk is designed to bounce back at us with a stylized, "off" quality, a tinniness further detaching us from reality, the way you hear words when you're high.

Roland Barthes once wrote an article in the fifties in which he compared the old movie spectator with someone "lying prone and . . . receiving cinematic nourishment rather in the way that a patient is fed intravenously." He then went on to praise the different situation in which CinemaScope placed the spectator: "Here . . . I am on an enormous balcony, I move effortlessly within the field's range, I freely pick out what interests me, in a word, I begin to be surrounded. . . ." It seems that we are back in a prone position, only now they are using harder stuff in the IV.

Those friends active in the industry tell me that the problems with American movies today begin with the structure of studio bureaucracy and decision-making. There has been a vast increase of studio functionaries, few of whom know how to read a screenplay, they say. It takes forever to get a script approved; and, on the other hand, some projects are approved without even reading the script because a validated name—a star or proven director—has expressed willingness to make it. (The aforementioned fiasco *Toys*, for instance, had Barry Levinson's and Robin Williams's guaranteed participation.)

More and more, I am told, action movies go into production without a final script; the gaps are patched over with last-minute wisecracks. In comedies, the whole process of screenwriting has changed drastically: it now resembles the *Saturday Night Live* method, with teams of gag writers sitting around a table bouncing one-liners off each other. *The Flintstones* had thirty-five writers working on it, and the result was not so much a shaped narrative as a series of riffs. At its best, like *Wayne's World*, this can be refreshingly anarchic, a postmodernist reproach to the well-made play; at its worst, say *The Flintstones*, you get an incoherent infomercial for marketed products, masquerading as a feature film.

But we must pull back from these sour, dyspeptic

thoughts. There is something in the discussion of the American movie industry as a whole that automatically distorts one's reflections in a pessimistic direction. Perhaps it is that the subject is too large to allow for nuanced discriminations. After all, films such as *Vanya on 42nd Street*, *The Hour and the Time*, *Schindler's List*, *Laws of Gravity*, *Quiz Show*, *Surviving Desire*, *Looking for Bobby Fischer*, *Fresh* and *Before Sunrise* all demonstrate signs of intelligent life in American movie-making.

One major source of intellectual complexity in American movies during recent years has been documentaries. I am thinking above all of the amazing dialogues between doctors and patients in Fred Wiseman's *Near Death*, of Errol Morris's wry explorations of the Dallas justice system (*The Thin Blue Line*) and Stephen Hawking's astronomical ideas (*A Brief History of Time*), of Ross McElwee's self-aware, probing autobiographical exposures, in *Sherman's March* and *Past Imperfect*, of Alan Berliner's brilliant family portrait, *Intimate Stranger*, and of Terry Zwigoff's extraordinary *Crumb*, about the cartoonist and his family. Good documentaries tend to make psychological connections between past and present that hip narratives shy away from: hence their more thoughtful, rounded context. Take *Crumb*: we not only see R. Crumb, but we hear the testimony of his excruciatingly articulate brother Charles, his mother, his ex-girlfriends, his children, and it becomes clearer how this hero of the New Vulgarity turned out the way he did. Such documentaries—marginal as they may be commercially—at least ensure the survival of intelligence in American films.

We are still faced with an anomaly. Why are they so much less afraid in Europe to make movies with intellectual discourse? Is it that the intellect is traditionally a less stigmatized, more alluring organ across the Atlantic, or is it a function of government-subsidized cinema? Whatever the answers, there can be no doubt that some heady films that tickle the mind as well as the heart continue to be made abroad, with comfortable audacity and without apology. For instance, Nanni Moretti's *Caro Diario* (which showed here briefly) is a delightfully nervy personal essay, in which the author muses on everything under the sun, like a modern-day Montaigne, complaining of his ailments, critiquing other movies, celebrating remnants of Roman urbanism. Moretti expresses his worldview through his tastes (high as well as low culture—Pasolini and *Flashdance*), which he defends in humorous or dyspeptic fashion. Eric Rohmer's *The Tree, the Mayor and the Mediatheque* contains long arguments between characters about ecology and town planning, without ever losing sight of the human drama. Indeed, the romantic sparks between a somewhat ill-matched couple (a provincial mayor, a Parisian novelist) get expressed mainly through their intellectual disagreements. The mind is perceived as an erotic organ, which requires its own stimulation, its own foreplay.

Rohmer has embodied for four decades a kind of happily intransigent, thoughtful movie *(My Night at Maud's, Summer, A Winter's Tale)* that permits extended dialogue, ideas, mental play. Equally important, Rohmer established the model for a low-budget, psychological cinema—restricted to a few characters, a few real locations, a contemporary story, no costly special effects or costumes—which scores of European films *(Un Coeur en Hiver, La Discrète*, virtually all of Jacques Doillon's and Rudolf Thome's work) have followed. The Rohmer model has also been taken up successfully by independent American filmmakers, such as Steven Soderbergh *(Sex, Lies and Videotape)*, Hal Hartley *(Trust, Simple Men, Surviving Desire)*, Richard Linklater *(Slacker, Before Sunrise)* and Jon Jost *(All the Vermeers in New York)*.

Both Moretti's idiosyncratic, personal essay style and Rohmer's psychological chamber drama are two approaches that American filmmakers might profitably follow if they are interested in seeing a less boastfully ignorant type of work onscreen. Or not. Maybe the solutions to this problem of cinematic brain drain will not come from mimicking Europe at all, but from our filmmakers finally coming to terms with the persistence of American intellectual life, its valid concerns, and the specific, Emersonian nature of the American mind.

This essay was contributed to a collection called Dumbing Down: Essays on the Strip-Mining of American Culture, *edited by Katharine Washburn and John Thornton. I was dubious about the volume's central premise, that American culture is getting dumber and dumber, which strikes me as somewhat reactionary; but I decided to participate anyway because I am so fond of Katharine and because this would give me a pulpit to express certain things I was brooding upon.*

Mary McCarthy once made the flip remark that "movies are one medium that cannot think." I think, as in many of her judgments about performing arts, that she was dead wrong; but it led me to wonder, How do movies think? and Do movies think? and How can we get them to think more? The attempt to answer those questions took the form of a trio of essays included here: this one, on resistance to intellectuality in the movies; another, on the essay-film; and a third, on the phenomenon of writer-directors.

IN SEARCH OF THE CENTAUR:
The Essay-Film

My intention here is to define, describe, survey and celebrate a cinematic genre that barely exists. As a cinephile and
personal essayist, I have an urge to see these two interests
combined through the works of filmmakers who commit essays on celluloid. But, while there are cinematic equivalents
to practically every literary genre, filmmakers tend to shy away
from the essay, and that in itself is intriguing. What it signals
to me is that, in spite of Alexandre Astruc's tempting utopian
term *caméra-stylo*, the camera is not a pencil, and it is rather
difficult to think with it in the way an essayist might.

Ever since I began looking for essay-films, the cinema
mavens I consulted were quick to suggest candidates that
seemed pretty far-fetched, given my idea of what an essay is.
I was told, for instance, that Brakhage's abstract film poems,
Jancsó's masterly tracking shots, Tarkovsky's transcendental
dramas, even the supposedly genre-subversive remake of *Little Shop of Horrors*, were all "essays" of one sort or another.
These examples suggested a confusion between a reflective,
self-conscious style and an essayistic one. While an essay
must reflect or meditate, not all meditative sensibilities are
essayistic. Take Brakhage: for all the mythic sweat of his writings or the lyrical satisfaction of his visuals, I am unable to

follow a coherent argument or know what he actually thinks about, say, the play of light on an ashtray for forty minutes. So let me propose that, rather than rushing in anxiously to fill the void, it might be important as a starting point to face the brute absence—the scarcity—of essay-films.

What exactly do I mean by an essay-film? To answer that I have to step back first and convey my sense of the literary essay. To me, the essay is as much a tradition as a form, and a fairly discrete one: prefigured by classical authors such as Cicero, Plutarch and Seneca, it crystallized with Montaigne and Bacon, thrived with the English familiar essay of Dr. Johnson, Addison and Steele, Hazlitt, Lamb, Stevenson, Orwell and Virginia Woolf, propagated an American branch with Emerson, Thoreau, Mencken and E. B. White, down to our contemporaries Didion, Hoagland, Gass and Hardwick. There is also a European strand of philosophical essay writing that extends from Nietzsche to Weil, Benjamin, Barthes, Sartre, Cioran and others; and a Japanese essay tradition that includes Kenko, Dazai, Tanizaki and so on.

It is easier to list the essay's practitioners than to fix a definition of its protean form. "A short literary composition on a single subject, usually presenting the personal views of the author," says the *American Heritage Dictionary*. While I defy anyone to boil down Montaigne's rambling late essays to a single subject or characterize them as short, I do agree that the essay offers personal views. That's not to say it is always first-person or autobiographical, but it tracks a person's thoughts as he or she tries to work out some mental knot, however various its strands. An essay is a search to find out what one thinks about something.

Often the essay follows a helically descending path, working through preliminary supposition to reach a more difficult core of honesty. The narrative engine that drives its form is "What do I *really* think about X?" not, "What are the conventional views I am expected to have?" For this reason the essayist often plays the nonconformist, going against the grain of prevailing pieties.

Essayists often cast themselves in the role of the super-fluous man/woman, the marginal belle lettrist. The obverse of this humility, Montaigne's "What do *I* know?" is a mental freedom and a cheekiness in the face of fashion and author-ity. The essayist wears proudly the confusion of an independent soul trying to grope in isolation toward the truth.

Adorno, in "The Essay as Form," saw precisely the anti-systematic, subjective, nonmethodic method of the essay as its radical promise, and he called for modern philosophy to adopt its form, at a time when authoritative systems of thought had become suspect. Nietzsche asserted famously that all philosophies were disguised psychopathologies. The essayist often begins with a confession of pathology, prejudice or limitation, and then in the best cases rises to a level of general wisdom that might be generously called philosophy.

Whatever twists and turns occur along its path, and however deep or moral its conclusions, an essay will have little enduring interest unless it also exhibits a certain sparkle or stylistic flourish. It is not enough for the essayist to slay the bull; it must be done with more finesse than butchery. Freshness, honesty, self-exposure and authority must all be asserted in turn. An essayist who produces magisterial and smoothly ordered arguments but is unable to surprise himself in the process of writing will end up boring us. An essayist who is vulnerable and sincere but unable to project any authority will seem, alas, merely pathetic and forfeit our attention. So it is a difficult game to pull off. Readers must feel included in a true conversation, allowed to follow thorough mental processes of contradiction and digression, yet be aware of a formal shapeliness developing simultaneously underneath.

An essay is a continual asking of questions—not necessarily finding "solutions," but enacting the struggle for truth in full view. Lukács, in his meaty "On the Nature and Form of the Essay," wrote: "The essay is a judgment, but the essential, the value-determining thing about it is not the verdict (as is the case with the system) but the process of judging."

I will now try to define the qualities that to my mind make an essay-film. Starting with the most questionable proposition first:

(1) An essay-film must have words, in the form of a text either spoken, subtitled or intertitled. Say all you like about visualization being at the core of thinking, I cannot accept an utterly pure, silent flow of images as constituting essayistic discourse. Ditto for a movie composed of images with incidental background noises, like Robert Gardner's exquisite *Forest of Bliss* or Johann van der Keuken's *The Eye Above the Well*; whatever their other virtues, these are not, to my thinking, essay-films. To be honest, I've never seen a silent-era movie that I could consider an essay-film. I have been told that Dziga Vertov's *Three Songs of Lenin* transmits its ideational content solely through its visuals. I grant that it delivers a clear ideological point, as does, say, Franju's *Blood of the Beasts*, but conveying a message of politics through images does not alone make an essay—or else we would have to speak of advertisements or political posters as essays. Both the Franju and the Vertov films seem (to use Vertov's label) "songlike," rather than essayistic.

(2) The text must represent a single voice. It may be either that of the director or screenwriter, or if collaborative, then stitched together in such a way as to sound like a single perspective. A mere collage of quoted texts is not an essay. There is nothing wrong with lots of citations or quotes in an essay (think of Montaigne), so long as a unified perspective is asserted around them. I know that Walter Benjamin used to fantasize writing an essay composed wholly of quotes, but he

never got around to it, and even if he had, it would not be what draws us to Benjamin, which is his compelling, tender voice and thinking process. When I read an Anthology Film Archives calendar description of an "essay-like" Japanese Super-B in which "some words are taken from Dostoevsky, others from Susan Sontag, Rimbaud, Bob Dylan, creating a string of overlapping images that ultimately build into an innate image," I don't even have to see it to know that it is not my idea of an essay-film.

(3) The text must represent an attempt to work out some reasoned line of discourse on a problem. I am not sure how to test this criterion; but I know when it's not there. For instance, Jonas Mekas's haunting text in *Lost, Lost, Lost* functions like an incantatory poem, not an essay.

By now it should be clear that I am using the term "essay-film" as a description, not an honorific; there are great cinematic works that do not qualify as essay-films, and highly flawed ones that do.

(4) The text must impart more than information; it must have a strong, personal point of view. The standard documentary voice-over that tells us, say, about the annual herring yield is fundamentally journalistic, not essayistic. Nor is Luis Buñuel's mischievous *Land Without Bread*, which parodies the faceless, objective documentary perspective while refraining from giving us Buñuel's own private thoughts about Las Hurdes, an essay-film. The missing element becomes immediately apparent when we contrast the film with Buñuel's lovely, idiosyncratic autobiography, *My Last Sigh*.

(5) Finally, the text's language should be as eloquent, well written and interesting as possible. This may seem less a category than an aesthetic judgment. Still, I include it because you would not expect to find, in a collection of the year's best essays, a piece written in condescendingly simple, primer diction; therefore you should not expect to hear such watered-down language in an essay-film. That such wonder-

ful writers of the thirties as Hemingway and Dudley Nichols should have, in attempting to reach the masses, used so cramped and patronizing a discourse in their narratives for Joris Ivens's *The Spanish Earth* and *The 400 Million*, when they could have written genuine essays, seems a sadly missed opportunity.

Those who regard the cinema primarily as a visual medium may object that my five criteria say nothing about the treatment of images. This is not because I mean to depreciate the visual component of movies; quite the contrary, that is what drew me to the medium in the first place, and will always hold me in thrall. I concentrate here on the value of the text, not in order to elevate words above visuals, or to deny the importance of formal visual analysis, but only because I am unconvinced that the handling of the visuals per se dictates whether a work qualifies as an essay-film. I will say more about the relationship between sound and image in this genre later. For now, permit me to look at a few examples.

My first glimpse of the centaur that is the essay-film was Alain Resnais's *Night and Fog* (1955). While watching it in college I became aware of an elegance in Jean Cayrol's screenplay language that was intriguingly at odds with the usual sledgehammer treatment of the Holocaust:

> Sometimes a message flutters down, is picked up. Death makes its first pick, chooses again in the night and fog. Today, on the same track, the sun shines. Go slowly along with it . . . looking for what? Traces of the bodies that fell to the ground? Or the footmarks of those first arrivals gun-bullied to the camp, while the dogs barked and searchlights wheeled and the incinerator flamed, in the lurid decor so dear to the Nazis?

The voice on the sound track was worldly, tired, weighted down with the need to make fresh those horrors that had so quickly turned stale. It was a self-interrogatory voice, like a true essayist's, dubious, ironical, wheeling and searching for the heart of its subject matter. "How discover what remains of the reality of these camps when it was despised by those who made them and eluded those who suffered there?" Meanwhile Resnais's refined tracking shots formed a visual analogue of this patient searching for historical meaning in sites now emptied of their infamous activity.

It may sound grotesque to say this, but I was more delighted with Cayrol's heady use of language than I was depressed by the subject matter—which in any case I knew all too well from growing up in Jewish Brooklyn. What stuck in my mind for years was that voice-over phrase: "The only sign—but you have to know—is this ceiling scored by fingernails." That "but you have to know" (mais il faut savoir) inserted so cannily in mid-sentence thrilled me like an unexpected, aggressive pinch: its direct address broke the neutral contract of spectatorship and forced me to acknowledge a conversation, along with its responsibilities.

A similar frisson occurred when, some years later, I was watching an otherwise conventional documentary, Nemec's Oratorio for Prague, about the events in Czechoslovakia in 1968. As the visuals displayed Russian tanks advancing on the crowd, the narrator said something like (I am paraphrasing from memory): "Usually we do not know where to pin the blame for massacres, we invoke large historical forces and so on. This time we do know who gave the order to fire. It was Captain ———," and the camera zoomed in on a Soviet Army man's head. Again I felt sort of an impudent tweak. Not that I had any idea who this Russian officer was, but I loved the sudden way the civilized elegy for Prague Spring was ruptured, and we were catapulted into that more basic Eastern European mentality of tribal scores to settle, long memories and bitter humor: that Russian pig may have mowed us down, but we hereby name him and show his face—just in case the millennium of justice ever arrives. I later identified that atypically malicious human voice on the commentary as an essayistic intrusion.

There are essayistic elements that color certain films by Chris Marker, Alexander Kluge, Jon Jost, Ralph Arlyck, Jean-Luc Godard, Jean-Pierre Gorin, Joris Ivens, Pier Paolo Pasolini, Dušan Makavejev, Jean-Marie Straub, Yvonne Rainer, Woody Allen, Wim Wenders, Hartmut Bitomsky, Orson Welles, Ross McElwee, Robb Moss; Alain Resnais's shorts, Fellini's *Roma*, Michael Moore's *Roger and Me*, Isaac Julian's *Looking for Langston*, Tony Buba's *Lightning over Braddock*, Morgan Fisher's *Academy Leader*, Cocteau's *Testament of Orpheus*, Louis Malle's *My Dinner with André*, Jonathan Demme's *Swimming to Cambodia*, and I'm sure many others that I've forgotten or overlooked. By no means will I be able to discuss all these in the limited space allotted. By zeroing in on a handful, I hope to convey a sense of the potentials and pitfalls of the form, as well as weed out the true essay-films from those that have merely a tincture of essayism.

The one great essayist in the film medium is Chris Marker. *Letter from Siberia* (1958), *The Koumiko Mystery* (1965) and *Sans Soleil* (1982) are his purest essay-films, though it seems that he has an inveterate essayistic tendency that peeps out even in his more interview-oriented documentaries, such as *Le Joli Mai*, or his compilation films, such as *Grin Without the Cat*. There is a tension in Marker's films between the politically committed, self-effacing, left-wing documentarist style of the thirties/Ivens tendency and an irrepressibly Montaignesque personal tone. He has a reputation for being elusive and shy—not the best qualities, on the face of it, for a personal essayist—and yet, perhaps because he evolved so diverse and complicated a self (ex-Resistance fighter, novelist, poet, filmmaker), he can emit enough particles of this self to convey a strong sense of individuality and still keep his secrets. He also has the essayist's aphoristic gift, which enables him to assert a collective historical persona, a first-person plural, even when the first-person singular is held in abeyance. Finally, Marker has the essayist's impulse to tell the truth: not always a comfortable attribute for an *engagé* artist.

A film such as *Letter from Siberia*, which seems at first the sympathetic testimony of a Western fellow traveler to the Soviet bloc, ends by coiling us in one contradiction after another. What keeps it on the Left is the good-humored, rather than sinister, tone in which Marker unveils the problematic aspects of Siberian life. In a characteristically witty passage, Marker interprets the same footage three different ways, based on three separate ideological positions, thus demystifying the spurious objectivity of documentaries, albeit with a lighter touch than that with which this operation is usually performed. The sequence also points to one of Marker's key approaches as a film-essayist, which is to meditate on the sound track, after the fact, on the footage he has shot. In Marker there is often a pronounced time lag between the quick eye and the slow, digesting mind, which tracks—months or even years later—the meaning of what it has seen, and this delay accounts for a certain nostalgia for the escaping present and a melancholy over the inherently receding reality of photographed images. It is like that passage in *Tristes Tropiques*, in which Claude Lévi-Strauss laments that the traveler-anthropologist always arrives too early or too late. In Marker's case, his camera arrives in time to record events, but his mind and heart take too long to catch up, not appreciating events sufficiently in the moment.

This time delay also allows Marker to project a historical understanding onto otherwise bland or neutral footage. The most dramatic instance of this occurs in the medal-bestowing ceremony in Cape Verde, Africa, shown in *Sans Soleil*. A year later, Marker tells us on the sound track, the President would be deposed by the man he is pinning a medal on. As he explains that the army officer thought he deserved a larger reward than this particular medal, we have the chilling sense that we are watching a bloody tragedy like *Macbeth* unfold at the moment the idea first crossed the upstart's brow. But as Marker tells us elsewhere in the film: "Ah well, history only tastes bitter to those who expect it to taste sugar-coated."

Sans Soleil is Marker's masterpiece, and perhaps the one masterpiece of the essay-film genre. How ironic, then, that Marker chooses the fictive strategy of a woman's voice (Alexandra Stewart's) reading passages from the letters of a friend, Sandor Krasna. This Krasna fellow is obviously a lightly fictionalized stand-in for the author, like Lamb's Elia. The film was assembled mostly during the seventies, a period when Marker was part of a political commune and preferred to downplay his auteurial signature (the line "Conception and editing: Chris Marker," buried in the long list of credits, is the only indication that it is his film), which may partly explain the diffident whimsy of hiding behind "Krasna." On the other hand, putting his comments in the third person has the distancing effect of giving a respect and weight to them they might not have commanded otherwise. As Stewart reads passages from Krasna's letters, prefacing them with "he once wrote to me" or "he said," the effect is almost like a verbal funeral portrait. Marker appears to be anticipating and celebrating, with mordant relish, his own death, projecting a more mythical figure of himself in the process.

"He wrote: 'I've been around the world several times, and now only banality interests me. On this trip I've tracked it like a bounty hunter.' " Place and homesickness are natural subjects for the essay-film: *Sans Soleil* is a meditation on place in the jet age, where spatial availability confuses the sense of time and memory. Unlike Wim Wenders, who keeps whining (in *Tokyo Ga* and elsewhere) that every place is getting to look like every other place—an airport—Marker has an appetite for geography and local difference; his lament is that, if anything, he feels at home in too many places. Particularly drawn to Japan, he visits his favorite Tokyo haunts, and the narrator reflects: "These simple joys he had never felt on returning to a house, a home, but twelve million anonymous inhabitants could supply him with them." Marker/Krasna is a man of the crowd, who revels in anonymity; a romantic who in San Francisco visits all the locations Hitchcock used in *Vertigo*; a collector of memories ("I have spent my life trying to understand the function of remembering") who explicitly associates recollecting with rewriting.

Marker's earlier Japanese film, *The Koumiko Mystery*, can be read as a sort of poignant power struggle between a lively young woman living in the present and a middle-aged filmmaker determined to turn her into past and memory through the process of infatuation. He sucks on her vitality, he "rewrites" her by meditating on her filmed image, thereby, perhaps, possessing her and her mystery in the only way he can.

Sans Soleil, a larger work, is about everything but the proverbial kitchen sink: time, emptiness, Japan, Africa, video games, comic strips, Sei Shonagon's lists, pet burials, relics, political demonstrations, death, images, appearances, suicide, the future, Tarkovsky, Hitchcock, religion and the absolute. What unites it is Marker's melancholy-whimsical, bacheloric approach to the fragments of the modern world, looking at them moment by moment and trying to make at least a poetic sense of them. "Poetry is born of insecurity," he says, "and the impermanence of a thing," at which point we see a samurai sword fight on television.

Given Marker's sterling example, and the video access "revolution," and with more and more conceptual artists and defrocked academics taking to Portapaks and cheap movie rigs, I half-expected to see a whole school of essay-films develop in the seventies and eighties. Not only did the technical potential exist, but a distribution circuit of underground venues, colleges and museums was in place, promoting "personal cinema" as an alternative to the commercial product. But the essay-film never really arrived. What took its place, instead, was an explosion of films that incorporated essayistic throat-clearings as but one of many noises in an echo chamber of aesthetic cross-reference that ultimately "subverted," to use current jargon, the very notion of a single personal voice.

It was the bad luck of the essay-film that, just as its technical moment arrived, the intellectual trends of the hour—deconstruction, post-modernism, appropriation art, the new forms of feminism and Marxism retrofitted with semiotic media criticism—questioned the validity of the single authorial voice, preferring instead to demonstrate over and over how much we are conditioned and brainwashed by the images around us. Not that these points are invalid, but they mute the essayistic voice: for if the self is nothing but a social construct, and individuality a bourgeois illusion intended to maintain the status quo, then the hip, "transgressive" thing to do is satiric quotation, appropriation and collage.

Some of the bright, experimental young filmmakers, such as Abigail Child, Laurie Dunphy and Anita Thatcher, produced "found footage" films, which mocked the patriarchy by deconstructionist editing. Others such as Trinh T. Minh-ha made what I would call "text films" (*Reassemblage, Surname Viet Given Name Nam*), which surrounded a subject such as colonialism or oppression of women through a reshuffling of voices and doctored footage. Steve Fagin's videos on Lou-Andreas Salomé and Flaubert's *Bouvard and Pécuchet* used Syberberg-like puppet stagings, with results that were intriguing, campy and elusive. DeDe Halleck and Anthony McCall dismantled and slyly reenacted Freud's Dora case in such a way that the filmmakers' politics were never in doubt, but their own interpretation of the case remained unclear.

These films are frightfully intellectual and effective up to a point in circling their chosen themes; and yet the last thing any of their creators would do is tell us directly, consistently what they actually think about their chosen subject.

A recent "collage film" by Yvonne Rainer, *Privilege* (1990), is a case in point: it mixes dramatic scenes, found footage, fake interviews, written texts, documentary sequences, and so forth, in a stimulating, braided exploration of menopause and racism. Jonathan Rosenbaum, defending this film in the *Chicago Reader*, wrote: "Approached as a narrative, Yvonne Rainer's sixth feature takes forever to get started and an eternity to end. In between its ill-defined borders, the plot itself is repeatedly interrupted, endlessly delayed or protracted, frequently relegated to the back burner and all but forgotten. . . . Yet approached as an essay, *Privilege* unfolds like a single multi-faceted argument, uniformly illuminated by white-hot rage and wit—a cacophony of voices and discourses to be sure, but a purposeful and meaningful cacophony in which all the voices are speaking to us as well as one another." Much as I sympathize with Rosenbaum's position, he is almost saying that all you have to do is recategorize some plotless stew as an essay and everything immediately belongs. Even essays have plots! Now it so happens that I admire Rainer's film, but I still cannot bring myself to accept a "cacophony of voices and discourses" as an essay. When I left the theater I was still unsure what exactly Rainer's argument was about menopause, or what she was trying to tell me about the relation between it and racism, other than that both involved feeling like an outsider. She would probably say, "I'm not trying to tell you anything, I'm trying to get you to think." Fine; so does an essay, but an essay also tells us what its author thinks.

Jon Jost is another independent filmmaker who has experimented on and off with essayistic elements. I recently checked out Jost's *Speaking Directly: Some American Notes (1972–1974)*, which the filmmaker himself refers to as an "essay-film," and found it insufferably irritating. In part my reaction is to Jost's solemn, humorless, self-hating, tediously lecturing persona. Granted, all essayists have the option to bring out the obnoxious aspect of their personality, but they usually balance it with *something* charming; in Jost's case I wanted to hide under the seat every time he came onscreen. Still, if he had made a true essay-film I could have applauded. But instead he created one more hybrid collage, with Vietnam atrocity stories and nightly-news broadcasts quoted simultaneously for ironic effect; with dictionary definitions suggesting something or other about linguistics; with fulminations against imperialism; cinema-verité interviews of his friends and lover; and large, smugly self-reflexive dollops informing us that this was a movie, as if we didn't know. Jost's autobiographical passages when he addresses the camera suggest the most potential for an essay-film; but he makes such vague, unprobing statements about his life or relationships—dismissing his parents in one sentence apiece as a war criminal and a cipher, respectively—that the self-analysis comes off as evasive and shallow. Perhaps all this is intentional; a self-portrait of an unlikable fellow. It finally seems to me, though, that Jost has not really attempted to understand himself, but simply subsumed his self-portrait in larger and more forgiving sociohistorical categories. (I am told that Jost redeemed himself with a much better essay-film called *Plain Talk and Common Sense.* If so, I suppose I look forward to being proved wrong.)

Clearly, the chief influence on early Jost, and indeed on most independent filmmakers who have selectively used essayistic maneuvers only to abandon or undercut them, is Jean-Luc Godard. Now, Godard may be the greatest film artist of our era, I will not dispute that. But strictly considering the

development of the essay-film, his influence has been a
mixed blessing. The reason is that Godard is the master of
hide and seek, the ultimate tease. Just when you think you've
got him, he wriggles away. When he whispers observations in
Two or Three Things I Know About Her, how can we be sure
those are really his opinions? He is too much the modernist,
fracturing, dissociating, collaging, to be caught dead expressing his views straightforwardly. (This raises an interesting side
issue: to what degree is the modernist aesthetic itself inimical
to the essay? Certainly the essay allows for a good deal of fragmentation and disjunction, and yet it keeps weaving itself
whole again, resisting alienation, if only through the power of
a synthesizing, personal voice with its old-fashioned humanist assumptions.)

Godard has often used the word "researches" in describing his filmic approach, particularly after 1968. "Researches"
implies a scientific attitude, enabling Godard to present, say,
deadpan ten-minute shots of an assembly line, ostensibly invoking, through "real time," the tedium that will encourage
us to empathize with the factory worker. (That is does not,
alas, but only makes us impatient with the screen, illustrates
what I would call the fallacy of real-time magic thinking.)
Generally speaking, "researches" is a good term for Godard's
nonfiction efforts, not "essays." The two possible exceptions
are *Ici et Ailleurs* (1974) and *Letter to Jane* (1972).

Ici et Ailleurs (Here and Elsewhere) is both Godard's surprisingly sincere effort to reflect on the frustration of making
a movie about the Palestinian struggle, and a typically modernist attempt "to weave a text and to tear it to pieces, to
build a fiction and to ruin its pretensions" (André Bleikas-
ten). Two voices, a "He" and a "She," chase each other on the
sound track, saying things like: "Too simple and too easy to
divide the world in two. Too easy to simply say that the
wealthy are wrong and the poor are right. Too easy. Too easy
and too simple. Too easy and too simple to divide the world

in two." Godard is here using the Gertrude Stein method of incantatory repetition and slight variation to create a cubist experience of language. It is effective in making us contemplate whether a truth is no less valid for being simple. But I would hardly call the text, with its blurted slogans undercut by verbal arabesques, an attempt at reasoned essayistic discourse.

Letter to Jane, on the other hand, is a closely reasoned, if nasty, provocation by two male-bonded ingrates, Godard and Jean-Pierre Gorin, against the female movie star who so generously collaborated with them on their otherwise un-budgetable feature, *Tout Va Bien*. There is something so pre-posterously unfair about their impersonal, didactic language as Godard and Gorin, like thought-police interrogators, critique the supposedly neocolonialist, ethnocentric angle of Jane Fonda's head as she appears to listen sympathetically to a Vietnamese peasant. *Letter to Jane* does open up new possibilities for essay-films, though, by audaciously resisting any pressure to dazzle the eye (the visuals consist mostly of the Fonda newspaper photo, with a few other stills thrown in), and allowing the voice-over to dominate unapologetically. Also, *Letter to Jane* solves one of the key problems of essay-films, what to do for visuals, by making semiotic image analysis its very subject. The result is, like it or not, an essay-film. And, for all its Robespierrean coldness, I mostly like it, if only because of its unshakable confidence in the power of expository prose.

Godard's ex-partner, Gorin, went on to develop a much more truly personal essay-film style in his own features *Poto and Cabengo* (1982) and *Routine Pleasures* (1985). In *Poto and Cabengo* Gorin takes as his departure point a seemingly sensationalistic true story about two sisters who invent their own way of speaking and turns it into a meditation on language acquisition. Just as Joan Didion and other New Journalism–trained essayists injected themselves into the story, so

Gorin's narration inserts his own doubts and confusions about what sort of film he is trying to make, thereby interrogating not only himself but the assumptions of the documentary genre. While it has become a cliché of the New Documentary to make the difficulty of getting the necessary footage the gist of the finished film, Gorin brings to this device a flexible, self-mocking voice (the expatriate filmmaker with the French accent, too smart and lazy for his own good) that is very engaging. In *Routine Pleasures* he dispenses entirely with a news "hook," cheekily alternating between two things he happened to take footage of, toy-train hobbyists and painter–film critic Manny Farber, and trying to weave a connection between these unrelated subjects (something about re-creating the world ideally?), if for no other reason than to justify his having spent European television-production money. The result is a perversely willed, unpredictable piece about the thin line between art and hobbyism (the film itself seems a demonstration of this), in which we learn still more about Gorin's inertial, seductively intelligent personality. By drawing closer to himself as a subject, however, he raises the ante of our expectation: for instance, having acknowledged Farber as his mentor, Gorin's discreet refusal to be more candid about Farber's personality and the dynamics of mentorship leaves one disappointed. In both features, Gorin seems hot on the trail of the essay-film, but is still too coy and withholding about sharing the fullness of his thoughts.

One of the natural subjects for personal essay-films is moviemaking itself, since it is often what the filmmaker knows and cares about most. There is already a whole subgenre of essay-films about the Movie That Could Have Been, Or Was, Or Could Still Be. Pasolini's *Notes Toward an African "Orestes"* (1970) is a sort of celluloid notebook into which the filmmaker put his preliminary ideas about casting, music or global politics for a project that never came to pass. Maybe by shooting these "notes," he used up the enthusiasm that might have gone into filming the classic itself. Given the murkiness of his *Medea*, I would just as soon watch an essay-film of Pasolini thinking about how he would do an *Orestes* in Africa as actually view the finished product. The opening sequences are promising: he casts by shooting passersby in the street, telling us, "This young man could be Orestes," shows a newsreel of an African military parade, saying, "These could be Greek soldiers," and conjectures hypothetical locations: "This could be the camp for the Greeks." He delivers ambiguous touristic impressions, such as "The terrible aspect of Africa is its solitude, the monstrous form that Nature can assume." He tells himself, "the protagonist of my film . . . must be the People," and keeps circling around the question of a chorus. So far so good. But then the film abandons these thoughts for ten minutes of Gato Barbieri noodling around in rehearsal, and an awkward, staged discussion in which Pasolini asks a group of puzzled African exchange students how they feel about the *Oresteia*.

What makes *Notes Toward an African "Orestes"* so tantalizing and frustrating is that a narrator of the intellectual and moral stature of Pasolini lets only slivers of his mind show through. Were he to have written an essay on the same subject, he would surely have struggled harder to pull his thoughts into focus. (Pasolini could be a very compelling and persuasive essayist). The final collage-form seems dictated clearly by the footage available at editing time, rather than any carefully evolved effort to understand. J. Hoberman sees it otherwise: "*Orestes* is a movie that requires an active viewer, the deconstructive narrative demands that you put Pasolini's film together in your head." I am all for the active viewer, but this seems to me letting Pasolini off the hook. "Deconstructive" should not become an all-purpose excuse for presenting unresolved, thrown-together footage.

A much more satisfying essay-film about the process of

moviemaking and what might have been is Orson Welles's *Filming "Othello"* (1978). This brilliant, if rarely seen, self-exegesis consists, for the most part, of Welles seated with his back to a television monitor, talking to the camera in order to have, as he puts it, a "conversation" about the making of *Othello*. Conversation is, of course, the heart of the personal essay tradition; Welles could hardly be naïve on this point, having claimed that he read Montaigne every day. He was certainly steeped in the French master's undulating, pungent discourse.

A famous raconteur and compulsively watchable actor, Welles through his own charisma solves the sticky problem of what to do about visuals in an essay-film, by simply filling the screen with himself talking. Suddenly we are face to face with our essayist, rather than hearing a disembodied voice. Cutaways to sequences of *Othello* (reedited), a relaxed luncheon discussion of the play between Welles and actors Michael MacLiammoir and Hilton Edwards, and footage of Welles addressing a Boston audience provide sufficient visual variety to his talking torso.

What is so refreshing about his talk is that he is speaking in an honest, maximally intelligent way about things he loves, Shakespeare and filmmaking. This Welles bears little resemblance to the arch poseur of late-night talk shows. Indeed, the audience is privileged to eavesdrop on a genius of the dramatic arts as he shares his thoughts and doubts about one of his most important productions. He is both musing to himself and seeming to dictate an essay aloud (though it was probably written out beforehand). On the other hand, he is also giving a performance, and we cannot help but judge him simultaneously as an actor, the way he whips his head from side to side or raises his eyebrows. Our awareness of the contrivance behind this seemingly artless conversation has been enhanced by Jonathan Rosenbaum's research on the making of *Filming "Othello"*: apparently it was shot over a number of years, with changing television crews operating under Welles's tight direction. (See Rosenbaum's "Orson Welles's Essay-Films and Documentary Fictions," *Cinematograph* 4, 1991.)

Welles tells us about the vicissitudes of filming *Othello*: how he was approached by an Italian producer who said, "We must make *Othello*"; how he had originally planned to shoot in a studio with fluid long shots and long takes, but after the Italian producer went bankrupt he was forced into improvised location shooting all over the map and quick editing to cover the shifts; how he had to hammer sardine cans into armor; and other war stories. He tells it exotically, "like a tale from Casanova," careening back and forth in his chronology, getting ahead of himself, digressing from meaty Shakespearian analysis to anecdote to critical response. "There is no way to avoid these—lapses into autobiography," he apologizes, as he begs our pardon later for rambling and failing to cite negative reviews. These apologies help to establish trust and rapport, in the classical manner of the personal essayist.

Vlada Petric notes (*"Filming 'Othello,' " Film Library Quarterly*, 1980) that, after reciting soliloquies of both Othello and Iago, as "a kind of compensation for the fact that the sound in the original print is poor," Welles "admits that his Othello 'does not do full justice to the play'; nevertheless he claims that the film is among his favorite works. . . . 'I think that I was too young for this part, and I wish I could have done it over again.' " The present film is, in a sense, the "doing it over."

Welles's other so-called essay-film, *F for Fake* (1975), is much less successful as such, largely because Welles seems more intent on mystifying and showing off his magician-Prospero persona than in opening his mind to us. I am never convinced that Welles is working hard to say all he can on the subject of counterfeit art; he is so taken up with a glib defense of artifice that he forgets to convey his own sincerity, something an essayist must do. He would rather have our tepid agreement that all art is a kind of lie than move us. Academic film critics, who overrate cinematic self-reflexivity and attention to the narrative "frame," adore the cheap joke he pulls on us when he promises that everything in the next hour will be true, then makes up some cock-and-bull story toward the end, without having told us the sixty minutes were up. Still, I'm grateful for *F for Fake*, because its florid, windbag Welles makes me appreciate all the more the wonderfully civilized, humane Welles of *Filming "Othello."*

Before he died, Welles was planning to make yet another cinematic self-analysis, *Filming "The Trial."* If you count in earlier Welles projects with essayistic elements, such as *Portrait of Gina* and *It's All True*, it is clear that he had become seriously devoted to the essay-film. Welles said himself in a 1982 interview: "The essay does not date, because it represents the author's contribution, however modest, to the moment at which it was made."

It could be said that all first-person narration tends toward the essay, in the sense that, as soon as an "I" begins to define his or her position in and view of the world, the potential for essayistic discourse comes into play. First-person narration in film is complicated by the disjunction between the subjective voice on the sound track and the third-person, material objectivity that the camera tends to bestow on whatever it photographs, like it or not. This tension has been cunningly exploited by the filmmakers who are drawn to the first person, such as Robert Bresson, Joseph Mankiewicz and Woody Allen. First-person narration in movies often brings with it a bookish quality, partly because it has so often been used in movies adapted from novels, but also because it superimposes a thoughtful perspective, looking backward on the supposed "now" of the film. Even an *I Walked with a Zombie* begins to seem studied and literary the moment we hear Frances Dee's narrative voice orienting us to events that began in the past.

First-person narrative also awakens the appetite for confession. Think of the strange accents of Meryl Streep's Isak Dinesen in the first *Out of Africa* voice-over: we wait for the shaky self-protectiveness of that voice to break down, become more unguarded, and the remainder of the film plays cat-and-mouse with this confessional promise (largely broken, it turns out).

One good place to start looking for shards of the essay-film might be movies with first-person narrators. Particularly autobiographical films, like Ross McElwee's *Sherman's March* and *Backyard*, Michael Moore's *Roger and Me*, Su Friedrich's *The Ties That Bind* and *Sink or Swim*, Ralph Arlyck's films, Tony Buba's *Lightning over Braddock*, Wim Wenders's *Lightning over Water* and *Tokyo Ga*, Cocteau's *Testament of Orpheus* and Joris Ivens's *Story of the Wind.*

Just as the diary is rightly considered a literary form distinct from the essay, so diary films such as *Sherman's March* and *David Holzman's Diary* obey a different structure than essay-films by following a linear chronology and reacting to daily events, rather than following a mental argument. Still, there are many overlaps between the two, as McElwee's thoughtful, digressive narrator in the wonderful *Sherman's March* (1986) demonstrates. Here McElwee plays with self-irony, ostensibly bidding for our sympathy while asking viewers to judge his bachelor persona as rationalizing and self-absorbed. Indeed, the last quarter of the film turns into a contemporary morality play in which the narrator relinquishes his power of judgment to his friend Charlene, who becomes the voice of wisdom and vitality, telling him what he is doing wrong with women. This pat turnabout does provide a conclusion, but it also reinforces the suspicion that McElwee wants us to read his "Ross" the way we would a fictional, self-deluding character.

Use of the first person invokes the potential for an unreliable narrator, a device we usually think of as reserved strictly for fiction; essayists from Hazlitt to Edward Abbey have toyed with a persona balanced between charm and offensiveness, alternately inviting reader closeness and alienation. The difference is that essayists keep the faith with their narrators, while McElwee finally leaves "Ross" hanging out to dry. It is an effective, even purgatively ego-slaying strategy, but it undermines the work's identity as an essay-film: however deluded he may be, the essayist must have the final word in his own essay.

Michael Moore's *Roger and Me* (1989) promises at first to be a model essay-film. The filmmaker sets up, in the first twenty minutes, a very strong, beguiling autobiographical narrator: we see his parents, the town where he grew up, his misadventures in San Francisco cappuccino bars. Then, disappointingly, Moore phases out the personal side of his narrator, making way for a cast of "colorful" interviewees: the rabbit lady, the evicting sheriff, the mystic ex-feminist, the apologist for General Motors. True, he inserts a recurring motif of himself trying to confront Roger Smith, GM's chairman, but this faux-naïf suspense structure becomes too mechanically farcical, and in any case none of these subsequent appearances deepen our sense of Moore's character or mind.

It is as though the filmmaker hooked us by offering himself as bait in order to draw us into his anticorporate capitalist sermon. The factual distortions of *Roger and Me*, its cavalier manipulations of documentary verisimilitude in the service of political polemic, have been analyzed at great length. I still find the film winning, up to a point, and do not so much mind its "unfairness" to the truth (especially as the national news media regularly distort in the other direction) as I do its abandonment of what had seemed a very promising essay-film. Yet perhaps the two are related: Moore's decision to fade out his subjective, personal "Michael" seems to coincide with his desire to have his version of the Flint, Michigan, story accepted as objective truth.

It must also be said that, unlike a true personal essayist, Moore resists the burden of self-understanding, electing to ridicule the inanities of the rich while not being hard enough on himself. The issue is not whether *Roger and Me* betrays the essay-film, a form that barely exists and that Moore may have no conception of. The real question is why filmmakers find it so difficult to follow a train of thought, using their own personal voice and experience to guide them? In Moore's case, there seems to be a more pressing political agenda. But another reason could be the huge difference between writing about and filming oneself. Filmmakers usually choose that career with the expectation that they can stay behind the camera, and I suspect that immense reticence or bashfulness may set in once a filmmaker who has taken center screen as the governing consciousness and main performer of an autobiographical film realizes how exposed he or she is. (And this exposure may far exceed what a literary essayist feels. Hence the dance of coyness and retreat, mentioned earlier in regard to Gorin.)

Roger and Me also raises the question of to what extent an essay-film can welcome and ingest interviews while still being true to its essayistic nature. At what point will the multiplicity of voices threaten a unified presentation of "the personal views of the author"? Of course, a film can be composed entirely of interviews and still exhibit a personal vision—Errol Morris's or Marcel Ophuls's documentaries, for example. But a personal vision is not necessarily a personal essay. Errol Morris's works, eccentric and personal as they are, do not seem to me essay-films. We can only guess what he is thinking as he exhibits the weird human specimens in *Vernon*,

Florida or *Gates of Heaven*, and our not knowing how we are supposed to interpret them is precisely the ambiguous point. Similarly, other nonfiction movies with essay flavorings, such as Marker's *Le Joli Mai* or Rouch and Morin's *Chronique d'un Été*, employ a degree of interview material that would seem, at least in my mind, to tip the scales away from the essay-film and toward the documentary.

The relationship between documentary and essay-film is uneasy at best. They are often mistaken for each other; frequently, a work starts off as an essay-film and then runs for cover in the protective grooves of the documentary. At times, however, they behave like two different beasts.

When Michael Moore made a splash with *Roger and Me*, he was at pains to tell reporters, somewhat churlishly, that he hated most documentaries and the standards of ethical documentary procedure. He also left the impression that he had invented a whole new type of movie, instead of acknowledging that there were other autobiographical filmmakers such as McElwee, Buba and Arlyck who had gotten there first.

To my knowledge Ralph Arlyck is, besides Marker, the one consistent essay-film maker. Arlyck, whose last two movies, *An Acquired Taste* (1981) and *Current Events* (1989), were both shown at the New York Film Festival (and hardly anywhere else), reported he was once on a panel discussion and described himself as a maker of essay-films, at which point some industry producer said with an incredulous sneer, "You mean like—*Thoreau?*" After that, Arlyck has been leery of using the term "essay-film," which may be even more box-office poison than "documentary."

An Acquired Taste is, in fact, a hilarious half-hour personal essay about the filmmaker's lack of commercial success, his jealousy and career envy, as seen against the American dream of rising to the top. Arlyck pokes fun at his pathetic go-getter attempts: there is one excruciating scene in which we watch him type out a grant application. "Increasingly I feel like the Ferdinand the Bull of filmmaking," he concludes. He prefers to stay home, play with the kids and make mild little films, while his wife flies off to France to defend her doctoral thesis. The Arlyck character comes across as a likable schlemiel, cousin to Woody Allen—not necessarily because he is influenced by Allen but because both are drawing from the same well of urban Jewish self-deprecating humor. (Indeed, listening to Woody Allen's digressive, epigrammatic narrators in films such as *Annie Hall, Hannah and Her Sisters* or his third of *New York Stories*, I have often thought that with a little push Woody could have ended up a natural essay-film maker—to the great chagrin of his bankbook. Perhaps his most original trick has been to smuggle contraband essayism into the fiction film.)

Arlyck, meanwhile, unabashedly and essayistically sticks to a single subject and presents his personal views about it. His feature-length *Current Events* tackles the question of how an ordinary individual should respond to the problems of the planet. It is essentially a film about a veteran of sixties protests—an over-the-hill ex-hippie, his sons call him— twenty years later, reflecting on the meaning of political commitment in the face of overwhelming world need and his own ideological skepticism. Since the subject is so much weightier than career vanity, the tone is more serious, and Arlyck strays further from home, interviewing people whose persistent commitment to doing good he finds exemplary—if impossible for him to imitate. He always brings it back, like a good personal essayist, to his own daily experiences, the examination of his own conscience. And there is the same intact Arlyck persona: the independent filmmaker and family man, puzzled, ineffectual, sardonic, decent and good-humored.

Of late, many women filmmakers have been making autobiographical films, using family memoirs as a springboard for personal reflection. Su Friedrich's *Sink or Swim* (1990), even more than her earlier *The Ties That Bind* (1984), is particularly noteworthy, in its complex, harrowing exploration of her relationship to her father. Though the film resembles a structuralist film-poem as much as an essay, Friedrich certainly demonstrates the possibility of making essay-films from a feminist perspective.

Another strong essay-film (or rather, videotape) is Vanalyne Green's A *Spy in the House That Ruth Built* (1989)—exemplary in its personal exploration of a subject (baseball), in the singularity of its first-person text and in its self-mocking humor and elegant language. Green weaves entertaining connections between the national pastime, erotic fantasies and the family romance. Here she is plotting her wardrobe for a shoot at the ballpark: "I wanted to go as a tramp, to look as if my head just left the pillow, and the gentle touch of a fingertip on my shoulder would topple me back into bed, where I would lie, framed seductively by the finest cotton and pastel pink sheets, smelling simultaneously of adult sex and a newborn baby's powdered bottom. . . . But how not to abandon that other part of myself—the adult woman with the twelve-page vita—while a child inside me was willing to whore her soul for a minute of eye contact with big Dave Winfield?" The visuals show us a witty assemblage composed of baseball paraphernalia, brief interviews and comically homemade, modest visual tropes. If the text seems wrenched at times into a too programmatically feminist line, Green recognizes the danger and stops herself, saying: "The more rhetoric, the less I said about me." In the end, she manages to say a lot about herself, in a manner that is broadly generous, forgiving and very appealing.

I began by pointing to the rarity of essay-films, without explaining why this was. Let me try to do that now.

First, there is the somewhat intractable nature of the camera as a device for recording thoughts: its tendency to provide its own thoughts, in the form of extraneous filmed background information, rather than always clearly expressing what is passing through the filmmaker's mind. True, the filmmaker may also register his thoughts through editing; but this does not remove the problem of the promiscuously saturated image.

Second, there may be, as Stanley Cavell has suggested, a sort of resistance on the part of motion pictures to verbal largesse. Screenplays today employ skeletal dialogue, following the received wisdom that the screen cannot "sop up" much language. Whether this is because of an inherent property in the medium, or because its limits have never been sufficiently tested (think of the novelty of Rohmer's *My Night at Maud's* when it first appeared—a real "talkie!"), the amount of rich, ample language a film can support remains uncertain.

Then there are commercial considerations: just as essay collections rarely sell in bookstores, so essay-films are expected to have little popularity; and films, after all, require a larger initial investment than books. Still, this uncommercial aspect hasn't exactly stopped the legion of experimental filmmakers, whose work often takes a more esoteric, impenetrable form than would an intelligently communicative essay-film.

Another reason has to do with the collaborative nature of the medium: it is easier to get a group of people to throw in with you on a fictional story or social documentary or even a surrealistic vision than to enlist their support in putting your personal essayistic discourse onscreen.

Of course, many independent filmmakers receive grants to make 16mm or video works that are ostensibly personal, and that they shoot or assemble alone; why don't *they* make more essay-films? I suspect there is a self-selection process attracting certain types of people into filmmaking as an art form: they revere images, want to make magic and are uncomfortable with the pinning down of thoughts that an essay demands. You would probably stand a better chance of getting a crop of good essay-films if you gave out cameras and budgets to literary essayists and told them to write their next essay for the screen than if you rounded up the usual independent filmmakers and asked them to make essay-films.

I anticipate a howl of protest: if what you are after is a polished literary text, why not simply write an essay? Why make a film at all? Don't you understand that the film medium has certain properties of its own? Yes, I do understand, but I continue to believe that it is worth exploring this underused form, which may give us something that neither literary essays nor other types of films can.

It seems to me that three procedures suggest themselves for the making of essay-films: (1) To write or borrow a text and go out and find images for it. I do not necessarily mean "illustration," which casts the visual component in a subordinate position. The images and spoken text can have a contrapuntal or even contradictory relation to each other. In Edgardo Cozarinsky's *One Man's War* (1984), the text, based on the late Ernst Jünger's diary as an officer in Hitler's army occupying Paris, is juxtaposed with archival footage from the period. The result is a stimulating clash between the ironic sensibilities of a left-wing émigré filmmaker and a displaced reactionary aesthete. But this is not really an essay-film, because Cozarinsky undercuts Jünger's words without providing a record of his own thoughts. (2) The filmmaker can shoot, or compile previously shot, footage and then write a text that meditates on the assembled images. This is often Marker's approach. (3) The filmmaker can write a little, shoot a little, write a bit more and so on—the one process interacting with the other throughout.

I do not know whether these processes, chance or the immaturity of the genre are to blame, but so far, almost none of the examples I would consider essay-films have boasted superlative visuals. Serviceable, yes, but nothing that could compare with the shimmering visual nobility of a dramatic

film by Mizoguchi, Antonioni or Max Ophuls. The one exception I know of is *Night and Fog*, a case in which the separation between visual stylist (Resnais) and screenwriter
(Cayrol) may have helped both images and text to reach the
same level of artistic ripeness. Even when a great cinematic
stylist like Welles tries his hand at an essay-film, the visuals
are nowhere near as interesting as those in his narrative features. *F for Fake* suffers from too much François Reichen-
bach, who shot most of its documentary material, and
Filming "Othello" is a conventional-looking, talking-heads
production made for German television. Marker employs a visual style that is notationally engaging and decentered (and
occasionally even mournfully beautiful, as in *Le Joli Mai*,
when he had the budget for better cameramen); but for the
most part, his visuals lack the syntactical rigor and elegance of
his language. Arlyck's texts have considerable complexity and
charm, but his visuals remain only one cut above the usual
neutral documentary or hand-held cinema-verité. It is almost
as though when the part of the brain that commands a sophisticated rational discourse springs into action, the visual
imagination becomes sluggish, passive and less demanding.

Here it might be argued by some that the power of cinematic images springs from the unconscious mind, not from
rational thought processes—that you need access to the irrational, the dreamscape, to make visually resonant films. I
wonder. So much of film theory is prejudiced in favor of the
oneiric that I doubt if I have the courage to take on these biases. All I know is that many of the film images that move me
most reflect a detachment, serenity or philosophical resignation toward the wakened world that I can only think of as rational. I do not want to sound too dualistic by implying that
essays are written only with the rational mind; certainly I am
aware in my own writing of tapping into unconscious currents
for imagery or passion. But I still say that the rational component predominates in the essay, which is a form par excellence

for the display of reasoning and reflection. So too should be the essay-film.

I am suddenly aware of many larger questions that my discussion may have failed to confront, and of my inability as a mere scribbler to answer any of them. Questions like: What *is* thinking? What is rationality? Is it possible to think exclusively in visual terms, or exclusively in language, without images? Will there ever be a way to join word and image together onscreen so that they accurately reflect their initial participation in the arrival of a thought, instead of merely seeming mechanically linked, with one predominating over or fetched to illustrate the other? Finally, is it possible that the literary essay and the essay-film are inherently different—the essay-film is bound to follow a different historical development, given the strengths and limitations of the cinematic medium? Have I been doing an injustice to the essay-film by even asking it to perform like a literary essay?

Look: it is perfectly all right if, after having read this, you decide to call a collage film like Makavejev's *WR*, or a duet in which the filmmaker disclaims agreement with the spoken text, like Cozarinsky's *One Man's War*, or a symphony of interviewed voices like Marcel Ophuls's *The Sorrow and the Pity*, or a dream vision like Brakhage's mythopoetic *Faust*, essay-films, just so long as you understand that you are using the term "essay" in a way that has very little relation to the traditional, literary meaning of the term.

I think this sudden frequency with which the term "essay-film" is being optimistically and loosely invoked in cinematic circles is not surprising. Right now, there is a hunger in film aesthetics and film practice for the medium to jump free of its genre corral, and to reflect on the world in a more intellectually stimulating and responsible way. When a good film with nonfiction elements comes along that provokes thought, such as Rainer's *Privilege*, it is understandably hailed as an essay-film. And it may turn out in the end that there is no other way to do an essay-film, that the type of essay-film I have been calling for is largely impractical, or overly restrictive, or at odds with the inherent nature of the medium. But I will go on patiently stoking the embers of the form as I envision it, convinced that the truly great essay-films have yet to be made, and that this succulent opportunity awaits the daring cine-essayists of the future.

Since writing this piece, I have seen a number of intriguing, thought-provoking nonfiction films that should be included in the discussion. There is Nanni Moretti's audacious Caro Diario *(see later discussion); Ross McElwee's skillful, moving, yet reticent continuation of his autobiographical musings,* Time Indefinite; *Alan Berliner's complex, funny documentary portrait of his grandfather,* Intimate Stranger, *about a man well loved by his colleagues but judged more harshly by his family; Patrick Keiller's* London, *an elegiac meditation on that city; Mark Rappaport's analytic reveries on Rock Hudson and Jean Seberg; and Godard's amazing, layered, multipart montage,* Histoire(s) du Cinéma, *which broods about the medium in an evocatively "essayistic" manner, insistently subverted by Brechtian distancings. Each of these works flirts with and hesitates to commit to the essay-film, bearing out my thesis that it is an increasingly tempting yet problematic form of our era. Finally, Marker's latest essay-film,* The Last Bolshevik *(1993), about the Russian filmmaker Alexander Medvedkin and the vicissitudes of mixing radicalism and art, triumphantly and confidently manages the form, reaffirming Marker's right to hold on to his title as "the cinema's only true essayist."*

WHEN WRITERS DIRECT

American movies today have charismatic actors, directors with cinematic panache, and production designers, cinematographers and special effects to die for. Where they fall down so often is their scripts. Many's the time one leaves the theater thinking: the screenplay just gave out—if only the characters had been fully drawn, the dialogue wittier, the plot better, more plausible.

One possible antidote—or at least hopeful tendency worth watching—may be found in the recent spate of motion pictures by writers-turned-filmmakers: ambitious, chewy, challenging pictures like John Sayles's *City of Hope*, David Mamet's *Homicide* and Paul Schrader's *Light Sleeper*. These films, whatever their defects, are blessed with more nuanced dialogue, social observation and psychological shadings than most. All of the above-mentioned *auteurs* developed their writing craft in forms other than or alongside screenwriting. Mr. Sayles is a prominent, prize-winning fiction writer; Mr. Mamet is probably our best contemporary American playwright; Mr. Schrader has two solid books of film theory and criticism to his credit. The diverse literary backgrounds of these filmmakers contribute, I would argue, to certain special assets—and problems—in their work.

The writer-turned-director is by no means a new phenomenon. Jean Cocteau, Marguerite Duras, Marcel Pagnol, Jean Genet, Bernard Blier, Preston Sturges, Norman Mailer, Susan Sontag, Sam Shepard, Peter Handke, Pier Paolo Pasolini come to mind. For purposes of argument, I am restricting the term "writer" to those who have penned books. If this seems high-handed toward screenwriters, I don't mean it to be. The pure screenwriter who goes into directing may be every bit as much a literary artist as the ex-novelist; but the training is different, and leads to different emphases. For instance, scriptwriters are taught to keep scenes short. A few lines of dialogue. Make your point and get out. A novelist or playwright, on the other hand, may be more inclined to let a scene meander and develop multiple points.

Such a scene occurs in John Sayles's *City of Hope*: a long, charming night walk during which Nick pays court to Angela, crossing half of Cincinnati in one continuous shot.

Sayles brings a broad novelistic canvas to *City of Hope*. His splendid novel, *Union Dues*, unearthed a coal-mining town. This time the social web is one of fragmented, warring urban "tribes"—construction workers, bosses, politicians, Blacks, Italians, Hispanics, gays, academics, cops—all at each other's throats, yet unable to ignore their interdependence. Presiding over all is the genially corrupt Mayor Baci, who says, "The next couple years in this town is gonna be one big yard sale, and then anybody with half a brain makes tracks and lets the Blacks and the Spanish duke it out over whatever's left." Baci is in the process of enriching himself further by tearing down poor people's housing to make way for a luxury development, Galaxy Towers.

Sayles, a progressive with strong working-class sympathies, seems drawn to an ensemble style for political as well as aesthetic reasons: he wants to examine the stresses on and endurance of community. Though his assessment of today's urban America may be grim, his amusement at each minor character's flamboyantly insistent presentation of self imparts an undercurrent of optimism and bounce to the film, making its title only partly ironic. Each of the fifty-odd speaking roles is written so as to be instantly distinct from the others. True, most are broadly outlined *types*. But if caricatures, they're shrewdly observed, live ones, like the goofy pair of bigoted housewife-complainers who make up the film's nitwit chorus. Everyone is given a little aria of expressive self-definition. Even Zip, an otherwise nondescript deadbeat arrested for a failed holdup, tells his partner, Bobby, who thinks maybe they're in Hell: "Naw. If it was Hell my mother would be in here with a copy of *USA Today* reading to us about which foods are mucus-producing when you've got a cold."

The most vivid parts of the film revolve around the African-American community, as their do-gooder councilman (brilliantly played by Joe Morton) attempts to satisfy both his impatient constituency and his conscience. The weakest parts, by contrast, center on young Nick (Vincent Spano), a drug-confused young man who is simply too much of a washout to carry as much of the meaning of the film as is ultimately deposited on his shoulders. This is not the fault of the actor, I think, so much as the writing. The whole "All My Sons" subplot, with its thick marinara of Italian family fights, father-son estrangements and the ghost of a dead all-Pro athlete brother who died in Vietnam, is maladroitly handled and unconvincing. What it suggests is that Sayles is better at presenting an expanding universe of new characters and milieux than he is at contracting it to a shapely conclusion and making us care about the fate of one individual.

In his book on film practice, *Thinking in Pictures*, Sayles writes: "Much is made of the difference between fiction and movies, yet in some ways they have more in common than movies and theater. It is possible in fiction to 'move the eye' around a setting, very much the way a tracking shot in movies does, by selecting and ordering details."

It must be said that Sayles has been better at this ordering of visual details in his fiction than his films. From the cinematic klutziness of *Return of the Secaucus Seven* and *Liana*
to the static postcardism of *Matewan*, Sayles has seemed—to
put it as charitably as possible—not a natural filmmaker.
There is very little pleasure to be derived in his movies from
elegance of framing, flow from shot to shot, or simply love of
objects and surroundings—the physical world in its material
aspect.

Mastering cinematic style can obviously be one of the
stumbling blocks for writers-turned-filmmakers (Preston
Sturges's visuals never did catch up with his wonderful
scripts). Previously, Sayles's two best-looking films were
Brother from Another Planet and *Baby It's You*. *City of Hope* is
a step up visually from anything he's done yet. It follows a
complex crisscross plan, tracking after one set of characters
and then pirouetting and following another set that crosses
the first one's path. The resulting simultaneity and overlap,
appropriately enough, helps to convey the excitements as well
as the stresses of big-city life. The pleasurable fluidity of the
visual scheme—derived more, one suspects, from *Hill Street
Blues* than *mise en scène* classics like *Rules of the Game*—unfortunately breaks down in individual scenes (as it does in
Hill Street) into mundane close-ups and two-shots, so that
there is nothing to mediate between the cinematically giddy
camera movements in the establishing shots and the routine
filming of the rest. It becomes a trick.

Sayles has written that "*Hill Street Blues* seemed a revelation when it first hit TV not only for the high level of the
writing and performance but for its successful grafting of the
soap-opera structure—repeating characters in parallel stories—onto the cops and criminals genre." What he doesn't
mention is the letdown when there's no commensurate payoff at the end of such shows for all the pulsating narrative
promise at the beginning. The same with *City of Hope*: as

long as Sayles keeps all the balls in the air, and the audience is kept moving from subplot to subplot, we are surprised or willing to suspend judgment. The problem is when the story has to be finally about something, when the filmmaker realizes he must make Something Bigger happen to pull it all together. So someone gets shot. And it feels melodramatic, rushed, expedient.

As a novelist, Sayles is well aware how to freight a narrative with a density of evidence, so that it springs with its own momentum into fateful consequence. But whereas a novel allows him time to gather his effects, the compressed temporal experience of film results in a spasmed, forced conclusion. Until that happens, *City of Hope* is enthralling.

David Mamet seems to have been an assured, "cinematic" filmmaker from his very first movie, *House of Games*. That debut film was a sinister, logical demonstration about con artistry, coolly refusing to manipulate audience empathy, and entirely successful on its own pleasurably Machiavellian terms. *Things Change*, Mamet's second feature, was rather lame, I thought, but again it looked terrific: not an ounce of visual fat on it.

Mamet, in his published screenplay *House of Games*, explains how he, as a writer, initially approached this problem: "The area in which I was most completely ignorant was, unfortunately, the visual. So I decided that in the absence of talent and experience, it would be good to have a plan. I decided to plan the whole movie, shot-by-shot, according to my understanding of the theories of Sergei Eisenstein." By this he means that, instead of trying to do anything virtuoso with the camera, he would film what he calls "uninflected shots," each meant to carry a simple action or piece of information, and let the emotions be generated by the editing.

In his own manual, *On Directing Film*, Mamet goes so far

as to say: "Always do things the least interesting way, and you make a better movie. . . . The more we 'inflect' or 'load' the shot, the less powerful the cut is going to be." (That's his theory, at least: the truth is that, from the start, Mamet's shots were uncommonly interesting, by virtue of their stylized lighting, crisp, weird framing and expressive use of decor.)

How odd that this hip, neophyte director should take up the theories of Eisenstein, which were developed for agitprop silent movies! But then, they dovetailed perfectly with his deadpan approach to directing actors, onstage or onscreen. "The acting should be a performance of the simple physical action. Period." The actor must not " 'help the play along' " by trying to inject motivation or hidden emotion, Mamet asserts. This may account for the slightly robotic look in many of Mamet's screen actors; their hands have been tied, they've been forbidden to project much character, because "there is no such thing as character other than the habitual action. . . ." Paradoxically, Mamet's people are often written with a psychological subtlety that almost invariably suggests a past, but which the aesthetic puritan or modernist in him suppresses. In *On Directing Film*, he scoffs at the whole notion of needing to know where a movie protagonist comes from, and stresses the crucial importance of withholding information, à la Hitchcock.

Mamet was on safer ground applying this deadpan, withholding approach to his first two films, which told claustrophobically small, logical stories. But his newest movie, *Homicide*—because it is warmer, deeper, more open to the real world, intellectually riskier—also points up the limitations of this style.

The film is about a homicide detective, Lieutenant Bobby Gold, who finds himself torn between his police force buddies—his "family"—and his conflicted, awakened loyalty to fellow Jews. The first half to two thirds of the movie is a high-wire act, brilliantly engrossing in its alternation of several police crises. Mamet seems utterly comfortable around law enforcement types and the police-procedural genre. When the two partners, played by those supreme deliverers of Mamettian patter, Joe Mantegna and William Macy, psych themselves up to break a case ("We'll be heroes. We'll strut"), we get both their jaded self-irony and the idealism that drew them to the profession in the first place.

Gold, investigating the murder of an elderly Jewish shopkeeper, is reluctantly affected by the fears of the Jewish community, who see the crime as part of a larger anti-Semitic pattern. Mamet's city is another, fiercer jungle of urban tribalism. One would dearly like to know something more about Lieutenant Gold's past, if only to understand how an apparently sophisticated big-city Jewish cop could have given so little thought before to his outsider status as a Jew. He seems so shrewd in matters of police work that his guilelessness and manipulation by a Jewish terrorist group is also hard to accept. He is asked by them to commit a crime: blow up the headquarters of a neo-Nazi group. That he does so, with so little advance motive, seems almost an *acte gratuite*—Mamet dares the audience to accept it on nothing but narrative faith. For the sake of so gutsy a film, I'm even willing. But it's harder to swallow that a cop as responsible as Gold is would then while away the time yakking in a diner and be late for a big stakeout, thus endangering his partner's life. That a homicide detective like Gold is capable of violence, I can accept; rank unprofessionalism and tardiness, no.

All this takes place within twenty-four hours. Could it be that Mamet's training as a playwright, respectful of the Aristotelian unities, led him to overcondense onscreen the amount of plot time necessary to bring about so huge a revolution in Bobby Gold's psyche? Unfortunately, for all of actor Mantegna's quiet ferocity, we see so little of Gold outside his job, learn so little about him, that we are left with the transformation of a cipher.

Homicide has such daredevil energy and intensity that it almost, but not quite, carries us past the many loose ends and red herrings that Mamet unleashes without knowing what to do with. Before the film starts to fall apart from its own conspiratorial complications, it manages to touch some very disturbing nerves on the theme of secular Jewry's guilt. It is to his credit that ultimately Mamet does not opt for a convert's polemic, but leaves us uneasily grasping the wrongness of all sides. The deeply disenchanted look on the face of the old black woman, the mother of a fugitive killed by Gold's botching of the stakeout, is a searing moment—a negative epiphany. But not entirely earned: too many shortcuts have been taken to get to that harrowing image.

Mamet's dialogue is both a glory and a disturbance. He has X-rayed the way we speak—the Ping-Pong slams, the herky-jerky stalls ("What I'm saying"), the odd abstractness of American talk, its class distinctions—with exactitude, so that Common Speech itself becomes a shadow character. On the other hand, the dialogue is so self-conscious that it cannot help but pull us out of the drama, if only to gasp in admiration. As with much minimalist fiction, the buzz of recognition derived from such demotic accuracy also undercuts the mimesis.

The metallic flatness of speech is foregrounded by Mamet's refusal to provide his characters with self-awareness. For all Bobby Gold's articulate street toughness, he is entirely unable to reflect on what is happening inside him. This total absence of introspection, of an inner life, puts a false ceiling on the drama.

Visually, *Homicide* is more sensuously fluid and freewheeling than Mamet's other films, tracking characters from room to room, interiors to exteriors. He has abandoned the Eisenstein theory of static, uninflected shots for continuous, long-duration takes. But, while making the switch, he has not altered that Mamet acting style which was devised for short shots and staccato beats; and the results have an eerie formality.

In essence, Mamet has come up with a filmic approach as stylized as Kabuki, while arguing in print that he wants only to make no-nonsense motion pictures and obey the KISS principle (Keep It Simple, Stupid). The disparity between his theories and outcomes makes for an awkward, not unappealing tension which is characteristic of writers-turned-directors. But then, Mamet cheerfully admits, "I've always been more comfortable sinking while clutching a good theory than swimming with an ugly fact." If he has yet to do something in film at the level of his best theater work, like *Glengarry Glen Ross*, he is nevertheless evolving a personal cinema which may yet stand comparison with that of anyone of his generation.

Paul Schrader is another writer-turned-director whose idiosyncratic films seem to point toward an imaginary, utopian cinema he would like to see made, but can only partly pull off himself. There is the whiff of theory in all nine of the features he has directed (including *American Gigolo, Cat People, Mishima, Patty Hearst* and the current *Light Sleeper*). Part of what makes them so tantalizingly original, if frustrating, is their struggle to reconcile perhaps irreconcilable polarities: between the contemplative and the violent, the demands of art films and commercial movies. It is as though Schrader were trying to yolk Robert Bresson to Sam Peckinpah in the same movie. His scripts for Martin Scorsese *(Taxi Driver, Raging Bull* and *The Last Temptation of Christ)* erupted with some of these same dichotomies, although Scorsese's nervously consistent style elided the schism.

Schrader began as a film critic in the sixties; his first book was a densely argued, groundbreaking study, *Transcendental Style in Film,* about such meditative directors as Bresson, Dreyer and Ozu. He has since published a second book,

Schrader on Schrader, which consists of his critical writings and statements on filmmaking. With Sayles, Mamet and Schrader—each the author of a manual on film practice—we are a long way from those wily old Hollywood veterans like John Ford or Raoul Walsh who clammed up about their craft decisions.

It is hard, in fact, to imagine a more articulate, honestly self-analytical filmmaker than Paul Schrader. Perhaps because he started as a film critic, his ex-colleagues have begrudged him his rightful place as one of our major directors. No doubt they are right in saying his films are flawed; but a flawed Schrader film tends to be meatier than the timid perfections of many others. And *Patty Hearst*, his best film, is that rarity: a pure, uncompromising American art film made with studio money.

Schrader himself attributes the "repressed" air of his movies to being raised in a strict Calvinist household and, unlike Spielberg or Coppola, watching very few movies as a child. "When Pauline Kael writes of me, as she did, that *Patty Hearst* is the work of a brilliant filmmaker who lacks the ability to make the audience feel, it's something I hate to hear and I certainly don't want to agree with it, but to the extent to which it is true it comes from the fact that I'm a filmmaker who never learned to feel about film during his formative years."

His film stories are usually about characters who themselves can't feel or love (like Julian in *American Gigolo*), are made numb (Patty Hearst) or act out hysterically (Travis Bickle, Jake LaMotta) to mask the problem of nonfeeling.

His new movie, *Light Sleeper*, is both an extension of this preoccupation and a breakthrough into greater emotional expression. It's about another of what Schrader calls his "lonely, self-deluded, sexually inactive people." John DuTour (Willem Dafoe) is an insomniac drug dealer spreading numbness, making his rounds through downbeat nighttime New York, reporting back to his boss (Susan Sarandon) to drop off the proceeds and order some takeout food, then going home to his empty apartment where he scribbles diaries in school notebooks, tossing them out when they're full.

But after running into his ex-wife Marianne (Dana Delaney), he comes alive with romantic ache, tries to woo her back, and the film takes on some of his desperate vulnerability. *Light Sleeper* is Schrader's least "cool" movie. In a poignant hospital cafeteria scene, Marianne disputes her ex-husband's claims that they used to be "magical" together: "You took off for three months without telling me and called once. That's how magical we were. You were an encyclopedia of suicidal impulses. . . . Nobody could clear a room like you, John. And the friends, you may have noticed, turned out to be mine, not yours. I envy you. A convenient memory is a gift from God."

The dialogue throughout is sharp and pungent. Schrader, who has always displayed a feel for the sleazy underside, captures the New York drug demimonde with moody, knowing details. The picture is stocked with memorable cameos, like a Hasidic money-launderer attracted to Susan Sarandon, a cokehead who wants to debate medieval theology, a skeptical Hispanic gun salesman and Marianne's gawky kid sister. Schrader's filmmaking technique is understated, mobile, skillfully precise; whatever problems he says he had in transforming himself from a word thinker to a visual thinker, both are clearly second nature to him now.

Which is not to say that *Light Sleeper* works entirely. Dafoe, who appears in every scene, finally gets on one's nerves with his haggardly morose one-note performance. Some of that is the script's fault: for all the evocative voice-over diaries given the main character, they tell us little about the guy. He is finally a passive, somewhat dumb, empty vessel awaiting a miracle. Schrader has expressed interest in the question: "At what point does the individual become archetypal?" Whatever the point, the character must first have been rendered as an individual.

Schrader's other, spiritual agenda is to build a movie around one "emotionally blinding moment. . . . That moment is the 'transformation' when all the bland characters, dull plots, and flat images can merge into the new images, which the viewer, now naked of 'screens,' will help to create. 'There must,' Bresson says, 'at a certain moment, be a transformation; if not, there is no art.' " But, as Schrader himself admits, this is hard to do if you are unwilling to go the Bressonian route of austerity and denial of spectacle. "One of the problems I've run into is that it doesn't really work in the commercial cinema because in order to get those blinding moments you have to deny so much, and if you do too much denial then you're out of commercial cinema. So what I've tried to do is a little bit of both. I've mitigated the denial, but then of course the blinding moments don't stand out so much."

There is, in fact, one blinding moment of considerable pain and power in *Light Sleeper*: Marianne's suicide. But then, Schrader feels obliged to settle scores with the "bad guys" via a Peckinpah-ish shootout. This morally murky revenge leaves one wondering about the protagonist's sanity. However, it does conveniently land DuTour in jail for yet another ending that allows Schrader to honor the finale of Bresson's *Pickpocket*, of which he wrote so enamoredly as a young film critic: "In a shatteringly tender scene he kisses her forehead, she his hand, and he says through the prison bars, 'How long it has taken me to come to you.' " The first time he quoted this redemption-through-grace finale was in *American Gigolo*, with Lauren Hutton rather absurdly standing in for the French girl, Jeanne. This time Jeanne is played by a savvy Susan Sarandon; but so little romantic chemistry has been generated earlier between Dafoe and Sarandon that the scene feels merely dragged in like the director's security blanket.

I find it curious that Schrader, Mamet and Sayles have all given us new films with superb minor characters but fuzzy, underconceived blobs for their protagonists. It is conventional movie wisdom, I realize, that if you want the audience to identify with the hero, a too specific main character might prevent that from happening. But I can't help wondering if, in wanting to make films with (theoretically) wide appeal, they were lured into writing dumber than necessary main characters. I hope their future protagonists will be more intelligent and self-aware: not necessarily intellectual, but worldly, onto themselves and others, as so many characters were in the best-written talkies of the thirties and forties.

It's also curious that all three of these thoughtful films come a cropper when they reach for violent plot solutions. It is as though Sayles, Schrader and Mamet have all bought the standard line that movies must be about "action." This is true, up to a point, particularly with American movies; but excessive faith seems to have been placed in the "magic" of movies to leap over gaps in narrative plausibility, simply by inserting an explosion. The pressure to "make something happen" has catapulted these three films into some very questionable third acts.

We have seen how screen narratives are just as likely to get derailed in the hands of writers-turned-directors as anyone else's. The problems occur not so much in the mechanics of directing as in the scripts themselves. David Mamet astutely says that "finally, the production is only as good as the script." The recruitment of writers into the directorial ranks is thus no insurance against half-baked screen stories. But it does seem to have produced a crop of films that are literate, complex and challenging.

THE IMAGES OF CHILDREN IN FILMS

Serious narratives about the inner lives of children tend to be rare onscreen, for obvious commercial reasons. They do not make good Friday night date movies. Studios shy away from projects without marquee names, and the days of the child star (Macaulay Culkin notwithstanding) are over. Those G-rated family entertainment movies built around children, such as *Home Alone* or *Honey, I Shrunk the Kids*, make no pretense of scratching beneath the surface of photogenic tykes. It is a truism of American screenwriters that you should give your best lines to the kid, the joke being that the child thinks like an adult—is an adult, for all intents and purposes, while camouflaged as a minor, like the overknowing Mr. Culkin, who perfected the art of resembling a malicious midget.

The usual problem with portraits of children in movies is the lack of individuated characters: each child is made to stand in for children per se, reflecting the filmmaker's warmly positive or hostile feelings toward this minority. Most often, the child is sentimentalized as an Innocent *(Forbidden Games)* refreshingly free from moral constraints, inhibitions, logic: "they live in a state of grace," to quote Truffaut's unctuous *Small Change*, which demonstrates the point by having a child fall out of a window without getting hurt.

The English are big on the child as Disenchanted Innocent, discovering that his parents or heroes have "feet of clay" (see *The Fallen Idol* or *Whistle Down the Wind*). Losey's *The Go-Between* at least acknowledges how quickly some children would like to lose their troublesome burden of innocence and get in on the adults' action.

Another archetype is the child as Monster, from W. C. Fields's wickedly comic clash with Baby Leroy in *It's a Gift* to actual horror movies, like the *Village of the Damned* series and *The Exorcist*, wherein the offspring acquire secret powers or run amok. In horror films, the child/dybbuk must be destroyed; in comedies, tamed. (The Taming of the Brat theme has a long tradition from *Ransom of Red Chief* to the more recent *I'll Do Anything*.)

The child may serve as an extension of the parent's ambition (*Bellissima*, *Bigger Than Life*) or merely as a kind of background static to adult life. In the latter, the child is brought in like a prop to intensify the adult protagonist's situation. If the hero is in a bad mood because of, say, money worries, his son bounces in asking him for a dollar. Conversely, if the marital-discord plot takes a conciliatory turn, their children are made to jump on the bed between the parents.

We must not forget the child as Victim, made to serve as emotional or physical pincushion for the world's casual cruelties. Postwar neorealist classics, such as De Sica's *Shoeshine* and *Bicycle Thief*, and Rossellini's harrowing *Germany Year Zero*, led the way in this street-urchin subgenre (followed by *Los Olvidados*, *Pixote*, *Salaam Bombay*, etc.). The child amateur, more seen than heard, lent the perfect semidocumentary presence to the neorealist aesthetic, walking through blighted war ruins with haunted, saucer eyes, taking it all in. Clearly, these films contributed to a grittier, less sentimental portrayal of childhood. Yet they also fostered a stylistic tic: the tendency to fixate (usually in close-up) on the kid's wounded baby face in the moment of being marked by life's lessons.

Many movies about children equate a child's suffering, consciously or unconsciously, with the Passion story. The cruel older sibling, the incontinent embarrassment, the parental rejection or unfair judgment, become childhood's stations of the cross.

Still, none of these qualifications are meant to deny that there has been a small, persistent tradition of quality movies centered on a child's perspective, which have managed to find an audience. Without being exhaustive about it, they include classics such as *Zéro de Conduite*, *Shoeshine*, *Bicycle Thief*, *The 400 Blows*, *Germany Year Zero*, *Mouchette*, *The Fallen Idol*, *Meet Me in St. Louis*, *A Tree Grows in Brooklyn*, *Pather Panchali*, *The Quiet One*, *The Little Fugitive*, *I Was Born But*, *Ohayu*, *Boy*, *Seven Up* and *Naked Childhood*, as well as more recent pictures like *Stolen Children* and *The White Balloon*.

Two thoughtful movies, recently released, underscore the richness of staying close to a child's point of view, as well as the potential risks involved. One is an Australian film, *The Quiet Room*, written and directed by Rolf de Heer, which focuses on a seven-year-old girl who stops talking, in response to her parents' open quarreling and threatened separation. The other, *Ponette*, is by the veteran French filmmaker Jacques Doillon, and it centers on a four-year-old girl after the death of her mother. Both are alternately painful and exhilarating to watch, evoking that experience of reluctant self-awakening that Thomas Mann called "disorder and early sorrow."

In *The Quiet Room*, we enter directly into the child's point of view through an interior monologue that is almost continuous. Never has extensive voice-over seemed more necessary: since the girl (acted with riveting sangfroid by the director's round-faced, blond daughter, Chloe Ferguson) has stubbornly taken a vow of silence, it is the only way we can be privy to her thoughts. We watch as she plays with her Barbies ("I'm a bit old for this really, but it's what I'm feeling"), parries her parents' attempts to get her to speak ("I'm not a baby that you can fool so easily") and reproaches them for their obtuseness to her and cruelty to each other. Lying in the dark, she tries to imagine herself elsewhere as they fight in the next room, enacting wrenching scenes from an unhappy marriage.

The girl in *The Quiet Room* wants a dog, hates the city where there's "no room for dogs to poo" and fancies that if they were to live in the country all their problems would be solved. She longingly recalls her earlier life, when she was an oblivious three-year-old, as a Golden Age for the family. It may be questioned how much she is idealizing this earlier time: no doubt some signs of her parents' conflicts were already beginning to show. Yet, because the narrative stays so close to the girl's viewpoint, offering no other source of information to correct hers, we are left with the impression that the filmmaker himself shares many of the girl's preferences: for country over city, naïveté over experience, children over adults.

What are we to make of the girl's superiority toward her parents, in thoughts such as "I wonder why adults don't have any imagination?" or "Why don't they listen to what makes sense?" Are these only hers, or the filmmaker's sentiments as well? There is something presumptuous to begin with about an adult's attempt to represent a child's point of view. In the effort to bridge the gulf that separates adults from children, a sympathetic filmmaker may be too glibly lured into ceding the moral upper hand to the child.

The main challenge for movies that adopt a child's point of view is that the filmmaker must insinuate some detachment from the child's subjective assessment of the adult world, or risk faux-naïve distortions. Accepting the child-hero's perspective uncritically, never questioning the validity of his or her judgment, seems to spring from a displaced adult narcissism, masquerading as exquisite sympathy for the child-surrogate. The child is made to act out the adult artist's fantasies of purity, spontaneity, victimhood and indomitability. The audience, meanwhile, is called upon to feel only pity (or cozy self-pity, for its own "inner child"), and to leave more complicated moral judgments at the door.

Films about children's inner lives tend to divide between those that merely abhor the loss of innocence and those that see the process as, in part, salutary and in any case, unavoidable. The better, more complex films tend to be the latter. Since most children do not feel themselves to be innocent, it falsifies to render them as guiltless. (Indeed, the best parts of *The Quiet Room* show the girl brattily manipulating her parents into fury or guilt.)

Another problem with trying to see through a child's eyes derives from the medium itself: that larger contradiction between following one character's viewpoint and the nature of film. Narrative point of view is subjective, whereas the camera always registers more of the objective, surrounding world than would correspond to an individual's consciousness. And if the narrator is seen in every shot, he or she cannot help but become objectified. In *The Quiet Room*, De Heer has employed various techniques to intensify the sense of being inside a child's head, from exaggerated lighting to upturned camera angles emphasizing adults towering over children. These somewhat coarse stylizations of subjectivity, together with the restriction of the action to one apartment, contribute to *The Quiet Room*'s claustrophobic ambiance. The result is a remarkably single-minded film—both its strength and weakness.

By contrast, *Ponette* seems promiscuously expansive in its minglings with the world. Director Doillon makes no attempt to restrict Ponette's compass: indeed, he surrounds his grieving protagonist with relatives, teachers and most important, other vividly observed children (cousins, classmates). As in his earlier films, Doillon's method is to stay on top of his characters, using an intimate, mobile camera attentive to daily crises and inner adjustments. With patience, warmth and a minimum of melodrama, the story of a child coming to terms with the harshest blow imaginable, the death of a mother, realistically unfolds.

"In grief the world becomes poor and empty," wrote Freud in *Mourning and Melancholia*. But the wonder of *Ponette* is that this impoverishment opens up unexpected vistas. At the heart of the film is a miraculously nuanced, affecting performance by dark-haired little Victoire Thivisol, who won the Best Actress award at the 1996 Venice Film Festival, as Ponette. Loyal to her mother, she tries to summon the absent parent with prayers, presents, magic words, songs, vigils. And, of course, denial. Since everyone tells her that her mother is with God, the little girl decides she needs a better relationship with Him, so that she can make a deal and get her mother back. Her father, charismatic and atheistic, alone takes a brutally straight tack with her: "Lying won't make the hurting stop." These father-daughter scenes have an electricity which shows the possibilities when adult and child characters are actually allowed to communicate with each other onscreen.

As Ponette threads her way through the advice and local superstitions regarding death, the film itself walks a thin line between belief and doubt, consolation and despair. Rather than trying to catch with tilted camera angles a child's point of view, it enters fully into the rhythms of childhood, where playing and reality merge. As one cousin puts it: "Ponette's playing at waiting for her ma." Ponette's precocious task is to come to terms with the irreversibility of time. When a teacher tells Ponette to be more like Jesus, who "is joyful as a child," the girl sensibly responds: "It's not joyous being a child."

Too often, children are pressed into film narratives as either emblems of joy or martyrdom. Deifying children, as in Bertolucci's profoundly silly *Little Buddha*, comes easily to adults and is ultimately patronizing. What is more difficult for the film artist is to render a child not as symbol but as complex, flawed individual, groping to make sense of the world. At the very least, *Ponette* and *The Quiet Room* give us two more examples to add to the gallery of cinematically memorable characters who happen to be underage.

THE 32ND NEW YORK FILM FESTIVAL

The word out of Cannes and elsewhere this year was: slim pickings. So I was pleasantly surprised at how strong, overall, the 1994 New York Film Festival turned out to be. Not that there were any masterpieces (save Tati's revived *Playtime*), but every one of the programs seemed absorbing enough to take seriously.

Movie journalists used to cushier junkets often carp that the NYFF is not much of a *festival*, in the bacchanalian or smorgasbord sense—that they can see the same films and much more at Cannes or Toronto. True, the NYFF is short on parties and venues, and offers only twenty-five or so programs; but this juried exclusivity, this narrowing to a presumed "best," permits a concentration in which every film counts, resonates against the others. It is not a clearinghouse; it performs a different, more austerely discriminating function, which inevitably puts more pressure on each film to deliver the goods.

I should explain that the New York Film Festival is one of the constants in my life, a seasonal ritual mixed up with the onset of fall, the Day of Atonement, new classes to teach and the climax of the baseball season (alas, no distraction this year). Complicating a lifelong habit as audience member is the fact that for four years I served on the NYFF's selection committee, which gave me an insider's perspective into its group processes, and friendships depriving me of potential sourness toward the institution. My judgment about the films themselves, however, has not been affected: I still love some, hate others and feel ambivalent about the majority—as I did when I was on the selection committee.

During that time, I came to understand, though the criteria were never spelled out, that there *was* such a thing as a New York Film Festival film. It had to have a certain gravity or density to hold an auditorium as large as Alice Tully Hall—not to mention opening and closing nights at the Philharmonic. (Occasionally, exhaustion and/or perversity would lure the committee into choosing something silly and light (like *In the Soup* or *Breaking In*; this year there were no "sillies"). Second, a film might be gaudily entertaining (like *Pulp Fiction*) but could not be merely commercial; it needed some pretensions to art, some pedigree. Third, attention had to be given to balance (geography, genre, gender, experimental, documentary, retrospectives). Fourth, the Festival has always tended toward progressive, leftish politics, all things being equal, and eschewed the Right.

Finally, the NYFF has had a built-in auteurist predisposition, a sympathy for filmmakers whose work has already been included in the festival (or its junior festival, New Directors/New Films)—as well as an atoning reflex toward those whose inclusion now seems overdue. (Hence Hal Hartley's weakest film, *Amateur*, in this year's list, after better efforts like *Trust* and *Simple Men* were snubbed.) Some auteurist favoritism is unavoidable: faced with thousands of films out there, the selectors can't help looking forward to a recognizable name—the new Atom Egoyan, say—with quickened anticipation.

There are two paradoxes in this auteurist policy, it seems to me. One is that many of the directors being promoted are not full-fledged *auteurs*, in the sense the word used to mean, so much as talented, up-and-coming practitioners still feeling their way. In the last decade, with a shrinking pool of mature, high-quality art movies—and with an increased responsiveness to parts of the globe beyond Western Europe—the NYFF has steadily poached on what used to be the province of New Directors/New Films. (I would include this year's visually stunning but corny South Korean film, *To the Starry Island*, and Tunisia's earnestly feminist melodrama *The Silences of the Palace* in my Previously Not Ready for Prime Time category.)

The second, largely unacknowledged paradox the NYFF faces is that it is promoting its new auteurism in a vacuum. When the Festival got rolling in the sixties and seventies, it was assumed that the directors spotlighted by it would become well known to American film audiences—if they weren't already art house staples. But the gap has widened between international festival cinema and the American public. Each year the NYFF introduces new work by prizewinning filmmakers respected abroad, such as Hou Hsiao-Hsien, Manoel de Oliveira, Abbas Kiarostami, Jacques Doillon, Idressa Oudriago, Edward Yang, Mani Kaul, Alexander Sokurov . . . and they remain unknown, undistributed, unpronounceable names here. If I assert that Kiarostami is Iran's greatest filmmaker, it already sounds funny—oxymoronic—to many people. But I'm not speaking only of the ethnocentric or incurious moviegoer: what does it tell us that even so sophisticated a film buff as David Thomson did not include any of the above in his recently revised *Biographical Dictionary of Film?* So we have a good faith but quixotic attempt on the part of the New York and other American festivals (Telluride, San Francisco, etc.) to introduce to the public the cream of world cinema, two weeks a year, and—because it does not get picked up, beyond the occasional "cutting edge" venue or college package—the understandably skeptical reaction that these selections are anything more than esoterica and pedantic multiculturalism. (For instance, this year's masterly *Satantango*, by veteran director Béla Tarr, aroused a certain incredulous derision simply because it was a seven-hour Hungarian movie.)

The truth is, we are living in an era without masters. No Renoir, no Ozu, no Rossellini, no Godard (I know Godard's still alive, but he's no longer a master). The last two masters of cinema were Fassbinder and Tarkovsky. Their ghosts hovered over the NYFF this year: Fassbinder directly, with the retrospective showing of his marvelous film *Martha*, and Tarkovsky indirectly, via his two main disciples, Sokurov and Béla Tarr.

For admirers of the late German director, *Martha* was a rare treat: vintage Fassbinder, among his ten best, I'd say. Fassbinder's perfect sense of control here allows him to wed psychological realism and Grand Guignol camp. What gives Fassbinder's narratives shape and point is their drive toward the revelation of human cruelty. In *Martha*, every cut, every composition, tightens the noose of cruelty. Margit Carstensen gives a tremendous performance in the title (Joan Fontaine *Suspicion*) role, asserting an odd, princessy willfulness beneath her anorexic masochism. A woman whose father won't let her touch him marries a sadist who forbids tenderness. Oddly enough, this depressing schema moves toward a certain reserved dignity, as the heroine evolves from a dreamy, self-deceiving romantic to one who comes at least to understand her fate. Karlheinz Böhm is also quite good in the "James Mason" role of cold, controlling husband. The film struck some critics as an unbelievably grotesque caricature of patriarchal marriage; but if you accept the premise that Martha is not entirely a victim, it plays out rather plausibly.

Béla Tarr has been compared to Tarkovsky, but his black-

and-white approach to long-duration, long-shot, *plan-séquence* filmmaking owes at least as much to Jancsó, his fellow Hungarian—and perhaps Angelopoulos as well. Tarr brings to this usually sombering technique a gallows humor: call it the comedy of bleakness. He stays so long in real time with these characters flailing futilely against their blasted, abandoned backwater environment that, through maddening repetition, something liberating or at least cathartic is achieved. Characteristic is the scene in which a tavern keeper smashes his own bottles in a backroom fury until, acting-out impulse exhausted, he thoughtfully sweeps up the damage. Tarr is great at directing an actor alone, not an easy thing to do: his isolates have the "I can't go on, I'll go on" extremism of Beckett figures. For me, the most compelling sequences are two "soliloquies" which occur around midpoint: the first shows a drunken emphysemic doctor spying on his neighbors, writing notes, falling down and trying to rouse himself to go out and buy some more schnapps. The second involves an idiot girl who, after watching a man enter the house of a woman (her mother?), decides to torture a cat. A weird, tranced scene ensues, excruciating to watch, in which she flaunts her power over the cat, hangs it upside down in a string bag and breaks its legs. In the end she staggers through the town at dawn and swallows rat poison.

What is Tarr getting at? Part of his concern seems to be about nothing more (nor less) than framing: his camera moves from far away to super close-up, like someone with alternate astigmatisms. The narrated texts and philosophic speeches have a giddy, self-contradictory quality, canceling themselves out in self-mocking, vodka cynicism. From Tarr's titles (*Damnation*, *Satantango*) one might infer a theological position that God may be dead but the Devil's existence is indisputable. For all its intense, powerful moments, there remains something turgid at the film's ideational center. It is devilishly clever, always fascinating, but not quite great art: the whole does not add up to something more than its parts, nor is its extraordinary length necessarily justified. And it does not so much end as stop. But *Satantango* introduces us to a major filmmaker.

Alexander Sokurov is another devotee of the oneiric, Tarkovsky-wet, *plan-séquence* aesthetic. His *Whispering Pages* belongs alongside Béla Tarr's epic in the NYFF's radical fringe. Last year the NYFF did itself proud by showing Sokurov's spectral, nonnarrative meditation on Chekhov, *Stone*. *Whispering Pages* continues in a crepuscular, poetic vein, this time glancing off Dostoevsky's *Crime and Punishment*. The best way to take in a film this visually gorgeous is just to watch it, without any narrative expectations. There is no one in cinema today crafting more luminous images than Sokurov. Unlike Tarkovsky, who had a futurist bent, Sokurov seems resolutely attracted to the past's aura: his images here resemble turn-of-the-century gum-bichromate still photographs by Stieglitz or Steichen. There are also hauntingly paranoiac scenes of a delirious Raskolnikov figure walking through knots of carousers, which recall the German Expressionist "street films" of the twenties, like *Warning Shadows*. Most remarkable is the sequence in which people keep jumping off a balcony to their deaths, and another in which the protagonist suckles the lap of a stone lion. The film falters only when it tries to be narrative, vomiting up hammy dialogues between Raskolnikov and Sonya.

What is Sokurov's message? Better not to ask. In interviews he talks all kinds of reactionary, Russian-mystic nonsense; but the man makes beautiful movies. In a sense, Sokurov embodies, even more extremely than did his mentor Tarkovsky, the problem of the visionary film artist whose fuzzy, schmaltzy "content" is hard to take seriously, even as his images are so seductive. Does it take having a cockamamie philosophy these days to make rigorous, visionary films?

One way to look at this year's NYFF was as a struggle between the "new cinemas" of *Pulp Fiction* and *Caro Diario*. Not that one necessarily has to choose; but I did, and for me, the breakthrough film was by Nanni Moretti, not Quentin Tarantino. One can see that Tarantino has a giant talent and that *Pulp Fiction* is a wonderful piece of filmmaking; I just don't happen to like it. I don't *dislike* it, but I can't respond wholeheartedly to all that recycling of fifties-to-seventies TV pop culture, or take seriously another violent film about the banal lives of hit men (warmed over from both Siodmak's and Siegel's *The Killers*).

Caro Diario is, on the other hand, that *rara avis*, a fully achieved, personal and personable essay-film—held together by nothing but the play of an interesting mind, going where it wills. Moretti already showed in his wilder, shaggier earlier films (like *Ecce Bombo* and *Sogni d'Oro*) a uniquely comic temperament—a Woody Allen with more rancor and bite. In this, his most poised film, he seems to have taken a leaf from Tati's episodic, abstract humor, and from Chris Marker's essayist manner. The steady display of an ironic intelligence provides tension enough: What will Moretti think to say next? In the first section, *On My Vespa*, the filmmaker-actor is a Vespa *flâneur*, riding through the streets of Rome, expressing his enthusiasm for building facades and dancing, his hostility toward slippers and other suburban incursions, his disgust at *Henry: Portrait of a Serial Killer* and by extension, all violent cinema, including Tarantino's. At one point Moretti stops his bike and tells a man in the adjoining car that he feels lonely, in a minority, and, even in a more politically perfect world, he would probably feel isolated. The driver of course speeds away. In a sense, *Caro Diario* is also a minority taste. Moretti is not embarrassed to make intellectual references: it's just another system of taste, like pop culture for Tarantino.

While all this commentary is occurring on the sound track, Moretti offers delightfully natural yet formally precise visuals. This first section, filled with brio and daring, and a Sunday sense of the city, ends with a melancholy, wordless visit to the site where Pasolini was killed. Part Two, *Islands*, conveys the uneasiness of leisure and travel, along with Moretti's critique of Italian bourgeois parents. Part Three, *Doctors*, takes us to the country of illness, telling the true story of Moretti's misdiagnosis and bout with cancer. The movement from rumination to narration, via a life-threatening experience, is very cunningly handled. I still like the first part best, for its mental freedom and exhilarating physical movement. But on the whole, as a lover of both movies and essays, this is a film I've been waiting for all my life.

Interestingly, both *Pulp Fiction* and *Caro Diario* seem part of a larger tendency in recent years for art movies to fragment into strings of short stories or essay segments. (Altman's *Short Cuts*, Jarmusch's *Night on Earth*, Giraud's *Glenn Gould* film). *Pulp Fiction* leaps back and forth between a subplot featuring fascinating performances by John Travolta and Samuel L. Jackson, and a dull, attenuated one with Bruce Willis. Jacques Audiard's *See How They Fall* attempts to complicate a rather traditional French crime movie terrain by shuffling two plots. *Chungking Express* follows one narrative, then, before it has been fully resolved, picks up another. Are we seeing the disintegration of single narratives in movies? Why has the short story, the vignette, acquired such a technically challenging allure for hip filmmakers?

• • •

This year, all four documentaries were excellent—and one, *Crumb*, was my favorite film in the festival next to *Caro Diario* (itself a kind of documentary, or nonfiction, film). Over the past few years, the documentaries seem to be getting not only more formally sophisticated, but more humanly interesting than the narrative pictures. Fiction films seem mired in plot exhaustion, which leads either to needlessly fractured post-modernist strategies or faux-naïf fairy tales. After an *Ed Wood*, whose stylistic panache and larky spirits cannot redress the one-note characterization of its eponymous hero, it comes as a relief to encounter the complex, uncontrived, believable human beings in these documentaries.

It's virtually impossible not to care about the two basketball aspirants in *Hoop Dreams*—not to cringe in sorrow when one of them, Arthur Agee, watches his father scoring crack on the playground. It's hard to resist the wacky, true story of the avant-garde composer/KGB scientist Leon Theremin in *Theremin*, with its knowing blend of movie excerpts featuring that unearthly instrument. And the new Marcel Ophuls cinematic inquest about the media in wartime, *The Troubles We've Seen*, manages to stay engrossing for every minute of its close to four-hour length.

Ophuls did well to make a movie not about Bosnia per se but about the war correspondents covering it. He knows journalism, is implicated in its mores and morals—which spreads the complicity around and saves the film from the heavy solemnity of other documentaries on war. Over the years, Ophuls has developed a free-associational approach which is so open-ended that questions of form become ultimately moot. Like Nanni Moretti, he is not afraid to follow his thoughts; and he has also learned to insert himself clownishly in the proceedings, risking bad taste but achieving a very personal, *provocateur* filmmaking. (See Ophuls's R&R with a Viennese prostitute in his hotel room—a bit of self-exposure that undercuts the saintliness of the *New York Times*'s John

Burns.) War correspondents may be brave, but they are also human, horny and ambitious, as this movie shows. Some of Ophuls's prankish Hollywood cutaways seem forced; and his insatiable historical curiosity leads him down so many digressive alleys you begin to wonder if the film has any center at all. But always there's a payoff; you learn something new (Robert Capa staged the famous "Death of the Spanish Republican" shot!). And even if you didn't, Marcel Ophuls would go his own way. He is one of the freest moviemakers alive.

The Troubles We've Seen is less a departure for Ophuls than a culmination. Terry Zwigoff's *Crumb*, on the other hand, is something new. I can't think of another portrait of an American artist on film that so reveals the trade-offs in that life. This is no soft-soap job. R. Crumb comes off in some ways as charmingly self-aware and dedicated, but in others as a selfish creep. What the movie demonstrates is that some artists never transcend their original traumas, they simply learn how to produce art out of them.

Crumb also suggests the way a successful artist can seem to use up all the creative oxygen in his/her family. The subject's sisters refused to be interviewed for the film, but his two brothers, Charles and Max, rivetingly testify to the dynamics of their competition. All three brothers grew up nerdily fixated on comic books; for all three, adolescence was a formidably maiming experience. Most articulate is Charles Crumb, the oldest brother, who speaks of his "wounded narcissism" and jealous, homicidal impulses toward Robert, even in boyhood. Charles emerges as both a wreck of a human being and a gentle, rueful soul whose suffering has produced self-understanding, if not self-forgiveness. Some of the most dangerous, enlightening moments in the film come when the two brothers are together in their mother's house, edgily trying to get at the truth about their upbringing. If *Crumb* is a more satisfying film, for me, than *Hoop Dreams*, it is finally because its subjects are so much more articulate and forthcoming. With *Hoop Dreams*, there is always the sense that its black teenage subjects are either too unaware or too shy about speaking their minds before white adult filmmakers, leaving the story interest to be generated by dramatic reversals wrought by time. In *Crumb*, thoughtful interviewees stare down the camera and compete to deliver the most honesty. *Crumb* is also shot in an artfully composed, stylized-lit manner reminiscent of Errol Morris's documentaries. The haunting ragtime piano in the background refers to Crumb's antiquarian love of early jazz and blues (ironically, he reviles the music of the scene that made him famous, sixties rock). Like *Ed Wood*, *Crumb* is about being stuck in a childhood obsession with pop images and id energies; but whereas Tim Burton celebrates this id fixation as goofy innocence, Terry Zwigoff explores the price of arrested development.

Two of the best narrative movies in the festival, Olivier Assayas's *Cold Water* and André Téchiné's *Wild Reeds*, were commissioned for a French TV project about adolescence, "All the Boys and Girls in Their Time." Directors of different ages were invited to tell stories set during their teenage years, using the pop music of the period. Would that American TV showed such initiative. Perhaps not coincidentally, these guidelines have resulted in Assayas's and Téchiné's best films.

Set in the early seventies, *Cold Water* is a disturbing film, because Assayas has chosen to make it existentially and subjectively from inside the teenagers' perspective; and one is not always sure to what extent he goes along with their indictment of the adults, or sees through this as the self-dramatizing posture of youth. A father tells his son to grow up and become an adult. A teacher loses his temper when the boy is unprepared and yanks him by the arm. Are we meant to think, "The Kids Are Alright"? What of the moment when the boy takes out a knife and cuts graffiti into a subway car? Or the girl shoplifts? I think Assayas is testing us, purposely not tipping his hand, waiting behind a dispassionate camera. The opening third is tense with stiff generational face-offs, while the camera lingers behind windows and doorjambs, afraid to intrude. The film breaks alive in the middle, with a long teenage party—one of the most extraordinary sequences in recent films—in which Assayas's camera does figure eights as it chases the running, fighting, partying kids hurling their parents' chairs onto a bonfire. This *Walpurgisnacht* of self-pity, ecstasy and self-destruction captures, nonjudgmentally, the utopian aspirations for tribal warmth underneath the kids' random, solitudinous behavior. It reminded me of Peter Marin's sixties essay "The Open Truth and Fiery Vehemence of Youth," which argued that teenagers needed rites of passage, opportunities to feel brave, and hated their parents for protecting them. Through drugs or other means, "adolescents provide for themselves what we deny them: a confrontation with some kind of power within an unfamiliar landscape involving sensation and risk." Certainly the wintry Midi landscapes of *Cold Water* carry a palpable meaning of ritual testing ground. The intentionally unresolved ending seems both effective and a bit of a cheat: does the heroine commit suicide, and if so, why? Assayas's narrative generates more issues than it resolves. But that's partly what makes *Cold Water* feel so rawly alive, even after it's over.

Wild Reeds is a much more classical, composed movie. Téchiné is one of the smoothest, most technically graceful film directors: he always knows where to place the camera and how to move it; but in the past I have been put off by his claustrophobic, contrived plots and hysterical yet bloodless characters. This time he has brought warmly to life a band of immensely attractive young people, in their intelligent fumblings and gravitations. Placed in the early sixties, with the Algerian War as backdrop, *Wild Reeds* is very much an ensemble piece, introducing a whole new generation of acting talent to the screen in one fell swoop. The lyrical mixture of political longing and sexual confusion, and the flowing *mise en scène*, made me think at times of Bertolucci's *Before the Revolution*. Except that that was a great film made by a young man with the pretended wisdom of youth, and this is a good film made by an older man with actual wisdom, utilizing the elegant perspective of memory.

Abbas Kiarostami is both a humanist filmmaker—in the tradition of De Sica, Rossellini's *India*, the Apu trilogy—and a playful formalist, with a penchant for complexly choreographed denouements. His method is to start with a skeletal script, which he embellishes on location with documentary and serendipity, giving the films a fresh, real-life texture. In *Through the Olive Trees*, as in the earlier two films of his trilogy, he has mostly used nonprofessionals, though the Director himself is played by a bearlike actor who looks nothing like Kiarostami. Ostensibly a film about shooting a movie in an earthquake-riven area, it evolves into a romantic comedy about a genial but illiterate, property-less ex-bricklayer, Hossein, who keeps asking for the hand of a girl from a better family. Hossein expounds the theory that social classes *should* intermarry, so that there will be more opportunity for mobility and cooperation: "Since I can't read, she could help our child with homework." As it happens, the girl ends up playing his mate in the film they are shooting. This leads to an enchanting scene in which Hossein, between takes, courts his taciturn beloved by telling her he would never act toward her as the Husband in their scene is doing toward the Wife.

As with the ending of *And Life Goes On*, the film's last shot is a stunning *tour de force*, merging landscape, title and plot in one braided whole. The camera, high above the olive grove, watches as Hossein chases the girl and finally catches up with her. We hear not a word of their dialogue; but the sprightly music and the alacrity of his gait as he runs off suggest that maybe she has finally said yes.

Among the charms of *Through the Olive Trees* is that it gives us a wonderfully inside, undefensive glimpse of Iran.

A side benefit of many NYFF offerings this year was, as always, anthropological: even when the films themselves proved less than artistically satisfying, they often brought us valuable news from elsewhere. *Strawberry and Chocolate*, for instance, told me more about daily life in Cuba, its ironies and avoidances, than any number of journalistic reports. I wish I could report that it was a return to top form of Tomás Gutiérez Alea, who co-directed with Juan Carlos Tabio. But *Strawberry and Chocolate* is soft ice cream. It's a harmless crowd-pleaser that revives the soapy premise of *Kiss of the Spider Woman*: sensitive queen helps teach insecure macho man how to feel. The gay art curator, Diego (magnificently played by Jorge Perugorria), keeps declaring, "When are they going to understand that propaganda and art are two different things?" Precisely—and it's true even of propaganda for tolerance and difference. Stylistically, the filmmaking has a shaggy laxness that seems a long way from Alea's earlier Antonioniesque masterpiece, *Memories of Underdevelopment*.

The best of the five offerings from Asia—and one of my favorite films in the festival—was Edward Yang's ambitious comedy *A Confucian Confusion*, set in today's prosperous, skyscraping, Americanized Taipei, where the characters are as apt as not to relax in T.G.I. Friday's, argue behind telecasts of NBA games and ads for BMW dealerships, and jump into Cherokee-red elevators. The film follows a dozen go-getters in their twenties and thirties, some uncertainly on the brink of marriage, others exiting that state, as they try to figure out what they really want from life. Yang keeps up a brisk directorial pace, especially in the frenetic night scene when everyone changes partners. But what really distinguishes the film is the tenderness and detached amusement he shows toward these somewhat spoiled, unhappy yuppies. Yang's screenplay, especially in the *tête-à-têtes*, has some wonderfully delicate writing, as farce and satire ripen into psychological nuance. One thinks of Wilder's *The Apartment*. I know dedicated Yangians will disagree, but I much prefer this film to his earlier work, including his highly touted epic *A Brighter Summer Day*. That story, about youth gangs, seemed too much under the influence of his great countryman, Hou Hsiao-Hsien; here, he really seems to know these yuppie characters better.

Chungking Express, a coterie favorite, lets us see surprising glimpses of Hong Kong. But its infectious, bravura love of filmmaking cannot distract us indefinitely from the thinness of the material. Wong Kar-wai took two coy, slender story ideas and rammed them together with sufficient doublings to make us wonder whether something deeper might be afoot. Alas, no. I see *Chungking Express* as primarily a proof of how internationalist has become YP (Young People's) Cinema: slapdash story, cute generic characters, slacker lifestyles, hip MTV surfaces, optics, all-important music sound track, passive Jarmusch-oid males fixated on this or that, perky gaminish girls. . . . It plays well, but an oldster like me may be excused for not being swept off my feet.

When Ken Loach is working at his best, he produces complex portraits of working-class life like *Raining Stones* and *Riffraff*. *Ladybird, Ladybird* is typical, not superior, Loach: which means powerful and exasperating by turns. How can it not shake you up, with such a powerhouse performance by Cissy Rock as Maggie, a working-class woman whose children keep being taken away from her by the British social services? On the other hand, as Oscar Wilde said about the death of little Nell, no one can watch the evil welfare workers coming to take yet *another* bairn away from Maggie without stifling a giggle. Doesn't this woman ever learn? More to the point, why is the narrative so stacked against the welfare bureaucracy that not a single caseworker expresses any opposition to these barbarities? Loach has the satisfaction of scoring Marxist points against the system; but in "raising" our consciousness, he falls into manipulative crudities. Formally, the film embraces the questionable assumption that the more graininess and jerky hand-held camera, the more *real*. Thematically, the problem is that there's no real tension between a mother's love and a monolithically uncomprehending State. It's only in the last (and best) scene, when Maggie and her saintly Paraguayan revolutionary lover Jorge turn on each other, that we get a true conflict between equals. By that time it's too late to save the picture from being more than entertaining agitprop.

One of the films I found most compelling in the Festival was Atom Egoyan's *Exotica*. That is, it stayed with me: I kept rethinking its situations and construction. The plot, a jigsaw puzzle of interdependence, interweaves a tax auditor who has lost his daughter and seeks assuagement of grief in a fancy strip club; a schoolgirl-costumed lap dancer who sees herself as his sexual healer; her ex-lover, the club's DJ, who is going off the deep end; a gay smuggler of parakeets, whom the accountant is auditing; and the bisexual club owner (played by Egoyan's perennial leading lady, Arsinée Khanjian, in hilarious Marlene Dietrich saloon keeper fashion). The real star of the movie, however, is the nightclub set: Egoyan, in a surprising Sternbergian vein, clearly had fun dollying and panning over every inch of it. This is his most cinematically fluid film; and the languorous rhythms build up an engrossing, sexy mood. Is all the angst, finally, authentic—or is it a trick? Are we to see the "look but don't touch" rule of lap dancing as a metaphor for moviegoing? The film seems to me, at bottom, about the hardening process: how people lose their bouncy innocence and potential and become the haunted, gaunt, damaged goods that allow for their and our compassion to grow.

Last year, it seemed to me, Egoyan had made a breakthrough with the personal, witty *Calendar*—a film more in the free spirit of *Caro Diario*. I still think I prefer his humorous, quotidian side *(Next of Kin, Calendar)* to the sleek, ominous narratives about sex games, voyeurism and repression, like *Speaking Parts, The Adjuster* or *Exotica*. For one thing, whenever Egoyan leaves the Armenian scene, his ordinary Canadians (his "goyim," you might say) are denatured, without history or specificity. Maybe he sees the tribal as innately comic, and the nonethnic person as generically spooky—which is why his creepy "horror" films are always about WASPs. But that's unfair to his non-Armenian characters; after all, they have humorous memories and families too, not just kinky obsessions.

Obsession gives a movie a quick audience hook, an appearance of energy; but it also risks becoming repetitious and static. *Exotica* avoids the trap—just barely—by its proliferating subplots. Steve McLean's *Postcards from America* takes the opposite path, doesn't even try for variety: it just lowers its head and concentrates on sex between men, as though no other activity existed on the planet. As a straight male viewer, I have to admit, I found it at first—well, estranging; it made me uncomfortable to watch this relentlessly ingrown, codified discourse. Every face, every figure, every landscape seems scrutinized purely for its erotic potential, according to a strict code that honors a cowboy-trucker grizzled look. Eventually, however, the film accumulates power through its very singlemindedness and strength of feeling. It progresses by fits and starts, intercutting overly stylized scenes from childhood (an abusive, hunky father) with more effective hitchhiking and urban vignettes in the present. The "glue" consists of an array of arty, film-school clichés for moodiness—the hustler-protagonist staring off into the anguished distance, walking, brooding—while the sound track quotes from the writings of David Wojnarowicz. Part of what makes the film so uneven is its source material: Wojnarowicz's prose shifts from lyrical to purple. The photography, by Ellen Kuras, is extremely good, conjuring up the forlorn truck-stop universe of Larry Clark's *Tulsa* photographs and Robert Frank's *The Americans*. For all the misery, anger, loneliness and illness portrayed onscreen, the film turns into a poem to the beauty of America: the landscape and the common American male linked, in neo-Whitmanian fashion, by an equation that asserts this country is a paradise of homoerotic desire, if not fulfillment.

There were a number of disappointing films from proven *auteurs* this year. Chief among them, Zhang Yimou's *To Live* struck me as a soggy, utterly conventional melodrama, the kind that could have used a good Dmitri Tiomkin score. I realize how ungrateful it may sound, given the trouble the director has gotten into for this film, to see it as a step backward into the realm of socialist realism. But its political criticisms are tame, and its psychology, especially in contrast to last year's *The Blue Kite*, seems stereotypical: the men are weak, the women are strong, the children suffer, and most of the commissars except for a few rotten apples are pretty good. There is also something wrong when a director as worldly as Zhang Yimou has to lean so heavily on crude folk humor, like practical jokes about giving someone tea with hot chili peppers. *To Live* tries so hard for universality that it gets sandbagged in "Family of Man" clichés.

Bullets over Broadway is subpar Woody Allen; it condescends to and insults the intelligence of its audience. After the tough, gloves-off honesty of *Husbands and Wives*, the genuine weirdness of *Shadows and Fog* and the amusing Keaton-Woody *pas de deux* in *Manhattan Murder Mystery*, I had thought we were in for an Allen renaissance; but he seems to have run for cover with this trite concoction of twenties gangsters, molls and dopey art-for-art's-sake playwrights. *Bullets over Broadway* is labored and boring.

I have been a fan of Hal Hartley in the past, appreciating the adroitness with which he walked a tightrope between originality and pretension. This time, in *Amateur*, he slipped—or was pushed by Isabelle Huppert and a larger than usual budget—into purest mannerism. Enough said.

I have saved the worst for last: *Red*. Krzysztof Kieslowski was once a good Polish director, but since *Veronique*, he has become a peddler of New Age sugar water for middlebrow audiences. His dialogue has turned unerringly phony ("You can't live your brother's life for him." "Who *are* you?" "Maybe you're the woman I never met"). Perhaps it's the problem of a displaced Pole with a tin ear for French nuances, coming on like Vox Europa, by sticking to portentous, pompous generalities. As for the story, it's so contrived I kept hearing Kieslowski's script conferences in the background: "Then we'll make her run into a dog, and take it to its owner, a misanthropic ex-judge...." Coincidences, soothsayings, women who are little more than fashion magazine projections (this time Irene Jacob gets the chic cipher role that Binoche played in *Blue*). "But it's meant to be a fairy tale!" you'll say. Then fairy tales are the last refuge of scoundrels, and "magic" a cloak for creative exhaustion. No wonder Kieslowski is quitting the business. Oh, yes, I almost forgot: the cinematography is exquisite, with its frames divided by color. The more polished Kieslowski's films get, the stupider. How to explain the fact that some very discerning film critics think so highly of *Red*? They have been, in a word, bamboozled.

The festival roundup is a very difficult kind of piece to pull off: no matter what motifs or crosscurrents you try to find, you can't help but end up with a choppy, fragmented compilation of mini-reviews. I have written wrap-ups of the New York Film Festival for the past four years, as well as "letters" from the Cannes, Berlin and Houston film festivals, and I don't think any of them works entirely. But I include the above as a sample of the genre, and as a sort of "mate" to my piece on the first New York Film Festival.

INTERVIEW WITH ABBAS KIAROSTAMI

I met the great Kiarostami, in town for his Film Society retrospective, at his hotel room across from Lincoln Center. Though he speaks some English, he had with him a translator, the film professor Jamsheed Akrami, who immediately shut the blinds, explaining to me that "sunlight was the enemy of Mr. Kiarostami." I noticed the director was wearing pinkish-tinted shades indoors. A trim man of medium height, wearing a crisp denim shirt and black jeans, he has the kind of civilized handsomeness that grows on you: warm, intelligent eyes and a sympathetic expression. Perhaps because he was used to getting general questions, when my comments addressed specific scenes he reacted with pleased surprise. Either that, or he was being exquisitely polite with me.

AK: It's best to talk only about films we love.

PL: Well, talk about some movies you loved when you were first becoming interested in films.

AK: In my country, my film education started with seeing classic American movies. Then, when I was fifteen, sixteen years old, there was an invasion of the Italian neorealistic films. This corresponded to the time when I could independently make decisions about what movies I wanted to see. My perception of the characters in American movies at the time was that they only belonged in movies, they didn't exist in reality. But the kinds of people we were seeing in neorealist films could also be seen around me, within my family, my friends, people I knew in the neighborhood. I realized that movie characters could also be real, that films could talk about life, about ordinary human beings.

PL: Did you also get a chance to see films by Ozu, Dreyer, Bresson? I ask because they have this quality of quiet and spirituality that is sometimes found in your films.

AK: Without a doubt, I think I have been influenced by all of them. But all those filmmakers were influenced and inspired by life, and so have I. If you see a similarity between my films and theirs, it's mostly because we looked at life in the same way.

PL: In *Homework* you use the word "researches" to explain what you wanted to do. This is the same word that Rossellini used for his historical films, and Godard, too. How much do you think of your films as "researches"?

AK: When I was making the film *Homework*, the only thing I was thinking about was my own problem, my kid's problem, I wasn't even thinking about movies at that point. I just had access to some negative film stock, and I put it together to shoot *Homework*. To call this movie a "research"— this is not the way you do research, it's not the right methodology. But if you were to call it "film," then it's not really film, it's more like "research." *(laughs)*

PL: What was your child's problem at this time?

AK: Let me start by saying that this was the most difficult film I ever had to make. My son was having this problem doing his homework, and that's why I decided to go to his school and see about a solution. But while doing that, I ran into so many other kids having similar problems, it was so alarming to just sit there and hear their problems. The film starts with my own son coming to the school. And he later reappears in the film, saying, "My father couldn't help me with my math problems."

PL: Children are so central to your films. Why, do you think?

AK: Partly by accident, because I was invited to start the filmmaking branch of this newly formed foundation called the Institute for the Intellectual Development of Children and Young Adults. That's how I got involved making movies about children; then gradually I developed an interest of my own.

PL: There's always a danger in making movies about children, of being sentimental or presenting the child as a martyr for adults' sins. Your portraits of children are not sentimental. How do you protect against using children too emblematically?

AK: Well, thank you for your comment. What really helped me in portraying children was that I could see my own two sons growing up right in front of my eyes. Plus the fact that my job was putting me in contact with children, and I developed this understanding that children aren't really sentimental, martyred or even innocent. They're adults to me. It's just that they aren't as formed or as knowledgeable as we are; but their understanding of life is sometimes deeper and healthier than ours.

PL: For instance, there's that scene in *And Life Goes On* when the boy makes a philosophical statement, and someone asks how he figured that out. He says, "One half I learned from history class, one half from my grandfather, and one half I figured out by myself." Three halves.

AK: Yeah, this kid was basically adding himself to those two halves.

PL: In *And Life Goes On*, the father at first seems irritable and impatient—everything his son does annoys him, but he tries to overcome this reflex. And I feel that this is something that runs all through your movies: this dialectic between frustration and patience.

AK: To me, the real guide in that trip was the kid, not the father, although the father has the steering wheel. In Eastern philosophy, we have this belief that you don't ever set foot in unknown territory without having a guide. And the reason I say that kids sometimes have a better and deeper understanding of life is that the kid here was acting more rationally, and the father was not rational. The kid has accepted the instability and the illogic of the earthquake, and he is just living on: he's thirsty, he's playing with the grasshopper.

PL: The funniest moment is when the man asks another boy, "What happened?"—meaning, on the night of the earthquake—and the kid starts telling about the soccer game that night.

AK: He doesn't talk about the disaster, he talks about what interests him in life.

PL: I still feel there's something intriguing about this balance between irritation and amusement. For instance, in *Through the Olive Trees*, the Young Man is complaining about romantic disappointments, and the Director is listening to this monologue as he drives. Sometimes he seems about to say, "Okay, I get it, enough already," but then he glances over and he seems amused by the Young Man. I think that you as a filmmaker sometimes toy with your audience, by making us go through something irritating—like the repeated incorrect takes in *Through the Olive Trees*—which also has an amusing side.

AK: I don't quite agree with you that those multiple takes are necessarily repetition. Because each time they're repeated, the audience's reaction to it is different. By the fourth time, they say, "Oh, enough of this."

PL: I guess what I'm really getting at is a question about your sense of pace. Your movies have these alternations of tension and relaxation, of stillness and conflict. Some scenes seem to go on a long time, and then at other times the drama is very condensed.

AK: That rhythm is based on Nature, Life: you know, day, night, summer, winter. The contrast between those things is what sustains our interest, because even if you love spring, you can't have spring all year long or you'd get bored. I think there is a pace to Nature, and if you adopt the same pace to your films, in the sense that you manipulate it—at some point caress it, at some point be rough with it—that will cause interest.

PL: I wonder if it's also a cultural difference, because American movies are becoming more and more constant action. You'd rarely get a sequence in an American film like the one in *Through the Olive Trees* where the two old men are philosophizing, since it doesn't "advance the plot," so to speak.

AK: I'm really enjoying this conversation. Because these are the kinds of things that I was always thinking about, but nobody ever brought them up. So I worry that maybe they don't understand. In the most recent example, *Through the Olive Trees*, we were making a movie about making a movie, but there were moments in the film when we weren't "doing" anything. I was even sometimes tempted to put black leader in between the scenes—because I was constantly hunting for scenes in which there was "nothing happening." That nothingness I wanted to include in my film. Some places in a movie there should be nothing happening, like in *Closeup*, where somebody kicks a can. But I needed that. I needed that "nothing" there.

PL: Do you need it for aesthetic or religious reasons? Or both?

AK: At one point those two intersect. If you bring out the aesthetic aspect, then maybe you'll see a reflection of the religious as well. The points where nothing happens in a movie, those are the points where something is about to bloom. They are preparations for blooming. Similar to a plant which has not emerged from the earth yet, but you know there are roots down there and something is happening. It's like when you read a novel: at the end of the chapter there's a blank where you can pause. That's the kind of thing I'm looking to create in my movies. With a novel, you can stop reading and do something else and then get back to it. But you don't have that kind of opportunity in a movie, you have to consciously work for pauses. So when people tell me "Your movie slows down here a little bit," I love that! Because if it doesn't slow down, then I can't lift it again. And that's the problem with American movies: it's all lifting and lifting and lifting.

PL: They used to have more variation. Like Howard Hawks would have these moments where everyone was sitting around—

AK: Or John Ford.

PL: Yes. By the way, I have an annoying question. In that scene in *Through the Olive Trees* where the Director has to do multiple takes because the Young Man keeps getting wrong the number of earthquake deaths—he keeps using his own family's deaths instead of supplying the figure in the script— why do they have to go to the start of the take each time? Why couldn't there just be a cutaway—as there is in the same scene when it appears in *And Life Goes On?*

AK: I wanted to use the kind of footage that usually ends up on the cutting room floor. And all that repetition also allowed me to get in the exchange where the Young Man is murmuring to the woman he loves, between takes.

PL: That's a great scene!

AK: And I really like that kind of stuff when somebody looks into the camera, and you think, "This guy's not very interesting," and he turns out to be surprisingly interesting. You have two types of material in a movie: the kind that is really strong, and maybe has an element of arrogance going with it—and the stuff that is subtle and not smug at all. That's the kind of material that I'm more interested in. The scenes that are less cinematically arrogant, they interest me more. When I edit my movies, I come upon perfectly framed, nice-looking close-ups, and I look at them and say, "This is too cinematic."

PL: You're an odd combination: a "humanistic" director, because of your neorealist lineage, and a self-reflexive, "formalist" filmmaker who's always playing with the fact that this is a movie, it's all artifice. For instance, at the beginning of *Through the Olive Trees*, the actor turns to the camera, "I am the man who is playing the director of this film." Just saying that creates a level of skepticism.

AK: Or like the scene in *And Life Goes On* where somebody says he needs some water. And then the script girl visually walks into the frame and gives him water! *(laughs)* The reason for that device was that my crew kept coming to me and saying, "This earthquake happened in summertime. But right now the leaves are turning yellow and we're losing the right season." I said, "Hey, we can't reenact that earthquake. We have to make our own earthquake. And our own earthquake is under control; we can monitor and check everything." To quote Godard: life is like a badly made movie. But when we make our movie, we can make corrections. So I choose when to make an earthquake, and maybe an earthquake in the fall is better than one in the summer.

PL: Yes, but you still want everyone to understand that it is a film, while they're watching the film. It's not like *Open City*, for instance.

AK: That's a film too.

PL: But Rossellini isn't showing us the microphone boom, or having an actor tell us that he's playing the director.

AK: I agree that you have to be absorbed by the film. But not to the extent that you forget that you're watching a film. Every film is ultimately a reenactment of reality, not that reality itself. I don't like movies to make their audiences react in a very emotional way. That's why, for example, I avoid using music in my movies.

PL: Let's talk about *Closeup*. It's one of my favorites of your films.

AK: This is a nice thing that we have in common. I have a strong feeling about that movie only. My other movies I have no opinions on, but I really like *Closeup*. The reason I like *Closeup* is: it was the kind of movie that didn't allow me as a director to manipulate or control it. I feel more like a viewer of that movie than the maker of it.

[Note: the film both documents the actual trial of a man named Sabsian who pretended to be the Iranian filmmaker Makhmalbaf, and also uses the figures in the case to reenact the deception on film.]

PL: I feel that it's a Dostoyevskian movie, in a way. I thought about the "hero," if you want, in terms of Prince Myshkin in *The Idiot*. He's like a Holy Fool. It's so strange because he's the impostor, but he comes across as much more sincere than the family he tries to deceive, who have this air of bourgeois inauthenticity.

AK: The reason you like that character is because he's an artist. That's why he can make up beautiful lies. And I like his lies better than the truth that the others have, because his lies reflect his inner reality better than the superficial truth that the other characters express. I think it's always the case that through people's lies you can draw closer, you can get a better understanding of them.

PL: Do you think it's an autobiographical film?

AK: At some points, yes. I resemble both Sabsian and that family. I have cheated on people and I have been cheated.

PL: Every young would-be artist starts out "impersonating" an artist, right? You have to bluff your way into art.

AK: Because when you're not happy with your real self, then you have to start imagining. That's what's really nice about having the power of imagination: everyone has a share of that power, but only artists can make the best use of it and bring that imagination closer to reality.

PL: Sabsian has this religious feeling about movies. He wants to take the family to see "his" movie together, as though at that moment he's a kind of religious guide. Do you think that film *is* a religion?

AK: I think so. But it depends on what movie.

PL: The ending of *Closeup*—

AK: It was so difficult to film that scene, after the trial, when we brought Sabsian back to the family's house. Normally when you shoot in a real house, the most difficult thing is to get the equipment in. But this time the difficulty was getting Sabsian, the character, in the house. Sabsian was just standing outside the door, kind of silent, because he felt that the kind of authority that had helped him get into the house the first time wasn't there anymore. So I went up to him and said, "Hey, don't be embarrassed. You didn't even lie to these people. Didn't you tell them you're going to bring your film crew to film them? That's what you did!" *(laughter)* So that took care of *his* problem. He felt better and he went in. But then I had difficulty just thinking about what I had done, what I had told him. I was about to cry. And I paced around the place where they kicked the can before I could go in. *(pause)* What happened in *Closeup* reminds me of the story of one of our poets. He was like a homeless guy with old, torn clothing. He was just passing by a religious school and he heard some people reciting from the Holy Book, the Koran, in a beautiful voice. So he stood there listening for a while, and then he was so fascinated that he banged on the door. They opened the door and he told them he had really enjoyed their recitation. "How did you learn to sing so beautifully?" When they looked at him, they thought this guy's nobody, so they tried to kid him, saying, "It's not a problem, all we did was go over there to that icy pool, we broke the ice and dove in. When we reemerged, we could recite like that." He actually followed what they told him and dove into the water, and when he came out they were worried that he was going to catch a cold or die. As they were drying him off, he said, "Okay, now you can bring me the Holy Book." He started reciting just as beautifully as they had. This is such a wonderful story, and I think something like that happened in this movie, in the sense that everybody got what he wanted.

PL: The ending is one of the most amazing I've ever seen. Usually in *Doppelgänger* stories, Stevenson or Dostoevsky, in all the literature about meeting one's double, there's an ominous, frightening feeling. But here the double embraces his model, Makhmalbaf, he hugs him on the motor scooter. I've never seen the *doppelgänger* and his model being so tender with each other!

AK: When I was making that scene, I praised the person who had invented that motorbike, because it enabled me to have this person hug his idol! As for doubles in general, sometimes your double becomes even more original than the original, because he's more devoted to the idea than the original is.

PL: Like a disciple.

AK: Yes. At one point the real director, Mr. Makhmalbaf, came to visit the family, to impress them in Sabsian's behalf, and the mother said to Makmalbaf when he was leaving the house: "Mr. Makhmalbaf, the other Mr. Makhmalbaf was more Makhmalbaf than you are." *(laughter)* I think the reason is that Sabsian wanted so desperately to be Makhmalbaf, but the real Makhmalbaf doesn't care to be Makhmalbaf anymore.

PL: If this movie had been made in America, it would have been about the culture of celebrity and how it empties everybody out.

AK: Which is why I made my movie in Iran. *(laughs)* No, I really don't mean to say that.

PL: I think it's curious that you made a movie about someone who impersonates Makhmalbaf, and then you got two different actors to play yourself in two later movies.

AK: I really didn't mean for them to play *me*, just any film director. Which is why the actor in the pretitle sequence of *Through the Olive Trees* says, "I'm playing the director." He didn't say, "I'm playing Abbas Kiarostami."

PL: Yes, but he's shooting a film with a sequence that's in *And Life Goes On!*

AK: But I don't think most audiences will remember that!

PL: *Closeup* is shot a lot in close-up. I have the impression that in your last few movies, you're placing the camera farther away, you're using fewer close-ups, there's a different, more complex handling of space.

AK: In *Closeup* we had two cameras in the courtroom scene. One is just a long shot to follow the proceedings of the court. The other one is our camera, an artistic camera, which is basically focused on Sabsian in close-up. The logic behind those two different shots is that the law always has to be in a long shot, meaning that you have to look after the interests of everybody. With that camera we can't get close to any individual. But the function of art is to get close to individuals. And through art you can get close to a person and then change the law. Sometimes you can realize that the frame created for one individual maybe is too tight and you have to extend it. And this is what Sabsian was trying to prove: that he needed a larger, an extended, frame. Every abnormal person would have that kind of a message: even sometimes by causing injury to themselves, they're saying, the law is too tight a frame for us.

PL: That's interesting. I also wonder: Do you have a preference for long shots, long-duration takes or close-ups?

AK: To me, a close-up doesn't necessarily mean that I'm close to the person. In every movie I made, the implication would be different. For example, in *And Life Goes On*, the use of long shots made more sense. If I were to use close-ups, it would have meant you were dependent on following one person. The Director character, in that movie, was irrationally obsessed with the close-up of the picture that he had [of two missing kids who had starred in his last movie], and he was showing the photo to everybody.

PL: The film was really more about a society rebuilding itself, so it's a long-shot movie.

AK: And that was what was also implied by the ending of the film, the final scene: that we need to look at things on a larger scale.

PL: You've now ended two movies, *And Life Goes On* and *Through the Olive Trees*, with these incredible shot-sequences, what the French call *plans-sequence*. Both are elaborately planned shots that are *tours de force*. It makes me think you're moving into another kind of filming.

AK: When I use a long shot it distances me from my cast and crew, and that affords them an opportunity to submerge themselves into the environment. That's also why I use a telephoto lens and pan with it. It's why I try to avoid tracking shots, because in tracking shots the whole crew stays too close to the actors and makes them self-conscious. It's my experience that when the camera is at a distance from the actors, they feel better, more like themselves, more able to relax into their characters. After the first one or two minutes of a shot-sequence, that's when the performances get interesting.

PL: Then why use only one shot-sequence in a film?

AK: My style is changing. In my future films you'll see more shot-sequences.

PL: This is probably too broad a question, but what has been the effect of the Iranian Revolution on your films?

AK: Actually, in many ways my films were the same before and after the political change. It's unfortunate that critics here haven't seen some of my more important prerevolutionary films. They weren't able to travel here because they're banned. Not by the censors, by the Ministry of Education. Sometimes for trivial reasons: in one, for instance, because a woman's hair was showing.

PL: Do you ever feel you have to censor yourself?

AK: Not at all. I normally choose subject matters that jump over the censors. But the censors aren't always very clever. Sometimes they cut stupid things. The censors' scissors have not cut any of my movies—yet. And I've never changed any of my movies because of the censors. But then again, I've never tried to deal with subjects that might provoke them. And I'm too old to feel honored or gratified if one of my movies were to be banned by the censors.

PL: Your films have performed the service of showing us a side of Iranian life which is different from the usual picture we get, since American media tend to demonize Iran.

AK: Believe me, sometimes when I am in this country I see images from Iran that terrify me. And I think, "Do I really live in a country like that?" I can assure you that the real Iranian society is much closer to my movies than the images you see on TV. It's all a question of what you want to emphasize: the sensational or normal life. In *And Life Goes On*, I had to decide: Do I want to emphasize the calamity of the earthquake, or the beauty of Nature and the character of the people? I'm so proud of my own people—especially when I'm away from them. When I was coming here from Iran, on my way to the Teheran airport I noticed a VW car's engine on fire and I stopped to help. Suddenly I saw fifty other people rushing from their cars to help. The man was trying to put out the fire with a raincoat. After the volunteers had extinguished the fire, they didn't stay around to be thanked. That's the kind of image that I have of my people, and that I'd like to put on film.

So often it is a mistake to meet one's heroes. One day I was brought into a hotel suite by a friend to be introduced to my idol, Roberto Rossellini, who was haggling furiously over the phone about money. When he hung up, he was cold and distracted; I found it difficult to associate the man before me with the creator of the sublimely wise Little Flowers of St. Francis. *Abbas Kiarostami, however, seems as wonderful a human being as he is a filmmaker. He exudes an approachable dignity, an open, candid receptivity; one is glad to be in the same world with such a whole, evolved person.*

I was dying to see his next film, and he did not disappoint: Taste of Cherry *is, to my mind, a masterpiece. I wrote about it as follows in my 1997 New York Film Festival piece for* Film Comment:

Taste of Cherry *solidifies Kiarostami's position as the most important filmmaker working today. In art-cinema terms (though Americans don't know it yet), we are living in the Age of Kiarostami, as we once did in the Age of Godard. Interestingly, both Godard and Kurosawa have publically "anointed" Kiarostami, given him their blessing, even as the Cannes jury awarded him the Palme d'Or. This cannot merely be a perversely esoteric or politically motivated response, based on anti-American sympathy for an Iranian filmmaker. No, I think it is because Kiarostami offers thoughtful, concrete solutions for the cul-de-sac of the art film, with his* cinema povera *which combines modest means with large themes and emotional power, which reinvents neorealism (amateur actors, slice-of-life stories) with self-reflexive, structuralist gestures, and which employs a polished visual style that fights free of prettiness.*

The festival's program note succinctly sums up Taste of Cherry's *plot: "A solitary man contemplating suicide drives through the hilly outskirts of Teheran in search of someone who will bury him if he succeeds, save him if he fails." The protago-*

nist, who has the dourly handsome looks of an Iranian Bruno Ganz, accosts in his search a laborer collecting plastic bags, a soldier, a security guard, a seminarian and finally an assistant taxidermist who alone is willing to assist him. In a sense, it's the same pattern as Kiarostami's script for The White Balloon: someone elicits help from a wide range of ordinary citizens— only this time, the cause is less benign. Kiarostami seems fascinated with this theme of the individual turning to the people, throwing himself on the mercy of the community. What makes it so piquant here is that the more they respond by wanting to help him survive, the more frustrated he gets. They can't really "hear," take in seriously, his wish to die, nor does he bother to give them the personal details accounting for his anguish, which in any case would only trivialize it. Kiarostami has enough respect for suicide as a valid option that he understands one can get to that point without having to demonstrate a lethal burden. He also knows that the suicidal prospect can have a willful, petulant side. When the seminarian starts saying that suicide is a sin against Islamic law, the driver cuts him off by retorting that if he had wanted a religious lecture, he would have asked someone who'd already earned his degree!

The genius of the movie is that it keeps in perfect balance the arguments for life and death. Optimism and pessimism are both seen as right—each side locked in its close-up isolation— and so the tension builds. Strange for a film about suicide, yet typically Kiarostamian, there are many comic moments, and fascinating topical digressions, such as one as about the Afghanistan and Iran-Iraq wars. The camera paces with the protagonist, sad and restless, backgrounded by construction pits and army maneuvers. Then night falls; and we watch in harrowingly beautiful long shot as the man sets out in a taxi through the hills to go lie in his ditch. This part is excruciating; I wanted the movie to end, I couldn't take any more, and then Kiarostami, as if appreciating my panic, offers his controversial postscript: black-and-white video footage of making the film, the man who played the suicide up and about, showing that "it's only a movie," showing that (the title of another Kiarostami film) "and life goes on." Would it have been better if the picture had ended in uncompromising bleakness, like Bresson's Mouchette? But then, Kiarostami is as much a humanist as an artist, and he could not bear to let his audience leave the theater, he explained at his press conference, in such a despondent mood.

WAS IT A MONTAGE
FOR YOU, TOO,
DEAR?

Of all the magical illusions movies have produced, none seems more durable than the illusion that the medium itself is steadily progressing toward a more realistic portrayal of love and sex. If this is true, how then can we explain the ridiculous phenomenon of the romantic montage, which only began stealing into films in the past twenty years? I refer to that succession of sentimental shots—calibrated to last the precise length of a Stevie Wonder forty-five—which is supposed to represent the habit-formation period of a love affair. Usually it occurs shortly after the hero and heroine have bedded down for the first time, and is offered as proof that the medicine has taken, so to speak.

A typical romantic montage consists of shots of the couple walking through nature, preferably by a beach; laughing as they transport grocery sacks; gazing earnestly at each other in bed, seen from the shoulders up; confessing something serious on a park bench (dialogue the audience never hears); the windblown motorcycle shot, woman holding man around the tummy; more shoulders in bed; and the pièce de résistance of amorous fun—getting someone wet. It seems there is nothing more devil-may-care and spontaneously hilarious than throwing one's lover fully clothed into a fountain or lake, unless it be to watch the other trip over and douse himself.

Am I alone in wondering, while being treated to these filmed inventories of leisure activities, what happened to the characters' respective jobs? Did each of their bosses give them several days off to enjoy the first fruits of sexual intimacy? Hardly my experience of employers.

Within the magic utopian bubble of the romantic montage, lovers' time stands still. Although the montage purports to be the cinematic equivalent of a sentence like "over the next few weeks the two grew closer," in fact there is no progressive arc of intimacy in the order of images, each moment being equally charmed and static. To make the point clearer, we might compare the romantic montage to more traditional passage-of-time montage sequences. Take, for instance, the "road-trip" montage, which alternates shots of moving train parts with newspapers or billboards charting the act's steady advance up the billing ladder. No narrative progression could be more graphically logical. For that reason, jaded audiences laugh at it today, while swallowing hook, line and sinker the romantic montage's slushier but less linear impressionism.

The technique of the romantic montage is simply that of a certain type of "lifestyle" television commercial: A woman rides her horse across green fields, twirls her child in her arms and rushes to her husband at the corral gate. (Such soft-focus, wordless ads are often slated for commercials in which dialogue might lead to embarrassing euphemisms, such as ads for tampons or toilet paper.) The iconographies of dating-service spots and TV–sales record packages also duplicate that of the romantic montage: sunsets, beaches, candlelight dinners, drifting canoes—fire and water. The easiest way to read a romantic montage is as a commercial for love. But why would love need its separate advertising campaign, when it is used to sell everything else?

Perhaps the romantic montage fulfills another function: letting film viewers with TV-softened attention spans "space out" from the strain of following a tense story line. It should not be surprising, then, that the images are banal (so banal that one suspects the second unit was sent out to fetch them as "filler"): they are intended as visual Muzak.

Besides, these postcard images are only background illustrations for the main text—the ballad on the sound track, whose diffusely inspirational lyrics advise the characters to "give love a chance" or "follow your feelings." (Feelings with a capital F, like the easy-listening hymn of that same name.) The platitudinous lyrics dissolve the heretofore singular protagonists in the general solvent of Lovers Everywhere. When a popular singer has been enlisted to supply new songs for the film, commercial considerations dictate a romantic montage every twenty minutes or less. With sound tracks that feature "golden oldies," the filmmaker gets a free ride on nostalgic personal associations the viewer brings to his or her beloved rock songs—a form of cheating already seen in Coming Home and The Big Chill, among others.

The idea of sequences dominated by a musical sound track is obviously influenced by MTV. Though the bludgeoning, cut-rate surrealism of some MTV is a far cry from the syrupy romantic montages, both have in common the subordination of film to the rhythms and time limits of recorded songs. The result of this procedure is usually a canned insularity which precludes all cinematic potential for some unguarded life from slipping through.

Given their triteness, one might expect romantic montages to be the refuge of desperate studio hacks. Yet they turn up, often as not, in "serious" little independent features with artistic pretensions. Whether it be Tender Mercies, Resurrection, Play Misty for Me or even Valley Girls, all these films are looking for a quick lyrical fix. But because the "behavior" in romantic montages does not spring from any fresh details of character or concrete milieu, these sequences lack genuine poetry. The shame is that they then go on to influence people in "real life," as we so hopefully call it—who place themselves in the appropriate paradisical setting at the appointed hour of sundown, and are baffled to find themselves hand in hand with an attractive other, yet still unaccountably miserable.

What most filmmakers do not know how to do at present is to look calmly and inquisitively at love, with that spiritual stillness that Carl Dreyer thought was part of the movie camera's mission: "to record the motions of the soul." Perhaps films of the twenties and thirties had better success at capturing this romantic field between lovers. Then there was greater faith in the power of glances and the language of faces—as well as an art of lighting more able to illuminate the inner life. The slow fires that burned in Garbo's eyes bespoke not only a different lighting style but a different amorous tempo. By contrast, the romantic montages of our largely underlit contemporary films betray a jittery shying away from the quiet dwellingness of love. Of course, franker social attitudes toward sexuality *have* quickened the romantic pace. But it remains to be seen whether sex itself is portrayed more realistically nowadays, or simply by a more anatomically exposed but equally artificial convention.

Traditionally, sex was led up to but never shown: a cut or fade-out would succeed the image of two people entering a bedroom, or (especially in French films) beginning to undress. Later, a symbolic vocabulary of ellipsis developed to represent the coupling itself: a camera pan across the room to a sudden crackling fireplace, a cut to surf crashing against the rocks, and other raucous manifestations of natural force. These are understandably greeted by derisive, campy amusement today. In their place, however, we now have the sex montage, close cousin to the romantic montage. (Indeed, the one sets up the other when they appear together in the same film.)

Determinedly "delicate" music on the sound track, usually a flute, piano or guitar, accompanies a series of shots of body segments. Often it is not clear at first which anatomical parts are being segmented, because the cinematography suddenly turns arty and dark, with shapes abstracted through fragmentation in the manner of a Weston still photograph. The fact that this same photographic style never appears again in the film testifies to the notion that sexuality is an activity that has nothing to do with the rest of life. It takes place in a realm where slow motion reigns: solemnity and rhapsodic wonder are the only tonalities allowable.

For the film editor, the problem is similar to that of the romantic montage: to make look sequential what is essentially a random collection of static shots. The sex montage usually opts for the sleight of hand of slow dissolves. These dissolves also suggest that in lovemaking whole chunks of time disappear, as though sex always and only occurs on the borderline of consciousness.

Such an approach neglects the ways that consciousness can often be intensified during sex, with lovers concocting their own "narrative" as they go along. One watches in vain for traces of that intelligent ordering, those canny progressions and causalities: this hand on that thigh, moving now to a better place (but why better?), the command to feed the passion one moment, or to slow it down for control at another. At the heart of actual lovemaking is a conversation, the messages passing from skin to skin or occasionally verbalized. This conversational element—with its Chekhovian misunderstandings and angelic forgivenesses, its awkward pauses, surprising confrontations, diplomatic transitions, its questions and reassurances, its idealizations and refocusings—is something I have rarely seen portrayed narratively onscreen. Perhaps it is impossible to do so. Yet the medium has found ways to convey so many other complex states of feeling. Surely there must be something between the sentimental flute montages with their hype of "the earth moving" and pornography, which sensationalizes and distorts in its own right by stripping sex of affection or vulnerability, reducing its participants to depersonalized puppets of lust. Both approaches seem very far from the way people ordinarily make love. The taboo would seem to be not sex per se but normal sexual pleasure-taking, shorn of melodrama.

I do not agree that old movies were "sexier" because "less is more," a view that implies that the unclothed human body is inherently unerotic. On the contrary, the freedom to show the beauties of flesh onscreen strikes me as a genuine advance, at least potentially. What stops contemporary movies from being more erotic—and more mature—is their avoidance of the dynamics of sexuality in their very exploitation of it. People can now watch bare bottoms and private parts and orgasm cries without blinking an eye, but we are still intensely embarrassed about taking in the act of love as it unfolds moment by moment. The montage of high points, in this particular case, is our puritanical shield.

It should be clear by now that the romantic montage and the sex montage have much in common. They spring from a similar embarrassment; they both treat mind and love as mutually exclusive; they posit a world that slips out of thinking's and history's grasp, a timeless utopian pastorale, unreal and therefore condemned to a barren circularity. It is a rare lover who loses entirely his or her sense of time passing; nor should a total collapse of temporal awareness be made the true test of love. Rather, our films should be willing to study the ways that love never steps out of the everyday world, but feeds on it, draws strength from it, with limitless opportunism, taking its time, in "real time." When that greater honesty arrives, perhaps these two montage conventions can be retired, and even allowed to acquire the naïve charm of other obsolete transitions—like calendar leaves self-ripping off a pad.

These essays appeared in the same or altered form in the following publications:

"Anticipation of *La Notte:* The 'Heroic' Age of Moviegoing" in *American Film.*

"The First New York Film Festival—1963" in *The Columbia Daily Spectator.*

"*Three on a Couch:* Jerry Lewis Adjusts" in *Columbia Magazine.*

"*Contempt:* The Story of a Marriage," "The Operatic Realism of Luchino Visconti," "Kenji Mizoguchi," "The Legacy of John Cassavetes," "When Writers Direct" and "The Images of Children in Films" in the *New York Times.*

"Antonioni's *Cronaca*" in *The Thousand Eyes.*

"*Diary of a Country Priest:* Films as Spiritual Life," "Sidney Lumet, or The Necessity for Compromise," "The 32nd New York Film Festival" and "Interview with Abbas Kiarostami" in *Film Comment.*

"Fassbinder's *Despair*" in *Lingo.*

"The World According to Makavejev," "Truffaut's *The Woman Next Door*" and "Was It a Montage for You, Too, Dear?" in *Houston City Magazine.*

"Fourteen Koans by a Levite on Scorsese's *The Last Temptation of Christ*" in *Tikkun.*

"David Lynch's *Wild at Heart*" in *Esquire.*

"A Taste for Naruse" in *Film Quarterly.*

Credits

"The Experimental Films of Warren Sonbert" in *Film Culture*.

"Three Ozu Films from the Fifties" in *Cineaste*.

"The Passion of Pauline Kael" in *New York Woman*.

"The Last Taboo: The Dumbing Down of American Movies" from *Dumbing Down: Essays on the Strip-Mining of American Culture*, edited by Katharine Washburn and John Thornton, W. W. Norton & Co.

"In Search of the Centaur: The Essay-Film" in *The Threepenny Review*.

INDEX

Index

Index

Index

ABOUT THE AUTHOR

Phillip Lopate is the author of the essay collections *Against Joie de Vivre, Bachelorhood, Being with Children* and *Portrait of My Body,* as well as the novels, *Confessions of Summer* and *The Rug Merchant.* He is the editor of the now classic *The Art of the Personal Essay* and is the series editor of *The Anchor Essay Annual.* His work has been included in *The Best American Essays* and the Pushcart Prize annuals and his film criticism appears regularly in the *New York Times.* He lives in Brooklyn, New York, with his wife and daughter, and teaches at Hofstra University.

Printed in the United States
by Baker & Taylor Publisher Services